FLOYD ON BRITAIN & IRELAND

KEITH FLOYD

BBC BOOKS

'What *is* jazz, Mr Armstrong?'
'Man, if you have to ask you'll *never* know.'

Photographs: Martin Brigdale
Food preparation: Berit Vinegrad
Styling: Andrea Lambton

Illustrations: William Hunt

Brocade curtains on cover
kindly loaned by
The Gallery of Antique Costume and Textiles

Published by BBC Books
a division of BBC Enterprises Ltd,
Woodlands, 80 Wood Lane, London W12 0TT

First published 1988
© Keith Floyd 1988

ISBN 0 563 20626 8 (Hardback)
0 563 20624 1 (Paperback)

Typeset in 11/13 Bembo by Butler & Tanner, Frome, Somerset
Colour originated by Technik,
and printed by Chorley and Pickersgill Limited, Leeds
Printed and bound by Butler and Tanner, Frome, Somerset

CONTENTS

ACKNOWLEDGEMENTS

When I wandered happily around the British Isles and Ireland looking for inspiration, information, love and help to compile this book I bumped and sometimes crashed into some marvellous people – they are all (I hope) listed below. Without their help the task would have been very difficult indeed, so thank you all very much. In the words of the great poet, 'I owe you one'.

MYRTLE ALLEN –
BALLYMALOE HOUSE, COUNTY CORK, IRELAND
STEVEN BONNAR – WHEELERS
SIMON BURNS – ISLE OF ERISKAY, SCOTLAND
CHRIS COPE AND CHRIS MONKMAN –
PLUMMERS RESTAURANT, BEDALE, YORKSHIRE
TIM DOUBLEDAY
GEORGE EMMETT – LINDEN HALL HOTEL, NORTHUMBERLAND
MRS WIN FLOYD
DAVID HARDING – BODYSGALLEN HALL, LLANDUDNO, WALES
SHAUN HILL – GIDLEIGH PARK HOTEL, CHAGFORD, DEVON
CELIA MARTIN
GEORGE McCALPINE –
RAMORES RESTAURANT, PORT RUSH, NORTHERN IRELAND
AIDAN McCORMACK – 19 GRAPE LANE, YORK
BILLY MACKESY – BAWNLEIGH HOUSE, COUNTY CORK, IRELAND
SIR FITZROY AND LADY MACLEAN –
STRACHUR HOUSE, ARGYLL, SCOTLAND
JIMMY MacNAB – THE CREGGANS HOTEL, ARGYLL, SCOTLAND
JANE AND MICHAEL O'CALLAGHAN – LONGUEVILLE HOUSE,
MALLOW, IRELAND
COLIN PRESSDEE – BARROWS WINE BAR, MUMBLES, WALES
THE PRESTIGE GROUP OF HOTELS
PAUL REED – THE CHESTER GROSVENOR HOTEL, CHESTER
MARGARET REES – COBBLERS RESTAURANT, LLANDYBIE, WALES
GARY RHODES – THE CASTLE HOTEL, TAUNTON

BARRY RICHARDSON
DECLAN RYAN –
ARBUTUS LODGE HOTEL, COUNTY CORK, IRELAND
KEVIN SCHOLEY – THE DANUM SWALLOW HOTEL, DONCASTER
MINNIE SELKIRK
JOHN SHEEDY – LONGUEVILLE HOUSE, MALLOW, IRELAND
MIKE SIMPSON – CULLODEN HOUSE HOTEL, SCOTLAND
RIC STEIN – THE SEAFOOD RESTAURANT, PADSTOW
JOAN VALSLER – QUILLS RESTAURANT, IPSWICH
MARGARET VAUGHAN – THE SETTLE RESTAURANT, FROME
ARTHUR WATSON – THE RIVERSIDE CAFÉ, WEST BAY, DORSET

PREFACE

Ten years ago it would have been impossible to imagine any self-respecting *bon viveur* sitting down to write a few honest words in praise of an anthology of recipes which celebrated British cookery and British chefs. Our reputation for good food has been miserable, and our continental cousins still look upon our restaurants as a huge joke. But at last all this is changing. The shadow of our puritan past and the politics of rationing which once conspired to promote a patriotic disapproval of the pleasures of the table are dissolving in favour of the fruits of post-war affluence and the rise of the yuppie culture.

Suddenly, the jaded palates of the media are being titillated and our weekend colour supplements are drunk with features on food and wine. New high-gloss magazines have appeared, elevating the food on our plates to fine art. Sainsbury's competes with Marks and Spencer to promote a wider choice of unusual fresh raw materials and a more exotic range of ready-to-eat foods.

With this hype has come a revolution in our restaurant kitchens. Suddenly, we are seeing the emergence of a vanguard of talented British cooks who are enjoying a status in society which was unheard of until now. Today top chefs are stars, because today food has become chic and fashionable.

But fashion breeds snobbery and this new-found trend in our life-styles has attracted a rich dollop of humbug and pretension amongst some of the protagonists and their camp followers. Much of what I read and see is so perfect, so fancy that it defies imitation – anyway, for most ordinary mortals. The foodie movement has put cookery on a pedestal when cookery is for the kitchen, the family and friends. Pedestals are for prima donnas, heroes and, perhaps, a handful of chefs. But cookery is for every day.

This is why I welcome this book. Keith Floyd is doing for food what Henry Ford did for the motor car. Food may be chic and trendy, but Keith makes it fun by stripping away the bogus mysteries of cookery which have intimidated people anxious to learn but too frightened to make a mistake. He is the only TV chef ever to acknowledge that mistakes can happen in the kitchen, and by having his own failures televised he breathes confidence into his audience and inspires affection – rather than awe – for his subject. If I were ever invited to write an irreverent epitaph for him, it might describe him as 'The only foodie who was never afraid to fart in public'!

However, Keith's book celebrates another – and altogether more wholesome – trend in food today: the revival of traditional British dishes. It took me the best part of fifteen years to recover from the trauma of a school diet of faggots, fishcakes, bubble and squeak, grease-laden stews with dumplings like cannon balls, a colourless vegetable flotsam called cabbage and a whole variety of revolting nursery puddings. But I recant and I confess that today some of these dishes – in name but *not* in the manner of their preparation at my school – appear regularly on the menu of The Castle at Taunton. Indeed, I recall vividly the day when I was first offered bread and butter pudding in my own restaurant. I was horrified and my chef had to beg me to try it. Yet since that day I have revelled in the glory of the British repertoire. It took me just a little while to understand that there was nothing wrong with those wonderful old favourites. It was only this nation's proud disinterest in food, expressed as carelessness in the kitchen, which had poisoned my mind and the perceptions of the whole world.

Sadly, and quite unnecessarily, providing good food in Britain today still tends to be the preserve of the more expensive restaurants. One of the great ironies of our time is that it took a Swiss chef, Anton Mosimann, to unveil the joys of our national cuisine to the cosmopolitan patrons of London's Dorchester Hotel. Meanwhile, in the more likely setting of the English country inn, where these dishes have a more natural home, the cooking, unfortunately, remains – for the most part – as disgusting as it was in my school days. Well, almost.

However, as I said at the beginning of this preface, times are changing. The best news is that in Keith Floyd, his books and his television programmes, Britain has discovered a marvellous ambassador-of-the-people who knows how to communicate the pleasures of good food honestly and enthusiastically to a greater audience than has existed in the past. Our kitchens are much brighter places for his influence.

Happy cooking and good eating.

Kit Chapman
The Castle at Taunton

British Cooking is
Alive and Well

'The essentials of English cooking are roasts of beef, mutton and lamb, the various meats cooked in salt water, in the manner of fish and vegetable . . . fruit preserves, puddings of all kinds, chicken and turkey with cauliflower, salt beef, country ham and several similar ragouts – that is the sum of English cooking,' says Antonin Carême, who clearly has not met the people I have. It is true that British cooking used to be a terrible joke all over the world but, happily, times have changed.

This is a personal and prejudiced book based on my own experience. It is not an exhaustive handbook or encyclopaedia of cooking in the British Isles – but I hope that it will help you to enjoy the new or re-discover the old tastes and aromas of good honest food.

In my view there are at present three levels or styles of British cooking. First there is the simple and traditional domestic cooking practised by a dying generation of cooks who set great store by honest ingredients – vegetables from their own garden, meat, fish and poultry carefully chosen from suppliers of repute who have no time for the battery-reared hen or the intensively farmed beast. These people also take advantage of nature's free harvest, whether it's blackberries from the hedgerows for jam, elderflowers for wine, or field mushrooms for breakfast. They would rather put an extra half-hour of love into a casserole than a stock cube, and you are fortunate to eat in their kitchens. In the course of researching this book and the television series of the same name I have been very lucky to eat this sort of food – boiled ham and butter beans with parsley sauce, Devon splits with clotted cream or a perfectly roasted free-range chicken with the kind of giblet gravy that, as a boy, I was brought up to expect in many homes.

Second is the cooking that has its roots firmly in the British farmhouse. It is based on the tradition of former times, but has been developed over a long period by enthusiasts of great talent and learning who have never had the need or desire to create fashionable or novelty food. They have not felt it necessary to ape French food to attract customers, being totally content and secure in the knowledge that here in the British Isles and Ireland we have on hand some of the finest food available in the world. True, it takes a little searching out, a bit of time and patience, but for those who love the craft of cooking and the joy of eating it is no trouble. The people who cook in this way (Myrtle Allen, Joyce Molyneux, Jane O'Callaghan, Sonia Stevenson, Margaret Vaughan and many more) take such pleasure in pleasing you that to sit at their tables is both a gastronomic and spiritually enriching experience. Myrtle Allen is not alone in being just as concerned about what the chickens she cooks eat as about what you eat. When such cooks have the time to talk to you about food, not only is your appetite excited, but your mind and heart are nourished too.

The third style of British cooking is new and exciting. It is the work of young cooks and chefs who have worked here and abroad under the acknowledged masters of the culinary art but, instead of becoming slavishly devoted acolytes to the style of their Svengali, they have cut loose like the guitarists of supergroups and started their own bands. They are the driving force of Formula One British cooking. They have absorbed the skills and lore of (usually) French modern cooking and applied the principles in a thoughtful innovative fashion in British food. They are, happily, too numerous to name and are proliferating in the provinces up and down the country. For me a perfect harmonious example of their labours is typified by one of Gary Rhodes' menus which says it all:

LUNCHEON

Cream of Leek and Potato Soup

Steamed Fillet of Mackerel with Sea Salt and Chives
on a bed of Marinated Vegetables

Slices of Melon, Grapefruit and Orange Segments
with a Yoghurt Dressing

❧

Today's Traditional Dish

The Chef's Speciality of the Day

The Castle's Roasts

Monday: Stuffed Loin of Veal	*Thursday:* Topside of Beef
Tuesday: Leg of Lamb	*Friday:* Turkey
Wednesday: Loin of Pork	*Saturday:* Corn-fed Chicken

❧

Traditional British Pudding of the Day

Hot Apple and Cinnamon Pies with fresh Custard Sauce

A Selection of Cheeses from the Board
served with Home-made Walnut Bread

❧

Coffee

MAIN COURSES

Lobster Consommé with a Spinach Parcel, light Fish Mousse
and a Collop of Lobster

A light Parfait of Chicken and Goose Livers served
with Caramelised Oranges, Corn Salad and toasted Brioche

A Fillet of Red Mullet sautéed in butter with an
Olive and Coriander Dressing

Five Loch Fyne Oysters lightly warmed in Butter
served in their Shells with a Champagne Sauce

A Rabbit Pithivier flavoured with Shallot and Thyme,
laid on a rich Rabbit Sauce

A Terrine of Duck, Veal Kidney, Pork Fillet,
Pistachio Nuts and Spices wrapped in Pastry, accompanied
by a Salad of Orange and Tarragon

A Sea Bass Mousseline garnished with Asparagus Tips wrapped
in Salmon on a light Lemon and Chervil Butter Sauce

A Fillet of John Dory cooked in Hazelnut Oil and served
with Spring Vegetables and Saffron Potatoes

Fillet of Beef in a Sauce of its own juices and the essence of Girolles

Breast of Corn-fed Chicken with glazed Apple and
toasted Almonds on a Cider Vinegar Sauce

Roast Best End of Lamb with a Fresh Mint and
Green Peppercorn Crust served on a Lamb Sauce
with Poached Currants

Fillets of Venison with a Celeriac Rosti and glazed Apples
on a Rich Game Sauce

Sweets and Cheese

Fresh Pineapple Mousse layered between two Meringue Biscuits
topped with glazed Pineapple Slices on a Plum Coulis

Glazed Apple Tart served with its own Sorbet

Home-made Prune and Rum Ice Cream served in a
Brandy Snap Basket with an Anglaise Sauce

A plate of three Chocolates – White Chocolate Marquise,
Fudge Terrine and a light Chocolate Cake
served with two Sauces

Hot Passion Fruit Soufflé served with a Passionfruit Sauce

A Selection of Cheeses from the Board served
with Home-made Walnut Bread

෴

Cafetière, Café Hag or a selection of Speciality Teas
and Chocolate Creams

Such a menu would have been inconceivable ten years ago and there is, of course, still a great tradition in hotels up and down the place where a stained chrome dome on silly carved legs is trundled up and down flock-and-fly wallpapered rooms with a grey slab of cold meat underneath, swimming in rich brown liquid under the banner of 'A Taste of Britain', God help us.

I have filled this book with many examples drawn from all three styles of British cooking – simple recipes for old favourites (and none the worse for that) like green pea soup, brawn or steak and kidney pudding, or fresh caught elvers from the Somerset Levels; refinements or variations on these traditional themes using the best home-grown ingredients such as a rabbit stewed in gooseberry champagne or roast chicken served with a tarragon-flavoured cream sauce; and plenty of the exciting gourmet dishes that our young cooks have been developing – try the light stew of Dublin Bay prawns and asparagus in a saffron soup on page 76, or the fillet of venison with celeriac and glazed apples on page 126. I have not placed the recipes in any particular order, beyond dividing them into their basic categories of soups, fish, ham and offal, game, poultry, meat etc. I hope you'll find your gastronomic journey of Britain and Ireland more exciting this way, with lots of unexpected halts and corners to browse in, and fresh discoveries to beckon you on round the next turning. And – who knows? – you may be tempted into trying, and finding you can cook, a really delicious concoction of contrasting flavours and textures that you would have passed by if it had been fenced off in an enclosure labelled gourmet food.

One important note – do *please* read the section on stocks and glazes (pages 150–153) in conjunction with the soup, meat, game and poultry recipes, and the section on fish stocks (page 87); and PLEASE take the times, temperatures and quantities as a guide, and not as an inflexible statement of mathematical fact!

Chefs or cooks – call them what you will – representing the three styles of British cooking have given me enormous help and encouragement in producing this book. My thanks to them all. Not only that, but they have also restored my faith in and given me hope for what must be one of the most important pleasures of life – eating. And, of course, cooking; but better yet – British cooking.

Eat your heart out, Monsieur Carême!

Keith Floyd
Ashprington, Devon

Fresh Pea Soup (page 32) and Stilton and Cauliflower Soup (page 29) with Flower Pot Bread (page 228)

IN SEARCH OF LUNCH

It is a Dorset summer bank holiday morning. Blue skies, no wind, and a big yellow sun is hot and high. In good spirits, we pile into my open-topped car and set off for the nearby agricultural and sports fair. We turn off the main road, its verges neatly trimmed and manicured by a concerned county council, into narrow lanes with overgrown hedges of ash and elder and banks of bracken and nettles strewn with the confetti of pink, purple and white wild flowers. Past fields of ripening wheat – small, friendly fields in which a thoughtful farmer has planted his grain to encircle the odd oasis of sentinel trees, rather than ripping them out to maximise his cereal-growing acreage.

It was in fields like these, thirty years ago, when corn was still harvested with a binder and extra hands were hired to stook the sheaves, that I would load the trailers with my Uncle Ken. Ignoring blistered hands and grazed knees, I would follow the binder round and round as it inexorably enlarged its swathe of destruction until, as the sun sank behind the hedgerow elms, only a patch of corn the size of a cricket square was left standing in the centre of the field.

It was the high point of the day. Our throats were dry from the dust and the chaff, but as the parcel of corn got smaller I would join the circle of farmhands, each holding a stick cut from the hedge, who stood waiting for the terrified animals – rabbits and occasionally a hare – which had taken refuge there from the path of the reaper. As each made its last desperate bolt for freedom, we'd run like hell after it, trying to club it before it reached the sanctuary of the hedgerow.

I earned seven shillings and sixpence that day. I was only fourteen and had broken my back, and had probably caused the farmer more trouble than I was worth by stooking the corn the wrong way up. But I was proud of my few shillings, and of the rabbit I'd caught. I spent the money on the latest Elvis Presley record and gave the rabbit to my mother to cook.

Anyway, that was years ago. Right now I'm feeling great as I sit behind the wheel of this sleek six-cylindered automobile and we turn

---

Clear Highland Game Soup (page 37) and Chilled Consommé (page 38)

into the field, neatly divided with ropes and stakes, that has been appointed the official car park for the show. Gentlemen in tweed jackets with faces as tanned, wrinkled and polished as their brogues wave us on to a space just beyond the stationary traction exhibition. We amble off past the stalls selling home-made jams, hand-knitted sweaters, Barbour coats and cartridge belts to the beer tent for a thirst-quenching pint served by a soft-spoken country woman, neat in a white blouse, black skirt and apron.

Refreshed, we go on our way to give money to polite young farmers inviting us to try our hand at walking on slippery barrels, or to heave balls at a coconut shy and not win one. We dodge the twelve-year-old Lucinda Greens of tomorrow as they canter blithely by on their ponies to the show ring to indulge in those curious but charming equestrian pursuits so beloved by the British. All those who haven't got a horse have dogs – Welsh springers, pointers, labradors, Jack Russells – the lot. There's another group of people here too, though less obvious than the Thelwell-pony and the pedigree-pooch-owning set. They have dogs as well, but these are the hell's angels of the canine world. I'm talking about that mystical band of men who own lurchers, sit quietly in groups wearing leather jackets and garish pullovers, and talk in whispers of the lore of coursing.

It is midday now, and time to eat, but we don't fancy half-cooked hot dogs and burned beefburgers or those ice-creams that spiral out of the machine and run down the four-buttoned cuff of your hand-made tweed jacket. So there is a council of war – and someone says that there is a brilliant pub that serves fine food and welcomes children only 8 miles away.

On this sizzling bank holiday Monday even the butterflies are taking a siesta and the bees and wasps are diving, Pearl Harbor-like, into the beers, Coca-Colas and orange juices clutched in the hands of off-duty stockbrokers and City analysts relaxing with their offspring on the floral terrace of the whitewashed coaching inn perched high on the side of a spectacular Dorset village. The tarmac of the car park sticks to the soles of our shoes and the smell of dry metal rises from the bonnets of the Volvos and BMWs. It is ten to twelve and beautifully designed signs proclaim the owner's intentions to welcome, water and feed us with the very best.

It's cool inside the bar and the black hand-painted boards offer a mouth-watering choice of dishes from dressed Dorset crab to home-made veal, ham and egg pie, not to mention the lasagnes, pizzas, curries, southern-fried chicken, vegetarian cutlets and other rubbish that passes for (and is accepted as) 'British food' these days. We order our drinks and a menu to check out further possibilities. By the time the staff have gone to look for more rice, change a barrel and found the straws for the kids, we have made up our minds. Too late. They tell us that the kitchen is closed.

Just another hot, lazy, dusty Dorset day, but I'd rather have been out cutting corn or baling hay and – if you'll pardon the pun – the whole British scene is as corny as Kansas in August.

Back home, hungrier and sadder, though wiser, I sit down and ponder what the hell I'm doing planning a television series on British cookery. It just doesn't exist. Does it? Well, the book's got to be written, so I set off on a 3,000-mile round trip of the British Isles looking for soul food and a place to eat it in! A gastronomic walk on the wild side.

I don't know for sure whether the restaurant on the river's edge at West Bay, Dorset, is actually called Arthur's Caff, but certainly this curious low white building is run by Arthur and his wife assisted by a band of happy helpers. And that's the name the locals give it.

Anyway, what's in a name? You'll find it easily enough – over a little bridge, just behind the hamburger and candyfloss stands on the harbour's edge. As a restaurant it defies classification – it's not exactly the Roux Brothers style, for sure. You can queue for milk shakes and fried chicken and chips, or you can sit by the big windows and watch holiday-makers on the water miserably rowing in the rain and declare, as I do every year, the lobster and strawberry season well and truly open. And you won't feel ripped off at Arthur's, believe me. I always have a cold boiled lobster with local new potatoes, a proper English salad of hearty lettuce, cucumber, spring onions and tomato with some good mayonnaise, then a bowl of strawberries with extra helpings of Dorset clotted cream – a modest enough snack, you'll agree, but usually by the time I've eaten the 'caff' is filling with people in raincoats and anoraks queueing for tea and cakes. I don't think the Michelin Guide will ever give it three stars, but if you're down that way and you've got a sense of humour and enjoy a bit of fresh fish – scallops, or whatever – give it a whirl, because it's one of those places that are happily just a little crazy and ever so British.

And that's what this little piece is all about: Britain and the brilliant things you can eat if, like I did, you wander aimlessly around these islands being whimsically self-indulgent in some of its restaurants and hotels. Especially in early summer when you hurtle past the yellow fields of rape under avenues of bright green beech and pink and white candled chestnuts or down lanes so overgrown that the flowers on the nettles kiss both sides of the old cabriolet and the occasional hawthorn branch tries to flip off the dark glasses. After Arthur's and a night at The George Hotel in Bridport where the breakfast is great and Tim the barman makes the best Pimms and strawberry daquiris in the entire universe, it is really good and very different, to say the least, to check into the Quantock suite at The Castle Hotel in Taunton (which has a fine perpendicular church in Hammet Street, by the way, if you're into that sort of thing).

Relax in a 900-foot-long bath, sip Champagne and wonder what to order for dinner. This is hardly a problem: my friend Gary Rhodes is a good cook (chef, I mean), and takes great pride in turning fresh local ingredients into dishes that are happily British, modern and light. Like the fillet of fresh herring with mustard sauce, the chicken consommé with shredded raw mushrooms, or the superb individual steamed orange pudding with orange syrup and clotted cream that I had.

After dinner Gary joined me for a drink. In my view he's one of the best – if not *the* best – examples of the new young breed of native-born British chefs working in these islands; one of those who are making a great impact on cooking and on eating out in this country, gradually disabusing the world of the notion that you can't eat well here. He's got a very sound background in terms of his technical ability with a deep understanding of his craft and is articulate in talking about it. And, on top of all that, he has the flair and creative ability that make all the difference between a regular good cook and one who is really very special indeed.

If I sounded jaundiced and bitter at the beginning of this introduction, it's because after spending nearly a year in France working on a food programme and researching a book, the shock of returning to England was terrifying. So I was amazingly excited by the standard of cooking I found at The Castle in deepest, darkest Somerset. Yet Gary Rhodes is not the son of a famous French chef whose family has been in the business for generations. He's twenty-seven with a punk hairstyle, bright eyes, keen looks and an autocratic attitude that could equally have gone with his being a rock-and-roll guitarist, a racing driver or a professional tennis player. No one else has ever been in catering in his family. They are ordinary, everyday people living in Kent.

Morning came – a sunlit English morning which I celebrated with a wonderful English breakfast. Saying goodbye to the wistaria-clad old Castle, much heartened I sped along the motorway on the next stage of my gastronomic tour. I cruised up the M5 past the curious peaty smell of Bridgwater and the life-sized model of a camel that some wag has abandoned on the edge of a field (why?), then across the Somerset Levels, that ancient kingdom of rivers where the fisherman was once king and eels and crayfish were staple fare, heading for lunch cooked by chef Paul Reed much further north at the Chester Grosvenor.

By now you must be thinking that my life is just a happy whirl, and yet I saw nothing of the city of Chester. No other British city has such well-preserved enclosing ramparts, in which places of the original Roman wall survive. I didn't see them; nor did I see any of Chester's famous galleried streets, known as the Rows, where shops open on to balustraded walkways reached only by steps from the road. I had no time to see the city's fine timbered inns and houses and no time for boating on the River Dee. I know about all these touristical goodies, my friends, because Judith, my secretary, who was with me on the trip, read about them to me from a book as we rushed by. I was reminded of the Frank Sinatra song which says, 'Let's take a trip to Niagara – this time we'll look at the falls.'

In the Grosvenor's pink dining room I made a light lunch of Paul's potted Cheshire cheese terrine: it's a perfect example of how the new breed of British chefs is developing British food by using local ingredients. After a quick tour of the kitchens and a brief rest, we hit the road again.

By late evening we'd made Scotland and the place names had reeled off the map like the football results: Motherwell 2, Hamilton Academical 2; Cowdenbeath 1, Stenhousemuir 0, etc, etc. Through Glasgow we sped as dusk began to fall, and the winding road around Loch Lomond was not as beautiful as I'd hoped. A Scots friend of mine said the only good thing about Loch Lomond is the song and that was fourth rate! Sounds like fighting talk: he said it, not me.

My spirits were beginning to flag as darkness fell – we were still miles from Oban. But we are true Brits, and a quick burst of 'Me and Bobby McGee' from the Country and Western Greatest Hits tape (much to Judith's horror) soon had the old works two-seater bouncing over the little bridge and on to the Isle of Eriskay – a 300-acre kingdom close by Mull where Robin and Sheena Buchanan-Smith have, for some bizarre reason of their own, chosen to turn their sombre granite home into a hotel.

The car crunched over the gravel, the house was dark and fore-boding – a few windows shone yellow in the night. It'd make a brilliant opening shot for a Hammer House of Horror film. The huge front door was opened, not by some black-clad ghoul with razor-thin lips, but by the jovial Robin. Inside a peat fire burned brightly and all was sweetness, warmth and light. And after a glass of old malt, which appeared by magic in my hand even before the formalities of registering were completed, all was well.

Over a dinner of smoked salmon sorbet served in a scooped-out melon, followed by simply poached fresh salmon and new potatoes, Robin, a former chaplain of the University of St Andrews, entertained us with tales of Scots lore, literature and ecclesiastical derring-do. And, of course, an impassioned sermon on the glories of malt whisky, many splendid examples of which he has conveniently to hand.

I awoke in the morning with childish excitement as I pulled open the curtains to see for the first time where I was. Across an uneven and slightly soggy lawn splashed with dark brown and green, a bit tundra-like, stood a copse of fine trees. Beyond them, profiled in the bright morning light, a yacht sailed by. The Morvan Hills looked fine and wagtails, sandpipers and eider duck wheeled and called in the clear skies. A big heron flapped awkwardly by.

Downstairs my host, resplendant in his kilt in front of the huge fireplace, said, 'Help yourself to breakfast from the sideboard.' Beneath battered silver domes lay kippers, kidneys, bacon and black pudding, accompanied by splendid home-made brown bread.

Day four of my gastronomic odyssey had begun and, heading east, Loch Ness was invisible in the driving rain as we made for Culloden House near Inverness for a feast of cullen skink, venison sausages in a piquant sauce, and some wonderful local raspberries. Japanese and American tourists watched in bewilderment as tartan-trousered and kilted officers of some of the old Scottish regiments were piped into a gargantuan feast taking place in the large dining room opposite.

After this the details of the succeeding days of the journey began to blur. Remember those black and white films in which the hero takes a trans-American train that tears through the night, and every second they flash up the name of the town it's passing through? It was all a bit like that. What day was it I had lunch with my friend John Noble at his Scottish baronial castle on the edge of Loch Fyne? I can't remember now, but I do remember the walk down the long drive, through the most perfect garden with its rushing river and just that air of neglect that brings real beauty into landscaped grounds. Around every corner a bird or animal would flutter up or dart in front of us to disappear into the profusion of red rhododendrons, pink, orange and red azaleas, white narcissus, yellow ponticum azalea, and chestnut, oak, rowan, yew and deodar trees. There was no mildewed butler to greet us, and there was dust on the banisters of the staircast that led to the dining room. Outside the windows below us Loch Fyne twinkled in the sun, and we feasted on oysters and boiled gigot of mutton.

Soon we were in England again – first port of call Northumberland and Linden Hall Hotel, where the genial George Emmett gave us superb roast beef and said that the best batter for fish was made simply of flour, water and vinegar. Then it was on to the elegant Middlethorpe Hall by the race course at York with no time for the 3.30, and even less to stop and stare at the medieval glories of this fine city. I remember the glories of Aidan McCormack's pan-fried chicken, though. (Aidan has now opened a restaurant of his own at 19 Grape Lane, York.) After lunch I turned west right across the spine of England heading for Bodysgallen Hall at Llandudno (who planned this crazy journey?). Knowing nothing of Llandudno (I think they may host political conferences there, and probably the *Radio One Road Show* goes there), I was delighted to discover this pretty Victorian town. And David Harding's crab tart with laverbread was most interesting. The gulls eggs, too, were curious, and the wild rabbit was supreme – but it was the cheeses that really took my fancy. There was the semi-hard Waun Gron and the soft Pantyllyn, a great goat's milk cheese called Maes Mawr, Caerphilly, of course, and a Gouda-type cheese called a Teifa.

Next stop was the Mumbles where we played at being Dylan Thomas, drinking Bass in the White Rose Pub which is a bit like a railway carriage and where the bottles are placed on mahogany shelves like confessional candles. No wonder Dylan used to gaze out at Swansea Bay and say it reminded him of Naples – he obviously spent too much time in the White Rose!

There were, of course, many more breakfasts, lunches and dinners along the way, some of them traditionally good, some excitingly original, and all of them cooked and served with an enthusiasm and skill that was unheard of in Britain a few years ago. There was the unforgettable breakfast on Exmoor of hog's pudding, a white sausage of groats and minced pork stuffed into natural skins, grilled until the skin had turned brown and split, served with laverbread fried in bacon fat until it was gooey and seasoned with a dash of malt vinegar and some freshly ground black pepper, then sprinkled with little crispy cubes of fried bacon.

It was great after such an exhilarating but exhausting trip to get back to London. We stopped at The Duke's Hotel and relaxed in the deep comfort of its polished mahogany and warm welcoming service. After a few of Salvatore's reviving Bloody Marys, we strolled into St James's for a dozen or so of the best Helford River oysters by way of an aperitif, before returning for an excellent lunch of grilled kidneys.

I fell in love with Ireland because a honey-tongued woman called Mairin Ahern persuaded me, against my will, to attend the Kinsale Gourmet Festival. This event, if my memory serves me well, lasted four days. Four days of eating, drinking, singing and dancing, during which time it seemed that nothing in this charming harbour town closed.

I fell into the wrong kind of company: Stan Gebler Davies and the Earl of Kingsale to name but two of its number, who in the pursuance of their art as writers have willingly sacrificed their livers for gastronomy. The immaculate blood-red rose worn in the lapel of Stan's white linen suit was still there when we boarded the plane for home four days later. I am not entirely convinced that he had undressed during that time – certainly the suit was somewhat wrinkled and his rose resembled those little pink blotting paper bombs we used to make at school by chewing the stuff and leaving them on the ceiling. Throughout the four days in this merry mayhem, the Cork City Jazz Band thumped out brilliant jazz and blues. If Billy Crosby, the band's pianist, isn't in the *Guinness Book of Records*, he should be. I reckon he played a straight six hours in one session without missing a note and, with a towel around his neck and a pint of Murphy's on the keyboard, this man really sang the blues.

As you drive into Cork city from the airport in the rush hour, news vendors dodge the traffic to sell you a copy of the *Echo* while you wait for the lights to change. The city is grey and seems to be coated in a fine layer of dust – it has an untidy air about it, but that impression quickly fades as you sit in the Long Valley Bar with a pint of Murphy's stout and a corned beef sandwich and watch the white-overalled bar staff dispense the stout with the reverence of nuns. A statue stands in the corner of this bar, with its oyster-coloured, glazed-brick floor, dark woodwork and nicotine-stained ceiling. It represents a former regular, finally banned for life from the bar after appalling drunken behaviour while living; now, however, because he was a poet and the Irish are generous and forgiving, he has been restored to stand for eternity on

Cockle and Mussel Chowder (page 48) and Cullen Skink (page 44)

the very spot where his Rabelaisian performances so offended in the past.

Tonight I will dine at the Arbutus Lodge where Declan and Michael Ryan select their local produce with care and cook it with consummate skill: dishes that range from nettle soup and tripe and onions to elegant creations of scallops, salmons and sweetbreads. One of the humblest dishes on their menu is my favourite: crubeens, or pig trotters, once served in pubs and, according to Declan, indispensable on a Friday or Saturday night after consuming 20 pints of stout. It's hard now to find them cooked in this way (rather like the faggots and peas of my childhood) but, believe me, they are delicious.

Ireland is rich in great cooks and characters, but there is one who stands out through sheer knowledge and understanding of all things culinary, and through the good humour and love with which she performs her craft, and that is Myrtle Allen. I lunched in her rambling hotel at Ballymaloe House in County Cork one hot day when the wistaria was mauve against the old grey walls and the gardens rang to the cries of dozens of children and parents celebrating their first communion with a magnificent buffet. Little girls in white dressed with veils of white lace and tiaras of daisies danced around the lawns, while the boys, uncomfortable in their neat suits, climbed trees and tried to get dirty and muddy. And we ate roast sirloin of beef with a golden crisp fat and flavour so fine that I cannot describe it. Even as the beef was being carved Myrtle popped into the garden to lift a root of horseradish to make the sauce to end all horseradish sauces.

I learned more from Myrtle about the selection of ingredients and the real lore of cooking that I ever have before. The taste of beef and that wonderful horseradish sauce lingered still on my palate as the train pulled into Belfast station. The big banner over the City Hall proclaimed: 'Belfast says no.' No to what? The streets were neat and thronged with some of the prettiest girls in Britain, but there were soldiers and Land Rovers on every corner. To my amazement, though, I discovered it was a lively, cheerful place, and the Ulster fry – the Irish breakfast – was great. By the time I had feasted on George McCalpine's fine food at Port Rush, visited the Bushmills distillery and dodged waves on the Giant's Causeway nearby, eaten potato cakes at the Folk Museum and colcannon and Irish stew in the Crown Pub, my spirits and my belief in mankind were lifted high. Ulster's OK.

Back in Kinsale to savour its specialities outside festive time, I spent

---

Devilled Crab (page 48) and Potted Shrimps (page 77)

a lot of time talking about food, cooking and chefs with my old friend Billy Mackesy who runs a great restaurant there called Bawnleigh House. After he had scrubbed the kitchen until it gleamed like the theatre of a BUPA hospital, we sat down to put the gastronomic world to rights, with the aid of the odd sip of Murphy's. Then it was into the old motor to bump and grind my way along the mighty Irish roads to Mallow, where I cheerfully submitted to the tender care and fine food of Jane and Michael O'Callaghan at the Longueville House Hotel. Next morning I pulled on my waders to toddle across the fields to the Black Water River, giving myself up to the mystical pursuit of the illusive salmon. I returned for lunch empty-handed, but there was no need to worry: others had provided for me.

To start with, there was a salad with at least five different types of lettuce delicately mixed with freshly picked asparagus, warm prawns and cubes of freshly poached salmon (possibly poached in more than one sense of the word). Then there was roast milk lamb, so succulent and pink that I had never tasted the like, reared on the O'Callaghan's rich pastures which are uncontaminated by pesticides or insecticides. The rhubarb tart with sweet, crumbly, buttery pastry and fresh cream completed an exquisite meal which was washed down with truly the last of the summer wine – the last few bottles of Michael O'Callaghan's superb white wine, Cois Moire, which he grows and makes on his estate, Ireland's only vineyard.

All Irish potatoes are great and those from the grounds of Longueville were superb, although Myrtle Allen might say that the best come from Ballymaloe. Others will claim that the spuds from Youghal are the best. If you happen to go on a potato tour and find yourself in Youghal, pop in and see my mate John Fitzgibbon in Aherne's Seafood Bar for a plate of prawns or some fresh fish and a few of his Irish coffees.

Well, I started this journey in despair but ended it full of optimism for British cooking. Some of the recipes that follow are personal favourites which I discovered whilst walking on the wild side.

It's a pity that the English language has no phrase directly corresponding to *bon appétit!* – enjoy your food!

1

SOUPS

Beautiful soup, so rich and green,

Waiting in a hot tureen!

Who for such dainties would not stoop?

Soup of the evening, beautiful soup!

Beautiful soup! Who cares for fish,

Game, or any other dish?

Who would not give all else for two

Pennyworth only of beautiful Soup!

Pennyworth only of beautiful Soup.

LEWIS CARROLL, *ALICE'S ADVENTURES IN WONDERLAND*.

JERUSALEM ARTICHOKE SOUP

2 lb (1 kg) Jerusalem
  artichokes, peeled and
  sliced
2 oz (50 g) butter
1 onion, chopped
Salt and pepper
2 pints (1 litre) milk
A little single cream
Chopped chervil
Fried bread croûtons

As you prepare the artichokes, pop them into a bowl of water to which you have added 1 tablespoon of lemon juice; this will prevent them from discolouring.

Melt the butter in a saucepan, put in the drained artichokes and the onion, and season lightly with salt and pepper. Cover and cook gently for 10 minutes. Add the milk and bring to the boil. Simmer gently for a further 10 minutes, then pass the soup through the fine disc of a vegetable mill. Return the soup to the saucepan, bring to the boil again and correct the seasoning. Before serving, add a little cream and chervil and fried croûtons.

BEAN SOUP

A heavy soup from Jersey with strong French influence, which would have kept farmers and fishermen happy and full on cold winter days.

4–6 oz (125–175 g) dried
  haricot beans
2 carrots, sliced
8 fl oz (250 ml) strong pork
  or beef stock
1 leek, sliced
2 potatoes, sliced (optional)
Parsley and thyme, chopped
Salt

Soak the haricot beans overnight, then drain. Bring to the boil and simmer for 1 hour in 2 pints (1 litre or so) of water, then add the carrots and continue to simmer for another $1\frac{1}{2}$ hours. Add some pork or beef stock and a few leeks and potatoes (if using). Bring to the boil again and simmer for a further 30 minutes. Add the parsley, thyme and salt to taste before serving.

STILTON AND CAULIFLOWER SOUP

$\frac{1}{2}$oz (15 g) butter
1 onion, chopped
1 cauliflower, broken into
   florets
1 pint (600 ml) light stock
1 bouquet garni
Salt and pepper
1 tablespoon cornflour
$\frac{1}{2}$pint (300 ml) milk
4 oz (125 g) blue Stilton,
   crumbled
Chopped parsley, to garnish

Melt the butter in a pan, add the onion and fry until soft. Add the cauliflower, stock, bouquet garni, and salt and pepper to taste. Bring to the boil, cover and simmer for 15 minutes; cool slightly. Remove the bouquet garni. Sieve or process in an electric blender until smooth. Blend the cornflour with 2 tablespoons of the milk. Add to the purée with the remaining milk. Bring to the boil again, stirring. Remove from the heat and stir in the cheese. Pour into warmed individual soup bowls and garnish with parsley. Serve immediately.

Photograph facing page 16

CUCUMBER AND CREAM SOUP

1 large cucumber, peeled and
   cut into pieces
1 large or 2 small pickled dill
   cucumbers, cut into pieces.
3 tablespoons lemon juice
3 tablespoons grated onion
6 fl oz (175 ml) double cream
Salt and pepper
1 tablespoon chopped dill

Put the cucumber pieces in a liquidiser, reserving 2 tablespoons for garnish, and blend with the pickled cucumber, lemon juice and onion. When the mixture is smooth, pour into a chilled tureen and stir in the cream, salt, pepper and dill. Garnish with the reserved cucumber and served chilled.

Leek and Potato Soup

This is a splendid winter soup if you cook it my way – a chunky, gutsy thing that, in fact, becomes a meal, and you just eat it with bread and drink some beer or wine. Alternatively, you can make it quite a refined little number for a starter for a carefully planned dinner party.

2 lb (1 kg) leeks
1 lb (500 g) potatoes
4 oz (125 g) butter
Salt and pepper
10 fl oz (300 ml) milk
Knob of butter
Chives to garnish
4–6 tablespoons cream

Use big winter leeks and cut off the top ragged green and the furry beard from the foot. This leaves you about 9 in. (23 cm) of leek. Strip off the coarsest outside leaves. Next slice the leeks into thin roundels and wash them and wash them and wash them under running cold water, at the same time spreading them into individual rings, until no grit or earth remains.

While these are draining – because they must be dry before you start to cook them – peel the potatoes and dice them into 1 in. (2.5 cm) cubes. Rinse them well under cold water and then dry them on some kitchen paper. Now take a big pot, melt the butter in it and throw in the leeks. Over a low heat – with the lid on – let the leeks soften; they will also reduce vastly in quantity. Now throw in your potato pieces, cover them with water and let them simmer for at least 30 minutes. Add a little salt and pepper and stir round with a fork so that the potato breaks up and you have a thick liquid almost like a purée. Next add the milk and simmer gently for another 30 minutes, until the soup is creamy and full of tender pieces of leek and lumps of potato. Season well with freshly ground pepper. Whisk in another knob of butter and serve.

That is the peasant version. You can refine it for your smart dinner party by following all of the above and leaving it to cool. Liquidise the lot in your food processor (you will now have quite a thick purée – not a soup – but you dilute this with a little chicken stock or more milk; O K, so you can use a cube, but you shouldn't really), and, of course, gently re-heat it. Serve sprinkled with finely chopped chives and with 1 tablespoon of cream poured into each bowl.

BARLEY BROTH

1 lb (500 g) stewing mutton
2 pints (1 litre) water
1 onion, diced
Salt and pepper
½ oz (15 g) pearl barley
2 oz (50 g) carrot, diced
2 oz (50 g) turnip, diced
2 oz (50 g) celery, diced
1 dessertspoon finely chopped
  parsley

Wipe and trim the mutton and cut into pieces. Place in a pan with the water, onion and salt and bring to boiling point. Skim well, then simmer for 2 or 3 hours. Wash the barley and add with the carrot, turnip and celery at least 1 hour before the end of the cooking time. Remove the meat and use it to make pasties – or take off the bones and return the meat, shredded or chopped, to the broth. Season the broth well, then add the parsley.

PEA AND MINT SOUP

Fresh peas and mint constitute the traditional summer flavours of British cooking.

4 oz (125 g) butter
1½ lb (750 g) fresh green peas,
  podded
2 oz (50 g) flour
2 pints (1 litre) chicken stock
Salt and pepper
Sprig of mint
A little caster sugar
5 fl oz (150 ml) double cream
Chopped mint to garnish

Melt 2 oz (50 g) of the butter in a pan, add the peas and cook gently, covered, for 5 minutes. Blend in the flour and gradually stir in the stock; season with salt and pepper and add the sprig of mint. Bring to the boil and simmer for 10 minutes or until the peas are tender. Reserve a few of the peas for garnish.

Rub the soup through a sieve or blend in a liquidiser. Return the soup to the heat; correct the seasoning and add sugar to taste. Stir in the cream, but do not let the soup reach boiling point. Serve the soup garnished with the reserved peas and chopped mint.

Fresh Pea Soup

If the peas are particularly young and fresh, water may be preferable to chicken stock as a cooking liquid. The heart of a small lettuce, finely sliced, may replace the onion for added freshness of flavour. This soup is also delicious chilled.

3 leeks, finely chopped
1 onion, finely chopped
2 oz (50 g) butter
2 tablespoons flour
3 pints (1.7 litres) chicken stock
1 sprig mint
2–2½ lb (1–1.25 kg) fresh peas, shelled
Salt and freshly ground black pepper
8 fl oz (250 ml) double or single cream

Sauté the leeks and onion in the butter in a heavy saucepan until tender. Sprinkle in the flour and stir to mix. Stir in the stock, bring to the boil and add the mint and peas. Cook, covered, for about 15 minutes, until the peas are tender. Remove the mint. Purée the mixture through a food mill or in batches in an electric blender. Return to the clean pan. Bring to the boil and add salt and pepper to taste and the cream. Re-heat. If too thick, add a little milk.

Photograph facing page 16

Green Pea Soup

The combination of dried peas and salted cured ham dates back to the Middle Ages when these ingredients were part of the staple winter diet. This soup was also known as 'The London Particular', being as thick as the dense fogs that once enveloped London and were colloquially termed 'pea soupers'. Thick pea soup was one of the most popular hot meals sold from streetbarrows.

2 oz (50 g) bacon, diced
4 oz (125 g) carrots, diced

Cook the bacon, carrots, celery and onions in the butter, under cover, for

2 oz (50 g) celery, diced
4 oz (125 g) onions, chopped
1 oz (25 g) butter
1 lb (500 g) dried green peas,
    split or whole
4 pints (2.3 litres) ham stock
Salt and pepper

5 to 10 minutes, Add the peas and cook for a further 2 to 3 minutes. Pour over the stock, add salt and pepper and bring to the boil; skim and simmer for 2 to 3 hours, skimming again whenever necessary.

Rub the soup through a coarse sieve or blend in a liquidiser. Return the soup to the pan and heat through; correct the seasoning. Serve with sippets or small pieces of bread to dip in; diced meat may be added to the soup, but this is not traditional.

Mike Simpson   *Serves 4*

CREAM OF OATMEAL AND ONION SOUP

2 pints (1 litre) chicken stock
1 lb (500 g) onions, diced
$3\frac{1}{2}$ oz (100 g) potatoes, cut
    into pieces
$2\frac{1}{2}$ oz (65 g) oatmeal
Salt and pepper
$\frac{1}{2}$ pint (300 ml) double cream

Bring the chicken stock, onions and potatoes to the boil and, when simmering, sprinkle in the oatmeal and stir. Season and simmer for 25 minutes, stirring frequently. Liquidise and pour back into the pan, add the cream, re-heat and serve.

Serves 4

NETTLE SOUP

1 onion, chopped
8 large handfuls young nettle
    tops, chopped
1 oz (25 g) butter
1 oz (25 g) flour
2 pints (1 litre) good chicken
    stock
Salt and pepper
Cream (optional)

Cook the onion and the nettle tops in the butter until soft. Add the flour and cook for about 3 minutes, stirring, then add the stock and season well. Bring to the boil, simmer for 5 minutes and then sieve. Re-heat, adjust the seasoning and add a little cream if desired.

MIXED VEGETABLE SOUP

In summer this soup may be served cold, topped with pieces of very lean bacon that have been cooked in it. Pork rinds may be substituted for the green bacon, and the soup may be enriched by the addition of some freshly grated cheese rinds – Cheddar or Cornish Yarg – just before the end of the cooking time.

$3\frac{1}{2}$ oz *(100 g) butter*
2 small onions, chopped
1 leek, chopped
$3\frac{1}{2}$ oz *(100 g) green bacon,*
  blanched and cubed
Bouquet of parsley, bay leaf
  and rosemary
7 oz (200 g) tomatoes
Salt and freshly ground
  pepper
$3\frac{1}{2}$ oz *(100 g) each potatoes,*
  carrots and courgettes,
  diced
$3\frac{1}{2}$ oz *(100 g) each broad beans*
  and peas, shelled
1 celery heart, finely chopped
7 oz (200 g) fresh haricot
  beans or 5 oz (150 g) dried
  beans, soaked and pre-
  cooked
4 pints (2.3 litres) veal or
  chicken stock
7 oz (200 g) rice
$\frac{1}{2}$ *medium green cabbage*
6 leaves basil
6 sprigs parsley
6 cloves garlic
Freshly grated Cheddar or
  Yarg cheese

Melt $1\frac{1}{2}$ oz (40 g) of the butter in a large saucepan and sweat the onions, leek, bacon and bouquet garni, covered, over a low heat for 15 to 20 minutes, without colouring. Discard the bouquet of herbs. Peel and chop the tomatoes, add to the pan and season with salt and pepper to taste. Heat the remaining butter in another pan and sweat the diced vegetables, the peas, broad beans, celery and the fresh haricot beans in it for 8 minutes. Add these vegetables to the first saucepan, cook for a few minutes, and pour in the stock and the dried beans, if used. Cover and simmer over a medium heat for 30 to 40 minutes, or until the haricot beans are tender and the vegetables are cooked but not mushy. Core and shred the cabbage. Raise the heat and add first the rice, then the cabbage. Cook, uncovered, over a medium heat for 15 to 20 minutes. A few minutes before removing from the heat, finely chop the basil, parsley and garlic and add to the soup. Serve with the cheese.

CREAM OF TOMATO SOUP

This is the real stuff – so sling out those tins of red liquid that I bet are in your larder!

1 oz (25 g) butter
1 onion, chopped
1 carrot, chopped
3 tablespoons flour
2 pints (1 litre) chicken stock
  or water
1 small clove garlic, chopped
2 leeks, thinly sliced
  (optional)
4 white peppercorns
1 teaspoon salt
1 tablespoon sugar
1½ lb (750 g) tomatoes,
  roughly chopped
1 chicken carcass (optional)
8 fl oz (250 ml) single cream
Croûtons or cooked rice to
  garnish

Melt the butter in a deep saucepan, add the onion and carrot and cook slowly until golden brown. Add the flour and mix. Add the stock or water, the garlic, leeks (if using), white peppercorns, salt, sugar, tomatoes and chicken carcass (if using). Cover and cook over a low heat for 1 to 1½ hours, skimming as necessary. Remove the chicken carcass and rub the soup through a fine strainer. Combine the strained soup with the cream, and correct the seasoning. If the soup is too thick, add a little more stock or some milk to obtain the desired consistency. Serve with croûtons or stir in a little cooked rice before serving.

CREAM OF MUSHROOM SOUP

8 oz (250 g) mushrooms,
  chopped
1 oz (25 g) onion, chopped
2 pints (1 litre) stock
2 oz (50 g) butter
1 oz (25 g) flour
8 fl oz (250 ml) single cream
Salt and pepper
¼ wineglass Sauternes

Put the mushrooms and onion into the stock and simmer for 20 minutes; pass through a sieve. Re-heat the purée. Work the butter and flour together to make a paste, and whisk this into the soup to thicken it. Season with pepper and salt and stir in the cream. Do not allow to boil. Add the wine at the last moment.

WILD MUSHROOM SOUP

You can use any edible mushrooms for this dish, but try to include ceps or chanterelles. However, when you tramp through the fields and woodlands on a fine autumn Sunday morning, be sure to bring your *Observer's Book of Mushrooms* with you – I can't afford to lose readers who poison themselves!

4 potatoes, thinly sliced
2 pints (1 litre) stock
1 lb (500 g) mixed wild
  mushrooms, sliced
1 oz (25 g) lard
2 onions, chopped
Salt and pepper
4 tablespoons cream
1 tablespoon finely chopped
  fresh herbs

Boil the potatoes in the stock until soft, then pass through a sieve into another saucepan. Sauté the mushrooms in the lard with the onions for about 10 minutes until soft, season with salt and pepper and add the mixture to the potato purée. Cover the soup and allow it to steep over a very low heat for 10 to 15 minutes – you must keep it well beneath simmering point. Before serving, add the cream and herbs.

CHICKEN BROTH

5–7 lb (2.25–3 kg) boiling
  fowl, trussed
1 large onion, stuck with 3
  cloves
2 carrots
1 large head garlic
1 bouquet garni
About 9 pints (5 litres) water
  or chicken stock
Coarse salt

Place the fowl, breast uppermost, in the bottom of an oval pot just large enough to hold all the ingredients. Place the vegetables and the bouquet garni around it. Pour on water or stock to cover, and slowly bring to the boil. Skim until no more scum forms on the top. As the fat from the bird melts and rises to the top, skim that off too. When boiling point is reached, add the salt and cover the pan, leaving the lid ajar. Reduce the heat and cook undisturbed at a slow simmer for $1\frac{1}{2}$ to 3 hours, depending on the age of the bird. Remove the bird and the vegetables from the pot and strain the broth through a colander lined with dampened muslin.

Clear soup was a way of feeding quantities of hungry mouths quite cheaply – it's the sort of thing to make for bonfire night when kids and parents need fortifying against the cold.

Serves 8 to 10

CLEAR HIGHLAND GAME SOUP

6 lb (2.75 kg) game bones
2 onions, halved
1 oz (25 g) butter
2 lb (1 kg) shin of beef, minced
1 set of game bird giblets,
* minced*
6 oz (175 g) celery, chopped
4 oz (125 g) white of leeks,
* chopped*
6 oz (175 g) carrots, sliced
1 bay leaf
6 parsley stalks
Salt
6 peppercorns
4 egg whites, beaten
* (optional)*
5 fl oz (150 ml) port wine
Diced cooked game meat, to
* garnish*

Brown the bones in a roasting tin in the oven; cook the onions in the butter until light brown. Put the bones, onions, beef, giblets, celery, leek, carrots, bay leaf, parsley stalks, salt and peppercorns in a large pan; pour over enough water just to cover. Bring to the boil and leave to simmer for 4 to 5 hours without stirring.

Strain the soup through a double layer of dampened muslin, and skim carefully to remove all traces of fat. If necessary, clarify the soup by pouring in 4 beaten egg whites on a very, very low heat. This collects any little particles left in the soup which can then be skimmed off.

Re-heat the soup, add the port and correct the seasoning. Serve the soup garnished with the diced cooked game meat.

Photograph facing page 17

GAME SOUP

1 lb 2 oz (550 g) green lentils
3 pints (1.7 litres) water
1 onion, diced
1 leek, white part only, sliced
1 sprig thyme
1 bay leaf
Salt and pepper
1 pheasant, singed and trussed
2 oz (50 g) butter, melted
4 fl oz (125 ml) double cream

Rinse the lentils and put them into a saucepan with the water, onion, leek, thyme and bay leaf. Season with salt and cook for 1 hour or until the lentils are very soft. Drain, removing the bay leaf and reserving the cooking liquid.

Season the pheasant with salt and pepper, pour the melted butter over it and roast at gas mark 4, 350°F (180°C), for 30 minutes or until slightly underdone. Cut the pheasant meat off the bones, setting aside the breast fillets. Pound the remaining meat in a mortar, and add the lentils. Pound again thoroughly until the mixture is perfectly smooth, rub it through a fine sieve into a saucepan and moisten it with the reserved lentil stock. Re-heat, add the cream and correct the seasoning. Dice the reserved pheasant breast fillets, place them in a tureen and pour over the soup.

CHILLED CONSOMMÉ

The addition of chopped chicken parts, particularly feet, provides extra gelatine to help set the stock.

5½ pints (3.2 litres) beef or
*   chicken stock*
1½ lb (750 g) lean chuck beef,
*   finely chopped*
1 egg white
2 oz (50 g) carrot, finely diced
3½ oz (100 g) leek, finely
*   diced*

In a tall saucepan, mix the broth with the chopped beef, egg white, carrot, leek and tomatoes. Bring to the boil, stirring. Reduce the heat, partially cover, and allow to simmer very slowly for 1 to 1½ hours. Add the tomato purée, if you are using it, at this point. Strain the consommé through a

12–15 tomatoes, halved,
  seeded and chopped
3 tablespoons tomato purée
  (optional)
Cayenne pepper (optional)

colander lined with a dampened
napkin, or several layers of dampened
muslin. De-grease the consommé
thoroughly, and season with a little
cayenne pepper if liked. Chill until
lightly set, and serve in chilled
porcelain cups.

Photograph facing page 17

Mike Simpson   *Serves 6 to 8*

SCOTCH BROTH

Scotch broth is very much what you make it. But its quality does
depend on obeying some simple rules. First, you must have lamb or
mutton stock, so this is the ideal winter soup to make the day after
you have had some roast lamb because you can use the bone to form
the basis of the stock. Put your lamb bone to simmer in 4 to 5 pints
(2.3–2.9 litres) of unsalted water while you prepare the other
ingredients. Second, make sure that your diced vegetables are all cut
into equal-sized pieces – about $\frac{1}{2}$ in. (1 cm) cubes. The addition of a few
ounces of chopped kale is a tip from a Scottish cook.

8 oz (250 g) carrots, diced
8 oz (250 g) turnips, diced
2 onions, diced
1 stick celery, diced
White of 1 leek, sliced
3–4 oz (75–125 g) pearl
  barley
4 oz (125 g) dried peas,
  soaked for 4–5 hours
Salt and pepper
About 4 pints (2.3 litres)
  lamb or mutton stock
Kale or other bitter winter
  greens, chopped (optional)

Add all the ingredients to the stock.
Simmer gently for a couple of hours,
making sure that the peas become
mushy and the barley expands and
becomes soft and white. If you wish,
add a few ounces of kale 10 minutes
before the end of the cooking time.
Check the seasoning and serve.

HARE SOUP

1 hare
2 oz (50 g) dripping
2 carrots, chopped
2 potatoes, chopped
2 leeks, chopped
2 sticks celery, chopped
2 onions, chopped
3 pints (1.7 litres) good stock
Bouquet of parsley, thyme and
  bay leaf
Salt and pepper
1 glass port
1 dessertspoon redcurrant jelly

Cut the hare into pieces, reserve the blood and break or chop the bones. Melt the dripping in a pan and when hot add the hare and brown slowly. Then add the vegetables, stock, herbs, salt and freshly ground pepper. Simmer slowly for about 2 hours.

When cooked, strain through a sieve, rubbing some of the meat through also. Pour into a clean pan and re-heat, adding the blood to thicken – do not boil. Add the port and redcurrant jelly, adjust the seasoning and serve.

BROWN WINDSOR SOUP

8 oz (250 g) shin of beef
8 oz (250 g) mutton
2 oz (50 g) butter
6 oz (175 g) onions, sliced
4 oz (125 g) carrots, sliced
2 oz (50 g) flour
4 pints (2.3 litres) brown meat
  stock
Bouquet of herbs
Salt and cayenne pepper
2 oz (50 g) boiled rice
5 fl oz (150 ml) Madeira

Cut the meat into 1 in. (2.5 cm) cubes. Melt the butter in a pan and fry the meat and vegetables until lightly browned. Sprinkle in the flour and cook until brown. Gradually stir in the stock; bring the soup to the boil, add the bouquet of herbs and simmer for 2 hours or until the meat is tender.

Season to taste with salt and cayenne pepper. Lift out the meat and remove the bones and skin. Return the meat to the soup and rub through a sieve or blend in a liquidiser. Re-heat the soup and add the rice and Madeira. Correct the seasoning and serve.

Light Stew of Dublin Bay Prawns and Asparagus in a Saffron Soup (page 76)

MEAT BROTH

This basic broth of beef, with the addition of chicken and veal, may be used in any recipe calling for beef broth, stock, consommé or *pot au bouillon*. Almost any veal, chicken or beef bones may be included; the exceptions are large marrow bones that take up too much room in the pot, obliging you to add too much water and thus weaken the resulting broth.

$2-2\frac{1}{2}$ *lb (1–1.25 kg) shin or leg of beef*

$2-2\frac{1}{2}$ *lb (1–1.25 kg) plate or short ribs of beef*

$2-2\frac{1}{2}$ *lb (1–1.25 kg) chicken pieces (backs, necks, wing tips)*

1 chicken carcass, raw or cooked (optional)

1 meaty veal knuckle, chopped (optional)

9 pints (5 litres) water

10 oz (300 g) carrots

1 large onion, stuck with 3 cloves

1 large head garlic

1 bouquet garni

Salt

Place a round metal grille in the bottom of your stock pot to prevent the ingredients from sticking. Tie thin cuts of meat into compact shapes with string. Starting with the largest pieces, fit all the beef, chicken and veal into the pot. Add the water and bring very slowly to the boil; it should take at least 1 hour for the water to reach boiling point. With a spoon or ladle, carefully lift off the surface scum as the liquid comes to the boil. Add the carrots, onion, garlic, bouquet garni and salt, and skim once more as the broth returns to the boil. Turn the heat down, cover the pot with the lid ajar and leave to simmer undisturbed for $3\frac{1}{2}$ hours if you wish to serve the beef afterwards, or for 5 hours if you wish to extract all the goodness of the beef into the broth. Strain the finished broth through a colander lined with dampened muslin. De-grease throughly with kitchen paper, or allow the broth to cool completely and then remove the solidified fat from the top.

Salad of Endive Lettuce with Steamed Red Mullet and Coriander Dressing (page 61)

KIDNEY SOUP

8 oz (250 g) shin of beef
1 lb (500 g) ox kidney
2 oz (50 g) butter
*4 oz (125 g) onions, coarsely
    chopped*
*1 dessertspoon chopped
    parsley*
*4 pints (2.3 litres) brown meat
    stock*
Salt and pepper
1 oz (25 g) flour
1 tablespoon tomato purée

Cut the beef and kidney into small pieces. Melt half the butter in a heavy-based pan and brown the meat and kidney, onions and parsley. Add the stock, salt and pepper and bring to the boil; skim well, cover and simmer for 3 hours, skimming occasionally.

Strain the soup and set some of the kidney pieces aside. Pass the remaining meat through a sieve or blend in a liquidiser. Melt the rest of the butter, stir in the flour to make a brown roux and gradually blend in the strained liquid, sieved meat and tomato purée. Bring to the boil and correct the seasoning. Serve the soup topped with the reserved kidney pieces.

MULLIGATAWNY SOUP

This highly spiced East Indian soup was extremely popular among British colonials and was brought to England in the nineteenth century. At that time it was sometimes served clear without any vegetables, but is today usually made as a thick soup.

4 oz (125 g) onions, sliced
4 oz (125 g) carrots, sliced
4 oz (125 g) turnips, sliced
2 oz (50 g) apples, sliced
2 oz (50 g) ham, chopped
2 oz (50 g) butter
1 oz (25 g) flour

Fry the onions, carrots, turnips, apples and ham in the butter until lightly brown. Mix in the flour, curry powder and paste, tomato purée and chutney. Gradually stir in the stock, add the bouquet of herbs, mace and clove. Bring the soup to the boil, skim and

1 dessertspoon curry powder
1 teaspoon curry paste
1 teaspoon tomato purée
1 tablespoon chutney,
  chopped
4 pints (2.3 litres) brown
  stock
Bouquet of herbs
1 blade mace
1 clove
Salt and pepper
5 fl oz (150 ml) double cream
Boiled rice, to serve

cook over a low heat for 30 to 40 minutes.

Remove the herbs, mace and clove and rub the soup through a sieve or blend in a liquidiser. Re-heat the soup, add salt and pepper to taste and stir in the cream, but do not let the soup come to the boil. Serve the soup topped with hot, fluffy, boiled rice.

Serves 8

Oxtail Soup

1½ oz (40 g) butter
1 whole oxtail, cut into small
  pieces
6 oz (175 g) carrots
6 oz (175 g) onions
6 oz (175 g) turnips
1 pint (600 ml) brown stock
3 pints (1.7 litres) water
1 shin bone
1½ oz (40 g) fine sago
Salt and pepper
Pinch dry mustard
2½ fl oz (60 ml) sherry
Cheese straws or bread sticks

Peel and roughly chop all the vegetables. Melt the butter and fry the oxtail and vegetables, turning frequently until brown. Add the stock and water with the shin bone; bring to the boil and skim. Cover and simmer gently for 3½ hours. Remove the bones from the oxtail and shred the meat.

Skim again and strain into a clean pan; add the sago and bring to the boil. Simmer gently for a few minutes until the sago is cooked. Season with salt, pepper and mustard. Add the sherry and serve at once with cheese straws or bread sticks.

...GER SOUP

..green peas are available, add 8 oz (250 g) of these to the soup
..ove the flavour.

..d tail of 1 conger eel

..bage, shredded
2 shallots, thinly sliced
8 oz (250 g) peas, shelled
  (optional)
1 bunch mixed fresh herbs,
  chopped
Parsley and thyme, chopped
Borage leaves, chopped
Marigold leaves, chopped
2 dessertspoons plain flour
2 pints (1 litre) milk
1 oz (25 g) butter
Marigold flower petals

Wash the head and tail of the conger thoroughly. Put them in a large saucepan, cover with water and add salt. Bring to the boil and simmer for 1 hour.

Remove the fish from the pan. Strain the liquid and return this to the pan, adding the cabbage, shallots, peas (if using), chopped mixed herbs, parsley and thyme, borage and marigold leaves. Simmer until the cabbage is tender.

Thicken the soup with the flour and cook for 5 minutes. Add the milk and butter and bring *nearly* to the boil. Throw marigold petals into the soup which is now ready to serve.

Jimmy MacNab *Serves 4*

CULLEN SKINK

Cullen is a small village on the Moray coast, and this thick fish broth – or skink – is the local speciality. Delicious it is too!

1½ lb (750 g) finnan haddock
  fillets
2 large onions, quartered
1 lb (500 g) boiled potatoes,
  sliced

Poach the haddock, onions and potatoes in the milk until cooked and all broken down. Strain and reserve the milk. Process the fish mixture in a liquidiser.

1½ pints (900 ml) milk
2 oz (50 g) butter
2 oz (50 g) flour
Salt and pepper
Cream
Chopped chives to garnish

Melt the butter and stir in the flour. Gradually add the reserved milk, stirring; add more milk if necessary. Then add the fish mixture and season to taste, taking care with the salt as the soup will already be fairly salty.

Lastly add the cream, being careful not to let the soup boil. Garnish with chopped chives.

Photograph facing page 24

Mike Simpson _____ *Serves 4 to 6*

CREAM OF SMOKED HADDOCK SOUP

A slightly more refined version of Cullen Skink.

2 finely chopped onions
1 lb (500 g) skinned smoked
 haddock, bones removed
 and cut into cubes
1 lb (500 g) raw potatoes,
 peeled and diced
3 pints (1.7 litres) fish stock
 (or water in an emergency)
8 fl oz (250 ml) milk
Double cream to garnish
Salt and pepper
Bay leaf and a sprig of parsley

Poach the fish, potatoes and onions in the fish stock or water until quite tender. Liquidise until very smooth, but do not strain through a sieve or you will lose all the nice little bits that give this soup its texture. Return the rather thick soup to a low heat and thin it down with the milk which has been warmed through with the bay leaf and parsley in it. Season to taste with salt and pepper and pour into bowls. Float a tablespoon of double cream on the top of each.

North Sea Fish Soup

4 scallops
3 oz (75 g) haddock fillet
3 oz (75 g) sea bass fillet
3 oz (75 g) hake fillet
3 oz (75 g) whole prawns
Lemon juice
Salt and pepper
2 pints (1.2 litres) fish stock
2 oz (50 g) shallots, finely
  chopped
2 egg yolks
2 tablespoons cream
1 tomato, skinned, seeded and
  diced
1 small bunch parsley, finely
  chopped

Cut the scallops and fish fillets into small pieces, shell the prawns and turn quickly in a little lemon juice. Season with salt and pepper.

Bring the stock to the boil and add the fish, shellfish and shallots. Just before it boils again, remove from the heat.

Mix the egg yolks and cream together and combine with the stock. Add the tomato and parsley. Serve the soup immediately.

West Bay Seafood Soup

The basis of this soup is a good fish stock which can easily be made using the slightly salted water that lobster or crab has been boiled in along with any shells and legs and a few lemon slices.

2 onions, chopped
2–3 cloves garlic, crushed
2 oz (50 g) butter
2½ lb (1.25 kg) mixed
  monkfish, cod, whiting,
  plaice

In a heavy saucepan, cook the onions and garlic in the butter until soft. Cut the fish into smallish pieces and add, with the shellfish, to the pan. Let this simmer, but not brown, add the tomato purée, tinned tomatoes, potatoes,

A few scallops and prawns
1 tablespoon tomato purée
1 × 14 oz (400 g) tin
  tomatoes, chopped
1 lb (500 g) potatoes, cubed
1 teaspoon cayenne pepper
1 bouquet garni
Lemon juice
1 glass dry white wine
Salt and pepper
4 pints (2.25 litres) fish stock
  or water

cayenne, bouquet garni, some lemon juice and the wine. Stir together gently and season to taste with salt and pepper, and more lemon juice if necessary. Add the fish stock, heat through, taste again and serve.

Serves 4

SCALLOP SOUP

2 pints (1 litre) water
6 fl oz (175 ml) dry white
  wine
1 shallot, thinly sliced or 1
  tablespoon thinly sliced
  spring onion
$\frac{1}{8}$ teaspoon powdered saffron
$\frac{1}{8}$ teaspoon curry powder
$\frac{1}{4}$ teaspoon dry mustard
$1\frac{1}{2}$ teaspoons salt
$\frac{1}{2}$ teaspoon pepper
8 oz (250 g) shelled scallops
4 tablespoons double cream
2 teaspoons chopped chives or
  $\frac{1}{2}$ teaspoon paprika

In a non-aluminium 4 pint (2 litre) pan put the water, wine, shallot or spring onion, saffron, curry powder, mustard, salt and pepper. Bring the liquid to the boil, cover and simmer for 15 minutes. Add the scallops, cover and simmer for just 5 minutes more. Purée the contents in a liquidiser, half at a time; the scallops do not purée completely but remain in tiny pieces.

Return the soup to the pan and add the cream; stir thoroughly. Re-heat, but do not boil. When ladling soup from the pan, make sure that you stir up the bottom to include pieces of scallop which will have collected there.

Pour into individual soup bowls and sprinkle with chives or paprika. Serve quite warm, but not hot.

GOWER OYSTER SOUP

A traditional Welsh way of economically combining easily available local ingredients. You could, of course, use chicken stock; but with so many sheep in Wales, mutton or lamb was more normal.

1 large onion, sliced
Pinch of mace
Salt and pepper
3 pints (1.7 litres) de-fatted mutton or lamb broth or stock
2 tablespoons butter
2 tablespoons flour
4 dozen prepared oysters
Croûtons of fried bread

Simmer the onion, mace, salt and pepper in the mutton broth for about 30 minutes, until the onion is quite soft. Strain the soup and reserve the liquor.

Heat the butter in a saucepan, stir in the flour and gradually add the strained broth, stirring well to avoid lumps. When smooth, let it simmer very gently for 10 minutes, put the prepared oysters into a tureen or into individual bowls and pour the boiling soup over.

Serve at once with triangles of crustless bread fried until golden in oil.

COCKLE AND MUSSEL CHOWDER

2 dozen cockles
2 dozen mussels
3 carrots, finely chopped
2 onions, finely chopped
Butter
2 medium potatoes, cut into $\frac{1}{2}$ in. (1 cm) cubes
Milk
Fresh thyme, marjoram, parsley and chives

Thoroughly clean and scrape the cockles and mussels, discarding any that do not close when tapped or are damaged or broken. Boil them in a little water until cooked. Remove from their shells and reserve the cooking liquid.

Fry the carrots and onions in a little butter. Add the reserved cooking liquid and the potatoes. Simmer for about 20 minutes.

Now add the cockles and mussels and a little milk. Finally add the fresh herbs and simmer for a further 20 minutes.

Photograph facing page 24

2

FISH

I could not restrain a wistful sigh. 'Jeeves is a
wonder.' 'A marvel.' 'What a brain!' 'Size nine-and-
a-quarter, I should say.' 'He eats a lot of fish.'

P. G. WODEHOUSE, *THANK YOU, JEEVES.*

COD IN CREAM SAUCE

Small new potatoes and fresh green summer vegetables would be ideal accompaniments to this delicately flavoured dish.

4 cod steaks or fillets
4 oz (125 g) butter
10 fl oz (300 ml) fish stock
1 tablespoon flour
2½ fl oz (60 ml) cream
½ dessertspoon lemon juice
Salt and pepper
Watercress to garnish

Wash and dry the fish carefully. Melt 1 oz (25 g) of the butter and fry the cod quickly on both sides without browning. Add the stock, cover and simmer gently for about 12 minutes. Lift out the cod, reserving the stock, and arrange on a hot dish. Melt 1 oz (25 g) of the remaining butter and stir in the flour; gradually add the stock and bring the sauce to the boil, stirring continuously. Simmer for 4 to 5 minutes. Add the cream, lemon juice, remaining butter and salt and pepper to taste; strain the sauce over the fish. Garnish with watercress and serve.

Billy Mackesy

SALT COD OR LING

Billy likes to serve this with fried potatoes and cabbage cakes – a version of Bubble and Squeak (see page 196) – though, of course, plain boiled potatoes would be very good too.

1 generous piece salt cod or
ling
Onions, sliced
Onions, whole and stuck with
cloves
Carrots, sliced
Parsley
1½ pints (850 ml) milk

Soak the salt cod or ling in cold water overnight, then rinse thoroughly under fresh water. Simmer the fish in fresh water for 10 minutes and strain.

Transfer the fish to a shallow tray. Add sliced raw onions and several whole onions stuck with cloves, sliced carrots and parsley (the quantities will depend on the size of the piece of fish). Cover with milk, add 2 cloves and some pepper and simmer for about 20 minutes, or until the fish is cooked and tender. Remove the fish and vegetables to a serving plate and thicken the remaining milk with a little nut of flour and butter mixed together. Strain this sauce over the fish and vegetables, and garnish with parsley.

Margaret Vaughan — *Serves 3 to 4*

COD'S CHEEKS AND TONGUES

This is an old West Country dish, and remarkably delicious. The cheeks are just as succulent as scallops, and only a fraction of the cost. Use the heads to make a fish stock (see page 87).

1 lb (500 g) cod's cheeks and
   tongues
Flour
Egg
Breadcrumbs
Butter

For the gooseberry and
   tarragon sauce:
4 lb (2 kg) gooseberries
1 pint (600 ml) water
2 lb (1 kg) sugar
3 fl oz (75 ml) tarragon
   vinegar

For the tailings:
1 lb (500 g) potatoes
Milk
Seasoned flour

Trim and thoroughly clean the cod's cheeks and tongues. Dip in flour, egg and breadcrumbs, then sauté in butter until golden brown.

Serve with hot tangy gooseberry sauce and tailings.

Top and tail the gooseberries and bring to the boil in the water. Simmer for 20 minutes. Add the sugar to the pulp and again bring to the boil. Simmer for a further 25 minutes, then leave to cool. Add the tarragon vinegar and pour into a sterilised earthenware jar. Seal and store for 10 days before using. You can serve the sauce hot or cold.

Using a potato peeler, peel the skins thickly from the potatoes. Dip the pieces of peel into milk and seasoned flour. Deep-fry until crisp.

DOVER SOLE

A fresh Dover sole is the finest flat fish there is. The flesh is firm and white, it comes easily away from the bone and is a pleasure to eat. A frozen fish is no substitute. I think that the two best ways to cook a really good sole are grilling or frying in butter. Either way you must first prepare your sole.

With a sharp knife make an incision under the black skin at the tail end and then, with a strong tug, rip off the skin. Turn the fish over and scrape the scales off the outer skin, cut an incision just behind the head and remove the innards and then, with a pair of scissors, trim off the tail and the little bits of fin and bone that run along the sides of the fish. If you want to grill or fry your sole in butter, but you don't like bones, which, as I have already said, are easy to deal with in this fish, then by all means fillet the little beauty, though in my view a sole must be cooked on the bone. (Incidentally, plaice, lemon sole and similar flat fish should be prepared in the same way, and it is worth bearing in mind, because sole is so expensive, that it is better to have a fresh plaice or lemon sole than a frozen Dover sole.)

First, then, to grill a sole. Prepare the flesh as I have described and, with a sharp knife, make a couple of diamond-shaped slashes in the white skin. Season with a little salt and pepper and brush with unsalted melted butter. Make sure that your grill is already very hot and put the fish under the grill, white skin side up. (If you have the kind of grill where the heat comes from underneath as in, say, a charcoal grill, place the fish white skin side down.) Keep the thin end of the fish – that is, the tail – furthest away from the heat so that it doesn't dry out before the thicker head end is cooked. A fish weighing about 1 lb (500 g), will probably need a cooking time of about 6 minutes on each side. After the first 6 minutes, turn the fish over, brush it with a little more butter and continue cooking. Add a little more salt and pepper.

You can serve this with a good wedge of lemon and some melted unsalted butter served separately in a jug; or, of course, you could melt parsley or anchovy butter over it. Alternatively, you can always serve it with a béarnaise or tartare sauce (see page 91). But to my mind it needs no more than just melted butter and the lemon juice. Serve it with the white skin side up – it will have been attractively charred by the bars of the grill.

For a sole fried in butter (sole *meunière*), prepare the fish as before. Wash it well and with fresh running water and dry it very carefully. Season the fish with salt and pepper and dredge it lightly in flour. In a pan large enough to take the fish, heat some clarified unsalted butter. (To make this, melt some unsalted butter in a saucepan and when the scum has floated to the surface, remove it and pour off the clear melted butter, avoiding the milky whey that has settled at the bottom.) Cook the fish in the clarified butter for 5 to 6 minutes on each side, taking care that the butter does not burn. Now take the sole out and place it on some kitchen paper to remove excess fat. Throw away the residue from the frying pan, clean it quickly and pop in a fresh lump of unsalted butter. As the butter begins to foam and turn very slightly brown, pop the sole back into the pan, add a squeeze of lemon juice and a pinch of finely chopped parsley, and eat at once.

These are simple ways of cooking a luxurious dish and they need little accompaniment – some new potatoes, one lightly cooked fresh green vegetable and, of course, the best white wine you can afford. It would be a pity to spoil the fish for a ha'porth of plonk.

Photograph facing page 73

Serves 3 to 4

STUFFED GURNARD

1–1½ lb (500–750 g) gurnards
3 oz (75 g) minced veal or chicken
Lemon juice
Coriander or parsley, chopped
Salt and pepper
1½–2 oz (40–50 g) melted butter
3 rashers bacon

Clean and wash the fish thoroughly; cut off the fins and remove the gills and eyes. Season the minced veal or chicken with lemon juice and chopped coriander or parsley to taste. Stuff the fish with the mixture and sew up the openings or secure with fine skewers. Season with salt and pepper. Curve the tails round and fasten in the mouths; arrange the gurnards in a buttered fireproof dish and pour the remaining butter over. Lay the bacon rashers over the fish; cover with a lid or foil and cook in the oven at gas mark 4, 350°F (180°C) for about 40 minutes.

HADDOCK WITH CHEESE STUFFING

4 haddock fillets
Lemon juice
Seasoned flour
1 egg, lightly beaten
Breadcrumbs and grated cheese
to coat
1½oz (40 g) melted butter
Parsley sprigs and lemon slices
to garnish

For the stuffing:
4 oz (125 g) grated cheese
2 oz (50 g) fresh white
breadcrumbs
2–3 oz (50–75 g) chopped
parsley
1 egg, lightly beaten
Salt and pepper

Pre-heat the oven to gas mark 5, 375°F (190°C).

Wipe the fish fillets, sprinkle with lemon juice and dust with seasoned flour.

To make the stuffing, mix the grated cheese with the breadcrumbs and parsley; bind with the egg and season with salt and pepper. Divide into four equal portions.

Spread the stuffing over the fish fillets and roll up, securing with wooden cocktail sticks. Brush the rolls with beaten egg and coat with breadcrumbs mixed with grated cheese. Lay the rolls in a buttered ovenproof dish and pour over the melted butter. Bake in the oven for about 30 minutes. Serve garnished with parsley and lemon.

KEDGEREE

Another stalwart of the British repertoire that was brought from India where it was a favourite among the loyal servants of the Empire.

2 lb (1 kg) smoked haddock
1 sprig parsley
1 bay leaf
2 lemons
Peppercorns
2 oz (50 g) butter

Put the haddock with the parsley, bay leaf, 1 lemon cut into slices and a few peppercorns into a pan; cover with water, bring to the boil and simmer until the fish is tender. Drain, remove the skin and bones from the fish and

4 oz (125 g) onions, chopped
1 lb (500 g) long-grain rice
2 pints (1 litre) fish stock
4 hard-boiled eggs
Salt and pepper
Curry powder or grated
    nutmeg
Chopped parsley to garnish

flake the flesh. Melt the butter in a deep pan and fry the onions gently for 5 minutes. Add the rice and fish stock; bring to the boil and simmer for 20 minutes.

Slice 3 of the hard-boiled eggs and stir gently into the rice with the flaked fish. Add salt, pepper and curry powder or grated nutmeg to taste. Add the juice of the remaining lemon. Pile the kedgeree into a hot dish and garnish with parsley and the remaining hard-boiled egg, chopped.

Myrtle Allen   *Serves 1*

PLAICE IN HERB BUTTER

1 plaice
Salt and pepper
$\frac{1}{2}$–1 oz (15–25 g) butter
1 teaspoon finely chopped
    mixed herbs (parsley,
    chives, fennel, thyme
    leaves)

Wash the fish and clean the inside thoroughly. With a very sharp knife cut through the skin, right round the fish, $\frac{1}{2}$ in. (1 cm) from the edge. Be careful to cut right through and make sure the side cuts join up at the tail or you will be in trouble later on. Sprinkle the fish with salt and pepper and lay it in $\frac{1}{4}$ in. (6 mm) water in a shallow baking tin. Bake in the oven at gas mark 6, 400°F (200°C) for 20 to 30 minutes, according to the size of the fish. The water should have just evaporated as the fish is cooked.

Meanwhile, melt the butter and stir in the herbs. Just before serving, pull the skin off the fish (it will tear badly if not properly cut) and spoon over the butter.

FISH AND CHIPS

The Great British Fish and Chips only came into being in the late nineteenth century after the dreaded French had invented the fried chip potato. Previously, battered and deep-fried fish was served with mushy peas, chiefly by street vendors. Curiously, the French, normally so disparaging about our food, adore the fish and the chips which they regard as uniquely British. No doubt many books have been written on the subject and even the editor of *The Good Food Guide* has wandered around the country looking for the perfect version. I offer you mine without prejudice or compromise.

First, the batter: Beat about 4 oz (100 g) best-quality plain flour into a smooth paste with about $\frac{1}{4}$ pint (150 ml) water *only*, then add a dash of finest malt vinegar. An alternative basic coating batter is described on page 92.

Second, the fish: Choose skinned fillets from a large, firm-fleshed, fresh North Sea cod, well washed and thoroughly dried.

Third, the fat: You must have a pan full of best-quality beef dripping.

Fourth, the chips: Cut these from firm, waxy-textured potatoes. We used to use Golden Wonder until they ceased to become widely available. First rinse them thoroughly under running cold water, and dry them very carefully.

Fifth, the method: Detailed instructions for cooking perfect chips are given on page 192. The important thing is to plunge the chips into hot fat (360°F, 167°C) until they are almost cooked, but not browned. Lift them out and strain them carefully. Now re-heat the fat, coat your fish in the batter and cook a piece at a time until it is crispy and golden. Then re-heat the fat once again and pop in the chips to crisp and brown off.

Like a perfect omelette, fish and chips should be served without delay or deference to the guests: as each individual piece is ready, serve it. Let your guests help themselves to the best sea salt and the finest malt vinegar.

Photograph facing page 56

Fish and Chips

ᴀ Bass with Fresh Salmon and Asparagus

1 lb (500 g) sea bass fillets
Salt and pepper
1 egg white
1¼ pints (750 ml) double
  cream
4 oz (125 g) unsalted butter
8 asparagus spears
8 small thin slices salmon
10 fl oz (300 ml) fish stock
2 glasses white wine
1 small bunch chervil
Lemon juice

Mince the fish. Place it with some salt in a pan over ice and beat. Add the egg white and continue to beat for a few minutes more. Slowly add 1 pint (600 ml) of the double cream, beating all the time. The mousse resulting should be light and should just hold its own weight when dropped from a spoon. Season with salt and pepper. Butter 4 ramekin moulds and fill with the mousse. Cover each with a piece of buttered aluminium foil.

Place the ramekins side by side in a roasting tin and add boiling water to three-quarters of their height. Place in a slow oven, gas mark 3, 325°F (160°C), and allow to cook for 10 to 12 minutes, until slightly firm to the touch.

To prepare the garnish, trim the asparagus spears so that they are all 4 in. (10 cm) long. Quickly blanch them in boiling water and refresh in ice. Roll the salmon slices around the asparagus spears, leaving the top and bottom showing. Place the spears in a buttered dish and cover with fish stock. Poach for about 2 minutes and strain off the stock and reserve.

To make the sauce, reduce the white wine, fish stock and chervil stalks until almost evaporated. Add the remaining 5 fl oz (150 ml) of double cream and cook to a sauce consistency. Drop in a few knobs of butter and flavour with lemon juice and salt and pepper to taste.

Turn out the ramekins on to 4 plates with the asparagus spears. Cover the mousse with the sauce and place a spring of chervil on top of each one. Serve immediately.

Roast Welsh Salmon (page 69)

POACHED TURBOT WITH GRANVILLE SAUCE

1 medium onion, finely sliced
2 tablespoons chopped parsley
4 thick turbot cutlets
Salt and pepper

For the Granville sauce:
1 shallot or small onion,
  chopped
1 tinned anchovy fillet,
  pounded
2 tablespoons sherry
2 teaspoons wine vinegar
6 peppercorns
Pinch each nutmeg and mace
1 tablespoon butter
1 tablespoon flour
6 tablespoons cream

Lay the onion on the bottom of a pan, add the parsley and put the turbot cutlets on top. Season well with salt and pepper and pour over enough water barely to cover. Lay some foil or a lid on top and poach very gently for 15 to 20 minutes, depending on the thickness of the cutlets. Leave in the water until needed.

Meanwhile, make the sauce by simmering in a double boiler the first 6 ingredients until the shallot is soft. In another saucepan melt the butter, stir in the flour and mix until smooth. Then add the first mixture and simmer, stirring all the time. When smooth and cooked, add the cream. Stir well, strain or liquidise and serve warm with the drained fish.

George McCalpine

ROAST TURBOT WITH LOBSTER SAUCE

1 carrot, finely diced
1 courgette, finely diced
1 leek, finely diced
1 shallot, finely diced
Butter
4 × 6 oz (175 g) turbot fillets
4 oz (125 g) caul
Fennel sprigs to garnish

Pre-heat the oven to gas mark 6, 400°F (200°C). Fry the diced vegetables in butter; allow to cool. Fold the fillets of turbot over and top with the vegetables. Divide the caul into 4, and wrap each fillet, with its vegetables, in a piece. Roast in the oven for 15 to 20 minutes or until cooked.

For the lobster sauce:
1 shallot, chopped
2 tablespoons dry white wine
8 fl oz (250 ml) lobster sauce
  (see page 91)
4 oz (125 g) butter

To make the sauce, sweat the shallot till brown. Add the wine and reduce. Add the lobster sauce and finally whisk in the butter.

To present the dish, strain a little sauce on to each of 4 plates. Place a roasted turbot fillet in the centre and garnish with a sprig of fresh fennel.

Aidan McCormack   *Serves 4*

FILLET OF TURBOT IN RED WINE SAUCE WITH SPINACH PASTIES

4 × 3 oz (75 g) fillets turbot
4 tablespoons olive oil

For the sauce:
6 oz (175 g) unsalted butter
2 lb (1 kg) turbot bones
4 oz (125 g) chopped shallots
2 oz (50 g) chopped
  mushrooms
1 pint (600 ml) red wine
1 pint (600 ml) fish stock
10 fl oz (300 ml) veal stock
2½ fl oz (60 ml) cream
Salt and pepper

For the spinach pasties:
4 oz (125 g) cooked spinach
1 oz (25 g) mushrooms, cut
  into julienne strips
1 oz (25 g) butter
6 oz (175 g) puff pastry
1 egg for egg wash

First make the sauce. Melt 1 oz (25 g) of the butter in a large pan and sweat the turbot bones, shallots and mushrooms for 5 minutes. Add the red wine, fish stock and veal stock, and reduce to one third of its original volume. Strain into a clean pan and reduce again until syrupy. Add the cream and bring to the boil. Whisk in the remaining butter, season and strain. Keep warm.

Pre-heat the oven to gas mark 5, 375°F (190°C). Mix together the spinach, mushrooms and butter for the pasty fillings. Divide the pastry into 4, and cut each piece out into a rectangle. Place a spoonful of the filling in the centre of each, brush the edges with egg and fold together to make a pasty. Glaze with the egg wash and bake in the oven for 10–15 minutes.

Fry the turbot fillets gently in oil. Pour a circle of sauce onto each serving plate and place a fillet in the centre with a spinach pasty to garnish.

POACHED JOHN DORY

2–3 lb (1–1.5 kg) John Dory
White wine and water in
equal parts
Lemon juice
Olive oil
Salt and pepper

Clean the fish and remove heads and fins. Place in a fish kettle and cover with equal parts wine and water; simmer gently until tender. Leave the fish to cool, then remove skin and bones. Arrange whole or in fillets on a serving dish and chill. Serve with a dressing made from two parts strained lemon juice to one part oil; season with salt and freshly milled pepper.

Paul Reed

SUPREME OF JOHN DORY WITH SPRING VEGETABLES

$\frac{1}{2}$ oz (15 g) courgette
$\frac{1}{2}$ oz (15 g) carrot
$\frac{1}{2}$ oz (15 g) turnip
$\frac{1}{2}$ oz (15 g) leek, white part
only, blanched
1 × 1 lb (500 g) John Dory
$\frac{1}{2}$ oz (15 g) blanched spinach
$1\frac{1}{2}$ oz (40 g) salmon mousse
1 oz (25 g) lamb's caul fat
(see page 62)
1 pint (600 ml) fish stock
4 fl oz (120 ml) lobster sauce
(see page 91)
$\frac{1}{2}$ oz (15 g) tomato pulp
Chervil

Cut the courgette, carrot and turnip into small even shapes and trim the leek, using the white part only. Blanch the vegetables.

Fillet the John Dory, leaving the tail and one bone intact, so as to keep both fillets on the fish. Place the spinach on the fillets, then sandwich the fish back together with the salmon mousse. Encase the fish with caul fat.

Steam the fish for 20 minutes over most of the fish stock and poach the vegetables in the small remaining amount. Place the fish on a serving dish, surround it with the Lobster Sauce and garnish with the cooked vegetables, tomato pulp and chervil.

Salad of Endive Lettuce with Steamed Red Mullet and Coriander Dressing

5 fl oz (150 ml) olive oil
2 cloves garlic
2 sprigs thyme
1 tablespoon coriander seeds
4 firm ripe tomatoes, skinned,
  de-seeded and diced
Salt and black pepper
2 medium red mullets, scaled
  and filleted
1 small endive lettuce

Photograph facing page 41

Make the dressing by warming the olive oil with the garlic cloves, thyme and cracked coriander seeds. Allow to cool and then remove the garlic and add the diced tomato. Season with black pepper and a little salt.

Steam the mullet until just cooked. Place it on a bed of endive lettuce and spoon the dressing over.

Elvers in Egg

If ever you find yourself one March midnight on the banks of the River Parret on the Somerset Levels and you see lots of shadowy figures with strange nets loafing about, you will know that the elvers (young eels) are running. And should you be lucky enough to acquire some, this is how you cook them – it's truly delicious! Be warned, however, that this is not a recipe for the squeamish.

8 oz (250 g) live elvers
Butter
6 eggs
Salt and pepper

I am sorry to tell you that you must kill the elvers by dropping them into boiling water for a second or two. Then drain and dry them carefully.

Melt a big knob of butter in a large frying pan. Whisk the eggs as for an omelette, add the elvers and tip the lot into the pan. Stir round till the eggs have set. Some like the finished dish to resemble an omelette, others prefer the eggs to be scrambled: the choice is yours, but I recommend the omelette way. Season with salt and pepper and serve with toast or fried bread.

CONGER EEL STEW

For this recipe a cut of conger eel from just behind the gut cavity is best, as this gives even, round 'steaks'. The conger is studded with slivers of garlic and wrapped in caul fat, which gives the fish a wonderful smooth moistness. The problem, of course, is getting caul fat – you need a good butcher. If you can get hold of it, buy plenty: it freezes well and you can use it for lining pâtés and as a casing for faggots. To make the caul manageable, put it in a bowl of warm water to which you have added a little vinegar. If you can't obtain caul, wrap 4 rashers of streaky bacon around the conger and secure them with string.

6 cloves garlic
2½ lb (1.25 kg) section of conger eel, skinned
Caul fat or 4 rashers of streaky bacon
4 oz (125 g) carrots
4 oz (125 g) celery
2 oz (50 g) butter
4 oz (125 g) button onions
Salt and freshly ground black pepper

Pre-heat the oven to gas mark 8, 450°F (230°C). Slice 2 of the cloves of garlic thinly, make incisions all over the fish and insert the garlic slivers. Wrap the fish in the caul fat or tie the bacon around it.

Chop the carrots and celery into $1\frac{1}{2} \times \frac{1}{2}$ in. (3×1 cm) pieces. Melt the butter in a heavy casserole, add the carrots, celery, onions, and the rest of the garlic and stew gently for 20 minutes or so with the lid on. Now add the conger, roll around in the butter and season with salt and pepper. Transfer to the oven and cook with the lid on for 20 minutes. Baste the fish with the butter twice during that time.

After 20 minutes, baste once more and remove the lid. Cook for a further 10 minutes with the lid off. Serve up like a joint of meat on a large oval dish, surrounded by the vegetables and with the juice poured all around. Carve it lengthways in long slices.

CONGER PIE

$1\frac{1}{2}$–2 lb (750 g–1 kg) conger
   eel, sliced
Salt and pepper
1 oz (25 g) flour
1 tablespoon chopped parsley
5 fl oz (150 ml) milk
2 hard-boiled eggs, quartered
8 oz (250 g) short or flaky
   pastry

Pre-heat the oven to gas mark 5, 375°F (190°C). Wash the slices of fish and cut them into squares about the size of an egg. Dry them and roll in seasoned flour. Place them in a roasting tin, cover with greased paper and bake for 20 minutes.

Let the fish cool, then put into a pie dish with the parsley, milk and hard-boiled eggs and cover with pastry.

Make a hole in the centre and decorate with leaves made from left-over pastry. Bake for a further 20 minutes.

CONGER EEL IN CIDER

$1\frac{1}{2}$ lb (750 g) skinned eel
$\frac{1}{4}$ lb (125 g) chopped onions
1 oz (25 g) butter
1 oz (25 g) flour
1 pt (600 ml) cider
Salt and pepper

Cut the eel into 3 to 4 pieces, wash and dry well. Fry the onions in the butter until golden. Add the eel pieces and brown lightly. Stir in the flour and cook until brown. Gradually stir in the cider, season with salt and pepper and cover the pan with a lid or foil. Bake in the oven for 1 hour. Serve the fish in the sauce, thickening it further with flour and butter if necessary.

ANCHOVIES, PILCHARDS, SPRATS AND WHITEBAIT

These small oily fish are all members of the herring family (pilchards are large sardines). They require little preparation before cooking and are good snacks or starters.

To grill these fish (with the exception of whitebait, which should only be deep-fried), simply scale them, then slit open the stomach and remove the intestines (something the French and Spanish don't do because they like the flavour of the liver and intestines – but we're a bit too squeamish for that!). Wash and dry them carefully, season inside and out with salt and pepper, brush with melted butter and pop under a very hot grill (or on a barbecue) for a couple of minutes on each side.

Serve with wedges of lemon or lime and brown bread and butter.

Serves 6 to 8

PILCHARD HOT-POT

3 lb (1.5 kg) pilchards
4 oz (125 g) butter
2 oz (50 g) flour
1 teaspoon tomato purée
2 pints (1 litre) milk
Salt and pepper
1 lb (500 g) parboiled
  potatoes, sliced
2 oz (50 g) Cheddar cheese,
  grated

Clean and scale the fish, split open and remove the bones. Lay the fish in a greased ovenproof dish.

Melt 2 oz (50 g) of the butter in a pan, stir in the flour and tomato purée, then add the milk, salt and pepper. Stir until the sauce boils and thickens. Pour the sauce over the fish and arrange the sliced potatoes on top; dot with the remaining butter and sprinkle with cheese. Bake in the oven at gas mark 4, 350°F (180°C), for 15 minutes. Place under a hot grill to brown just before serving.

ANCHOVIES IN EGG AND BREADCRUMBS

12 anchovies
Milk
2 oz (50 g) seasoned flour
1 egg
2 oz (50 g) white breadcrumbs
Butter and oil for frying

Wash and dry the fish thoroughly; dip them in milk and then in seasoned flour. Next coat them in beaten egg, then in breadcrumbs. Fry until crisp and golden brown. Serve at once.

SPRATS IN BATTER

2 lb (1 kg) sprats
1 quantity basic batter (see
  page 92)
Fat or oil for deep-frying
Parsley sprigs to garnish

Wash and dry the sprats; dip in the prepared batter. Deep-fry in hot fat or oil until brown and crisp. Garnish with deep-fried parsley sprigs.

DEVILLED WHITEBAIT

2 lb (1 kg) whitebait
Milk
2 oz (50 g) seasoned flour
Fat or oil for deep-frying
1 teaspoon cayenne pepper

Wash and carefully dry the whitebait, then dip them in the milk and coat with seasoned flour. Deep-fry in hot fat or oil until crisp and sprinkle with cayenne before serving.

MACKEREL WITH GOOSEBERRY SAUCE

The combination of mackerel – fried, grilled or roasted – and gooseberry sauce is reputed to have been brought to England at the time of the Norman conquest.

4 medium mackerel
Salt and pepper
1½ oz (40 g) butter
Gooseberry sauce (see page 90)

Gut and clean the fish and place in a buttered ovenproof dish. Season with salt and pepper and dot with butter. Cover with buttered greaseproof paper or foil and bake in the oven at gas mark 4, 350°F (180°C), for 20 to 30 minutes.

Remove from the oven; split the mackerel and remove the backbones. Serve with hot gooseberry sauce and small new potatoes.

Photograph facing page 72

HERRINGS AND APPLES

Herring enthusiasts are sharply divided in their views on when this delectable fish is at its tastiest. Some maintain the lean spring herring is the choicest, others that only in the fattened fish in early autumn can the true flavour be appreciated.

4 large herrings
Salt and pepper
2 oz (50 g) onion, finely chopped
8 oz (250 g) dessert apples, peeled, cored and grated
½ oz (15 g) sugar
3 oz (75 g) white breadcrumbs
2 oz (50 g) melted butter

Clean and bone the herrings, leaving them whole, and season with salt and pepper. Mix the onion and apples with the sugar and two thirds of the breadcrumbs. Divide this mixture into 4 portions and stuff into the herrings. Secure the openings. Lay the stuffed herrings in a buttered ovenproof dish, sprinkle with the remaining breadcrumbs and pour over half the

melted butter. Bake in the oven at gas mark 4, 350°F (180°C), for 20 minutes. Pour over the remaining butter just before serving.

FRESH HERRING WITH MUSTARD SAUCE

1 herring per person
Salt and pepper
Melted butter

For the mustard sauce:
10 fl oz (300 ml) fish stock
1 glass wine
10 fl oz (300 ml) double
  cream
English mustard
Butter

Season the herrings with salt and pepper. Brush with melted butter and grill for a few minutes on each side until the fish is a golden brown colour.

To make the sauce, put the stock and wine in a pan and reduce to about one third of its original quantity. Add the cream and cook until of a sauce-like consistency. Add a little mustard to taste and a few knobs of butter for richness and adjust the seasoning. Strain the sauce through a fine sieve and serve separately.

Serves 4

HERRING BAKE

In really fresh herrings, the backbones come away easily if first pressed lightly along their length on the skin side.

4 herrings
1 oz (25 g) butter
Salt and pepper
¼ teaspoon made mustard
1 teaspoon tomato purée
10 fl oz (300 ml) single cream

Clean and fillet the herrings. Divide the butter equally into 8 pieces and place a piece on each fillet; roll up, skin side outwards. Stand the herring rolls upright in an ovenproof dish and season with salt and pepper.

Mix the mustard, tomato purée and cream to a smooth sauce and pour over the fish. Bake in the oven at gas mark 4, 350°F (180°C), for 20 minutes.

PICKLED HERRINGS

A favourite fish course, delicious served with brown bread and butter. Salting was the traditional way of preserving herrings when they were plentiful. Be sure to start these at least 11 days ahead.

4 lb (2 kg) salt herrings
3 large onions, chopped
1 tablespoon mixed herbs
1 tablespoon rosemary
1 tablespoon sweet paprika
1 tablespoon crushed chillies
Dill
Black and white peppercorns
6–8 cloves
3 tablespoons allspice
*2 pints (1 litre) good-quality
   malt vinegar*
*1¼ lb (625 g) dark brown
   sugar*

Cut the herrings in half, taking out the back fin as you go. Soak the fish in cold water for at least 36 hours.

Chop the herrings into 1–1½ in. (2.5–3.8 cm) pieces and mix well with the chopped onions. Next mix in all the other ingredients except for the vinegar and sugar and leave for 3 hours.

Boil the vinegar and sugar in a pan until the sugar has dissolved completely. Place the herring mixture into sterilised pickling jars and pour over the sweetened vinegar. Leave for 4 days, turning each jar upside down once daily to ensure that the vinegar penetrates all the fish. The herrings can be eaten after 4 days, but improve in flavour if left for longer.

BUTTERED TROUT

4 × 6 oz (175 g) trout
Salt
1 oz (25 g) seasoned flour
4 oz (125 g) unsalted butter
Lemon juice

Clean the fish; sprinkle with salt inside and out and leave for about 1 hour. Wipe the fish and coat with seasoned flour. Fry the trout in half the butter for 2 to 4 minutes on each side. Dry the trout on kitchen paper and clean the frying pan. Melt the rest of the butter and when it is foaming pop the trout back in with some lemon juice.

ROAST WELSH SALMON

This Welsh recipe is a delicious way of serving salmon hot.

1 × 4–5 lb (2–2.5 kg) salmon
grilse or 1 × 3 lb (1.5 kg)
tail-end
Salt and pepper
½ teaspoon grated nutmeg
2 bay leaves, spread with
butter
1 in. (2.5 cm) sprig fresh
rosemary
2 cloves
4 oz (125 g) plus 1 tablespoon
butter
½ large orange, finely sliced
½ lemon, finely sliced
1 tablespoon vinegar

Season the salmon well inside and out with salt and pepper and rub in the nutmeg. Tuck the buttered bay leaves, rosemary and cloves into the gullet or, if using a cut of salmon, put the bay leaves underneath and then the other spices and herbs on top. Rub the 4 oz (125 g) of butter all over, cover with paper or foil and roast in the oven at gas mark 4, 350°F (180°C), for 20 minutes to the lb (500 g), basting at least once with the juices. When cooked, remove the fish to a warmed dish and peel off the skin.

Put the tablespoon of butter, cut into small pieces, the slices of orange and lemon and the vinegar into a saucepan. Let the mixture boil up quickly and reduce on a fast flame until the fruit slices are soft and slightly brown at the edges and the gravy is reduced by about half. Serve separately in a sauceboat, first removing the lemon and orange slices and placing them alternately along the back of the fish.

Photograph facing page 57

COLD POACHED SALMON

The best way I know to enjoy cold salmon. There is no point in using frozen salmon: if you can't buy a fresh one, don't bother. Better a few fillets of fresh cod with anchovy butter or a good old-fashioned tinned salmon sandwich with cucumber and vinegar.

1 × 10 lb (5 kg) salmon
About 8 pints (4.5 litres) fish
  stock
1½ pints (850 ml) mayonnaise
2 cucumbers

Clean the salmon, put into a fish kettle and cover with the cold fish stock. Bring to the boil and simmer very gently for 10 minutes. Turn off the heat and leave to cool with the lid on the fish kettle.

Lift the cold salmon carefully from the liquid and remove the bones and skin from the body – leave the skin on the head. Arrange the fish on a suitably grand dish and coat with mayonnaise. Peel the cucumbers, cut in half lengthways, de-seed and slice thinly in crescent shapes. Lay the cucumber slivers, overlapping, on the mayonnaise to resemble fish scales.

Serves 4

PERCH WITH PARSLEY SAUCE

This dark green fish of lakes and rivers is distinguished by the broad black stripes on the skin and the fact that its scales are difficult to remove. It should be scaled at once after being caught; failing that, plunge the fish into boiling water for a few minutes, after which the skin can be peeled off complete with scales.

4 × 8 oz (250 g) perch
2 oz (50 g) butter
½ oz (15 g) onion, chopped
10 fl oz (300 ml) fish stock
1 tablespoon vinegar
½ teaspoon anchovy essence
1 bay leaf
Bouquet of herbs (thyme,
  parsley)
1 clove
1 oz (25 g) flour
Cream
½ oz (15 g) chopped parsley
Juice ½ lemon
Salt and pepper

Scale, gut and clean the fish and cut off the fins and gills. Melt half the butter in a pan and gently fry the onion until golden. Add the stock, vinegar, anchovy essence, bay leaf, bouquet of herbs and clove. Simmer for 10 minutes, then add the perch and cook gently for 10 minutes. Keep the fish warm.

Melt the remaining butter, add the flour and cook for 2 to 3 minutes. Gradually stir in the strained cooking liquid and bring to the boil, then simmer gently for 10 minutes, whisking all the while. Add a little cream and the parsley, lemon juice, salt and pepper. Pour the sauce over the fish and serve.

LLYN PADARN CHAR WITH BACON AND A PARSLEY SAUCE

Llyn Padarn is a very deep lake near the town of Llanberis in the Snowdonia mountain range. It's full of char, a fish belonging to the trout family – you could use small brown trout instead, unless you're lucky enough to have a fisherman in the family!

4 × 8 oz (250 g) char
12 rashers streaky bacon
Salt and pepper
Vegetable oil for frying
1 onion, finely chopped
Butter
10 fl oz (300 ml) cream
1 bunch parsley, chopped

Gut and wash the fish and pat dry with kitchen paper. Remove the heads if desired. Wrap each fish with 3 rashers of bacon and season with a little salt and pepper.

Heat the oil in a pan and fry the fish for approximately 10 minutes on each side.

Make the sauce by cooking the onion in a little butter until soft, add the cream and parsley and bring to the boil. Check the seasoning. Pour the sauce over the fish and serve immediately.

SUFFOLK PERCH

4 × 8 oz (250 g) perch
4 tablespoons cooking oil
4 tomatoes, skinned and
  chopped
2 medium onions, chopped
Sprig of thyme
Salt and pepper
4 oz (125 g) soft herring roes
2 oz (50 g) fresh brown
  breadcrumbs
15 fl oz (450 ml) dry Suffolk
  cider
2 teaspoons chopped parsley

Clean and gut the fish. Heat the oil in a flameproof casserole and add the tomatoes, onions, thyme, salt and pepper. Simmer over a low heat for 15 minutes. Mix the roes and breadcrumbs in a bowl. Add 1 tablespoon of the tomato and onion mixture, mix well and season. Stuff the fish with this mixture and place on top of the remaining mixture. Add the cider. Bake in the oven at gas 4, 350°F (180°C), for 40 minutes. Sprinkle with parsley.

NORTH SEA FISH PUDDING

10 oz (300 g) plaice fillets
10 oz (300 g) salmon fillets
10 oz (300 g) monkfish tail
1 egg white
3 teaspoons chopped chervil
* and parsley*
2 fl oz (50 ml) double cream
Juice of ½ lemon
1 fl oz (25 ml) dry white wine
Salt and pepper
3 large scallops
1 oz (25 g) melted butter

Trim the fish fillets and monkfish tail, place on a tray and chill in the freezer for 30 minutes: this will firm the flesh of the fish for slicing.

Cut 2 oz (50 g) of each type of fish and place in a food processor with the egg white, herbs, cream, lemon juice, wine and salt and pepper. Blend until the mixture becomes a firm mousse. Transfer to a bowl and put aside.

With a sharp filleting knife, slice the remaining fish fillets lengthways as thinly as possible, allowing 2 or 3 slices of each fish for each of 6 darioles or ramekins. Slice the scallops in half.

Brush the darioles with the melted butter. Inter-layer each dariole with the fish slices and the mousse, alternating each variety of fish and placing a scallop slice in the middle. When each dariole is full, seal with foil and with a fork prick several holes to ensure that steam escapes.

Place in a roasting tin holding enough hot water to reach halfway up the darioles. Cook in the oven at gas mark 7, 425°F (220°C), for 20 minutes. Turn on to a serving platter and serve with a sauce of your choice.

Mackerel with Gooseberry Sauce (page 66)

POACHED MIXED FISH

8 oz (250 g) turbot fillet
8 oz (250 g) salmon fillet
8 oz (250 g) monkfish
8 fresh scallops
8 mussels
8 fresh prawns

For the sauce:
1 shallot, chopped
1 glass Champagne
5 fl oz (150 ml) fish stock
5 fl oz (150 ml) double cream
1 oz (25 g) butter
Salt and pepper

To garnish:
Diced tomato flesh
Chopped chives
4 sprigs dill

Cut the turbot, salmon and monkfish into pieces the size of an average scallop. Lightly poach with the scallops and the mussels and the shallot in the Champagne and fish stock. Add the prawns to heat through. When cooked, remove the fish from the sauce and keep warm.

Reduce the cooking liquid, add the cream and boil vigorously until thickened. Lastly whisk in the butter and season with salt and pepper.

Arrange the fish in a mound in the centre of the serving plate. Strain and pour the sauce round the fish and garnish with tomato, chives and sprigs of dill. George makes elaborate nets from cucumber peel to complete the garnish, but I'll let you off this!

Grilled Dover Sole (page 52)

GRILLED SEAFOOD

In this recipe you can use 12 Mediterranean prawns or 36 North Atlantic prawns instead of the Dublin Bay variety. You can also substitute quite a few other types of fish for the grey mullet – steaks of conger eel, dogfish, tope or shark; or whole small mackerel, red mullet, sardines, pilchards, black breams, small John Dory, gurnard or sea bass.

2 × 1 lb (500 g) cooked
lobsters
24 Dublin Bay prawns
4 × 4 oz (125 g) monkfish
steaks
4 × 3 oz (75 g) grey mullet
steaks
Lemon wedges

For the marinade:
2 fl oz (50 ml) olive oil
1 teaspoon chopped fennel
3 bay leaves, cut into pieces
Salt and freshly ground black
pepper
Juice of $\frac{1}{4}$ lemon

For the fennel dressing:
5 fl oz (150 ml) olive oil
1 fl oz (25 ml) red wine
vinegar
$\frac{1}{2}$ teaspoon salt
Freshly ground black pepper
1 tablespoon chopped fennel
$\frac{1}{2}$ small onion, finely chopped

Mix all the dressing ingredients together.

At least 1 hour before cooking, put all the marinade ingredients in a shallow dish and add the fish steaks. Turn over in the marinade two or three times during the hour. Prepare and light your charcoal grill at least 40 minutes before cooking. Cut the lobsters in half lengthways and crack their claws.

Cook the fish steaks for about 3 minutes on each side. The lobsters and prawns, being cooked already, don't need to go on the grill for very long: they should just be warmed through. This also slightly chars the shells, giving the grillade a spectacular aroma which is one of the best attractions of the dish. Brush the shells with some of the marinade that you used for the fish and put the lobsters on the grill for about 2 minutes per side, prawns for about 1 minute.

Serve everything on one large serving dish. Add any of the marinade left to the dressing and pour over the cooked fish. Serve with lemon wedges and plenty of French bread to mop up the dressing.

DUBLIN BAY PRAWNS

Known also as prawns, langoustines or Norway lobsters, these shellfish have very little to do with Dublin Bay. It was simply that when the fishing boats which had accidentally caught them arrived in Dublin the fishermen sold them to street vendors there who peddled their wares from baskets – street traders of the kind immortalised by Julie Andrews – whoops, sorry, I mean Molly Malone – in her greatest hit, 'Alive, alive-oh'.

Dublin Bay prawns, rather like sole, salmon and lobster, certainly fall in that category of food that should be bought as fresh as possible and tampered with as little as possible. When you have the chance to buy fresh, live prawns, run home with them at once and plunge them into slightly salted boiling water. Let them boil until a foam or mousse covers the top of the saucepan. Switch off the heat straight away and leave the prawns in the hot water for a minute or two. Strain them, rinse them under warm water and eat still tepid with home-made mayonnaise or aïoli (garlic mayonnaise).

Alternatively, you could grill them. Simply cut them in half lengthways, brush the fish with a little melted butter and possibly a hint of finely chopped garlic, sprinkle with finely chopped fresh parsley and pop them under a very hot grill until the flesh turns from translucent to milky white.

That, in my view, is all you need to do with fresh prawns. They can be served as a starter or with a bowl of wonderful fresh salad to make a fine lunch. Grilled prawns with a little savoury rice are a delicious supper dish. It's up to you, but in any event they must not be overcooked.

On the other hand, you could try Paul Reed's sophisticated stew of prawns – but first you must make some fish consommé. For this, make some basic fish stock (see page 87), then strain it through muslin and continue simmering (remove any scum that floats to the surface from time to time) to reduce it to one third of its original volume. Then add a generous pinch of saffron to it to give flavour and colour. Now read on ...

A Light Stew of Dublin Bay Prawns and Asparagus in a Saffron Soup

*4 large Dublin Bay prawns,
  with head and claws on,
  but body peeled*
*5 fl oz (150 ml) fish stock (see
  page 87)*
*5 fl oz (150 ml) saffron fish
  consommé (see page 75)*
*½ oz (15 g) each carrot,
  courgette and turnip,
  shaped and blanched*
*8 heads English asparagus,
  blanched*
Salt and pepper
1 sprig each red and green basil

Photograph facing page 40

First poach the prawns in the fish stock. Remove and keep warm. Add the saffron consommé to the stock and re-heat. Add the vegetables and asparagus. Adjust the seasoning.

Arrange the prawns on a dish and pour over the saffron consommé with the vegetables and asparagus. Garnish with basil.

Crowns of Prawns with Fresh Tomato Sauce

For the tomato sauce:
6 tomatoes, chopped
A few sprigs of basil
A drop of olive oil
Salt and pepper
1 teaspoon sugar

For the crowns:
4 leaves filo pastry
1 oz (25 g) melted butter

To make the tomato sauce, combine all the ingredients and cook gently until mushy. Pass through a liquidiser and then strain. Allow to cool.

To make the crowns, brush the filo pastry with melted butter and fold to make a double layer. Place over the base of small, upside-down quiche moulds – about 4 in. (10 cm) in diameter and trim into the shape of a

Mixed lettuces
Walnut oil
Salt and pepper
16 Dublin Bay prawns,
  shelled
Butter
Sprigs of fennel to garnish

crown. Cook in the oven at gas mark 5, 375°F (190°C), until light golden.

Carefully remove the pastry from the moulds and set on a plate surrounded by tomato sauce. Toss the lettuces in the walnut oil and place in the pastry crown.

Lightly season the prawns and fry in butter. Arrange the prawns on top of the salad and garnish with sprigs of fennel.

Serves 6 to 8

POTTED SHRIMPS

'Potted' shellfish is one of the great delicacies of all time when freshly made. Here is a recipe using shrimps, but you can adapt it slightly for crabs or lobster – use the juice of 1 lemon instead of anchovy essence. So simple, so British, so good.

1 lb (500 g) fresh shrimps
5 oz (150 g) clarified butter
2 teaspoons anchovy essence
$\frac{1}{4}$ teaspoon mace
$\frac{1}{4}$ teaspoon cayenne pepper
Salt

Pre-heat the oven to gas mark 4, 350°F (180°C).

Put the shrimps in boiling water and cook for 2 minutes. Cool and remove from their shells. Melt 3 oz (75 g) of the clarified butter with the anchovy essence, mace, cayenne and salt. Put the shrimps in an ovenproof dish and pour over the seasoned butter. Bake for 30 minutes. Remove from the oven, drain, reserving the butter, and leave to cool.

Pack the shrimps into small jars and pour over the strained butter in which the shrimps were cooked. Leave to set, then cover with the remaining 2 oz (50 g) clarified butter – it should be about $\frac{1}{4}$ in. (6 mm) thick.

Photograph facing page 25

SEAFOOD PIE

6 scallops, cleaned and cooked

About 2 lb (1 kg) of equal
  quantities of white crab
  meat, lobster (optional),
  mussels and cockles (or any
  other shellfish), cleaned
  and chopped

6 oz (200 g) mushrooms,
  cooked

A little spring onion

Parsley, chopped

Salt and pepper

10 fl oz (300 ml) white sauce

For the flaky pastry:

3 oz (75 g) butter

8 oz (250 g) flour

Pinch salt

Cold water to mix

First make the pastry. Chop the butter and divide into four portions. Sieve the flour and salt and rub in a quarter of the butter. Mix to a stiff paste with water and knead until smooth. Roll into an oblong and cover two thirds with small bits of another quarter of the butter. Fold the unbuttered piece of pastry over, then fold the piece covered with fat over that, making a three-fold piece. Press the edges and turn the pastry half-way round. Fold to the right. Roll into an oblong again and repeat twice more, using up the rest of the butter. Chill at least 1 hour, roll out and line a 10 in. (25 cm) flan dish. Bake in a hot oven at gas mark 6, 400°F (200°C) until golden brown. Add the fish ingredients, mushrooms, spring onion, parsley and seasoning to the sauce and fill the pastry case with the mixture, letting the sauce spill gently over the edge. Warm gently and serve on a bed of rice with a side salad.

Alternatively, the same mixture is nice put into the (well cleaned) scallop shells with mashed potato piped round the edge. Sprinkle with cheese and brown under the grill.

Scallops in Fans

4 leaves filo pastry
1 oz (25 g) melted butter
16 scallops, shelled
Salt and pepper
4 oz (125 g) finely chopped
  carrots and leeks
4 sprigs dill to garnish

For the sauce:
1 shallot, chopped
1 oz (25 g) butter
2 tablespoons fish glaze (see
  page 87)
4 fl oz (125 ml) white wine
5 fl oz (150 ml) double cream
Pinch saffron
Salt and pepper

To make the fans, brush the pastry with melted butter and fold each leaf to make a double layer. Continuously fold the pastry every $\frac{1}{2}$ in. (1 cm), concertina-style; pinch at the bottom and spread out at the top to make a fan shape. Cook in oven at gas mark 5, 375°F (190°C), for about 4 minutes.

Season the scallops and fry in butter until cooked. Lightly blanch the carrots and leeks.

To make the sauce, lightly sweat the shallot in the butter and add the fish glaze and wine. Reduce, then add the cream and saffron and boil briskly until thickened. Season to taste.

To serve the dish, strain the sauce on to 4 plates. Place 4 scallops and some of the carrots and leeks in the centre of each. Top with a filo pastry fan and garnish with a sprig of dill.

Oysters

Some people fall ill the first time they eat oysters. The first time I ate them – I got arrested. It's a long story, your honour, and in no way was it my fault that the companion I lunched with was so incensed by the stale lobster served to him that, seeking poetic retribution, he decided to remove one of the eighteenth-century prints from the flock purple walls of the main staircase. A policeman of more mature years might have taken a different view. After all, the print was returned, and the gents' lavatory restored to its former state.

However, such an unpropitious start to the pleasure of oyster eating has not diminished my enthusiasm for one of the greatest delights on earth. Despite the fuss in September when the first oysters of the year become available, I believe that these shellfish, like sprats and Brussels sprouts, should not be consumed until the weather turns cold and the frosts set in. Over the years I have devoured many dozens in many places. In France during the weeks leading up to Christmas, oyster sellers set up trestle stalls in front of cafes. There is nothing finer in the early morning of a Provençal winter's day than to breakfast off oysters and white Châteauneuf-du-Pape while sitting round the oil stove in some derelict bar where old men in slippers deal the first hand of cards to while away another day. Where in England can you wander into a pub with a dozen oysters and be offered a plate, pepper and lemon as you order your drink?

Nor was there anything finer than sitting on a November morning on the banks of the Helford River, drenched to the skin with fine drizzle, talking with Len Hodges at his Duchy oyster farm and swallowing dozens of the sweetest (without prejudice!) little dreams in front of the BBC camera for my series on fish. Len kept me spellbound and unaware that my chair was sinking deeper into the soft grass. I eventually fell over backwards – wine, oysters and all.

I must say that I love oysters simple like that, but for those of you who like them cooked, here are some recipes from my mate Steven Bonnar of Wheelers.

Serves 2 to 4, depending on appetite

GRILLED OYSTERS

24 oysters, opened
2 oz (50 g) shallots, finely
  chopped
Freshly milled black pepper
24 knobs butter
Lemon halves and parsley
  sprigs to garnish

When you have opened the oysters, leave them in the deep shell. Sprinkle with the shallots and black pepper, then put a knob of butter on top of each one and cook under a very hot grill for a few minutes. Garnish with half a lemon and a sprig of parsley and serve immediately.

OYSTER AND DILL TARTLETS

6 oz (175 g) shortcrust pastry
24 oysters
2 oz (50 g) spring onions,
  trimmed and finely chopped
2 egg yolks
6 fl oz (175 ml) double cream
Chopped dill
Salt and pepper

Roll out the pastry and use to line 6 individual fluted 4 in. (10 cm) flan cases. Bake blind in the oven at gas mark 6, 400°F (200°C), for 15 minutes until just set. Place 4 oysters in the bottom of each flan case. Divide the spring onions equally among the flan cases. In a bowl mix the egg yolks, cream, dill and salt and pepper. Pour into the flan cases to cover the oysters neatly. Reduce the oven temperature to gas mark 3, 325°F (160°C), and bake the tartlets for a further 20 minutes until set.

David Harding   *Serves 4*

MUSSELS WITH SAFFRON AND ORANGES

3 lb (1.5 kg) mussels
1 glass dry white wine
1 pint (600 ml) fish stock
1 shallot, finely chopped
1 carrot
1 leek
1 stick celery
4 fl oz (125 ml) cream
Pinch saffron
Grated rind and juice of 1
  orange
Salt and pepper

Clean the mussels of barnacles and de-beard. Discard any which are open. Place them with the wine, fish stock and chopped shallot in a large saucepan. Cover and cook over a high heat until all the mussels have opened. Remove the mussels from the pan, strain the liquid and reduce by half.

Take the mussels from their shells and check that the beards have been removed. Cut the carrot, leek and celery into thin strips.

Add the cream, saffron, vegetable strips, orange rind and juice to the reduced liquid in the pan and bring to the boil. Add the mussels and adjust the seasoning. Serve immediately.

GRILLED LOBSTER

1 × 1½ lb (750 g) live lobster
Pinch fine sea salt
Black pepper
4 oz (125 g) best unsalted
  butter
Juice of 1 lemon
1 bottle Château Grillet 1970
  or 1976

With a sharp 12 in. (30 cm) cook's knife, kill the lobster with a sharp plunge through the back of the head. Then cut it in half lengthways. Remove the black or greenish sac from the head and the black or green thread which runs the length of the body.

Pre-heat the grill. Place the lobster on a grilling tray, season with salt, pepper and little knobs of butter and cook under the hot grill for 10 to 15 minutes, or until the shell on the claws has turned pink.

Upon your finest polished table, set the crystal and silver; there will be silver jugs of melted butter and lemon juice. Before eating, check that the petals have not fallen from the red roses that add the only colour to the otherwise cool and sombre room. If the telephone rings, ignore it. A smile of satisfaction is quite in order as you pour the pale greenish Château Grillet into a large glass and sip in silent splendour as you contemplate the milky flesh of your lobster. Eating alone has its compensations.

BOILED LOBSTER

I prefer grilled to boiled lobster, but a cold lobster salad is really rather good. Pop the unfortunate live lobster into a pot of salted, violently boiling water, put the lid on firmly with a weight on top and leave to boil for about 15 minutes – until the lobster has turned completely pink. Turn off the gas and leave for another 10 minutes or so before straining carefully.

Cut the lobster in half and serve warm with melted butter. To eat cold, reduce the boiling time by 5 minutes and allow the lobster to cool in the water in which it was cooked.

CRAB SALAD

8 oz (250 g) white crab meat
2 tablespoons vinaigrette
1 teaspoon chopped chives
1 tablespoon tomato flesh,
    diced
Salt and pepper
Fresh chervil to garnish

For the sauce:
4 oz (125 g) brown crab meat
8 fl oz (250 ml) vinaigrette
2 tablespoons double cream
Salt and pepper
Dash cayenne pepper

In a bowl combine the white crab meat with the vinaigrette, chives, tomato, salt and pepper. Leave to cool in the refrigerator.

Meanwhile make the sauce. Place all the sauce ingredients in a blender and blend until fine. Pass through a sieve.

To present the dish, put a ladle of sauce on each plate with a mound of crab meat in the centre. Garnish each with a sprig of chervil.

DRESSED CRAB

15 oz (425 g) crab meat
    (about 3 crabs)
6–7 oz (175–200 g) soft
    breadcrumbs
$\frac{1}{2}$ tablespoon white wine
    vinegar
2 tablespoons chutney
1 oz (25 g) butter
Generous pinch dry mustard
    or 1 level teaspoon French
    mustard
Salt and pepper
4 fl oz (125 ml) white sauce
4 tablespoons fresh white
    breadcrumbs
1 oz (25 g) butter

Scrub the crab shells. Mix all the ingredients except the buttered crumbs together. Check the seasoning and adjust if necessary. Pack into the shells, top with the crumbs and dot with butter. Bake in the oven at gas mark 6, 400°F (200°C), for about 20 minutes, until heated through and brown on top.

SPIDER CRAB AND AVOCADO TERRINE

Spider crabs make the best terrine, but ordinary crabs make a very pleasant one too.

1 × 1 lb (500 g) spider crab
4 fl oz (125 ml) double cream
1 egg, separated
1 leaf gelatine or 1 level
    teaspoon powdered gelatine
1 teaspoon lemon juice
Salt
Cayenne pepper
Groundnut or sunflower oil
¼ avocado per serving
Endive, to garnish

For the shellfish reduction:
½ oz (15 g) butter
1 oz (25 g) carrot, chopped
1 oz (25 g) onion, chopped
1 oz (25 g) celery, chopped
2 oz (50 g) tomato, roughly
    chopped
½ teaspoon tomato purée
1 fl oz (25 ml) dry white
    wine
12 fl oz (350 ml) water

First pick the meat out of the crab, reserving all the pieces of shell.

To make the reduction, melt the butter in a pan and cook the carrot, onion and celery in it until beginning to colour. Add the crab shells, tomato, tomato purée and white wine and stir over a high heat for 2 or 3 minutes. Add the water, bring to the boil and simmer for 40 minutes. Strain through a sieve into a second saucepan. Reduce this liquid down to 2 tablespoons by rapid boiling. Allow to cool a little.

To make the terrine, bring half the cream to the boil, then take it off the heat. Whisk the egg yolk with the shellfish reduction and add the hot cream. Stir constantly with a wooden spoon over a moderate heat till the savoury custard starts to thicken. Take off the heat and add the gelatine. Cool the pan by setting it in a bowl of iced water. When it is tepid, add the crab meat and lemon juice, and season if necessary with salt and a pinch of cayenne pepper.

As the crab mixture gets colder, it will begin to set. Before it sets too hard, whip the remaining cream until thick and soft but not stiff, and fold it into the mixture. Then beat the egg white to soft peaks and fold that in too. Pour the mixture into a terrine mould oiled with groundnut or sunflower oil. Leave to chill for at least 3 hours in the refrigerator.

Turn out by inverting the mould and bringing it down on to a tray with a firm tap. Repeat until it slips out. The coating of oil should be enough to slide it out, but if it fails to move, dip the mould briefly into hot water.

Slice the terrine with a thin-bladed knife first dipped into very hot water. Accompany each serving with a quarter of avocado, peeled, sliced and dressed with an olive oil dressing, and a couple of leaves of dressed endive.

Serves 3 to 4

DEVILLED CRAB

Served in small individual dishes with fingers of hot buttered toast, this makes a good first course.

1 oz (25 g) onion, finely
  chopped
¼ green pepper, diced
½ oz (15 g) butter
½ oz (15 g) flour
5 fl oz (150 ml) milk
4 oz (125 g) crab meat
1 oz (25 g) fresh white
  breadcrumbs
Dash Worcestershire sauce
½ tablespoon made mustard
2 oz (50 g) cheese, grated
Salt and pepper
Finely chopped parsley to
  garnish

Photograph facing page 25

Fry the onion and green pepper gently in the butter for 10 minutes, without allowing it to take colour. Add the flour and cook for 2 to 3 minutes, gradually stir in the milk and bring to the boil. Add the crab meat, breadcrumbs, Worcestershire sauce, mustard and 1 oz (25 g) of the cheese. Season with salt and pepper and spoon into individual dishes. Sprinkle with the remaining cheese and bake in the oven at gas mark 5, 375°F (190°C), for 20 minutes, or until lightly brown. Garnish with finely chopped parsley and serve.

COCKLES WITH LAVERBREAD

Laverbread is a rich green seaweed that you can gather from seashore rocks. If you have picked your own you must wash it thoroughly several times to remove all grit and sand, then boil it in a little water in a covered pan for up to 6 hours, stirring regularly to prevent it sticking. Allow any excess liquid to evaporate. (It may be pressure cooked for about 1½ hours.) You may buy a tin of laverbread, or possibly get it fresh from your fishmonger. Waun Gron is one of several Cheddar-like cheeses made in west Wales.

Laverbread, cooked
Cockles
Breadcrumbs
Waun Gron, grated
Garlic butter

Put some hot laverbread into the bottom of a gratin dish and spread evenly. Place some fresh cockles on the laverbread and sprinkle the breadcrumbs and grated cheese on top with a little garlic butter. Pop under the grill for 3 or 4 minutes until golden brown.

Serves 4

ORMERS IN CASSEROLE

Ormers are large molluscs rather like an elongated limpet. Once the staple fare of the common people, they are now a highly-prized delicacy, especially in the Channel Islands.

12 large ormers
4 oz (125 g) butter
1 oz (25 g) flour
8 oz (250 g) onions, chopped
8 oz (250 g) carrots, sliced
Parsley, chopped
Salt and pepper

First clean the ormers by removing them from their shells. Discard the entrails and the 'eyes'. Scrub well until all the black is removed. Beat the ormers to tenderise them, wash them again, dry and prick with a fork. Fry them in the butter on both sides until golden brown. Place in a flameproof casserole. Add the onions and carrots. Blend the flour with the water remaining butter in the pan, add approximately 1 pint (600 ml) and heat, stirring, till the sauce thickens. Pour the sauce over the ormers, add the parsley, season, cover and simmer for 3 hours.

STOCK AND SAUCES
FOR FISH DISHES

FISH STOCK

Use trimmings from any white-fleshed fish – such as sole, turbot, whiting, conger eel and so on – to make this stock.

2 lb (1 kg) fish bones and
   heads
5 oz (150 g) carrots, sliced
5 oz (150 g) leeks, chopped
2 oz (50 g) spring onions,
   chopped
2 oz (50 g) butter
4 fl oz (125 ml) dry white
   wine
3½ pints (2 litres) water
1 bouquet garni

Remove the gills from the fish heads. Soak the bones and heads in cold water for 3 to 4 hours. Roughly chop the fish bones and heads. Sweat the vegetables in the butter. Add the fish pieces, then pour on the white wine. Increase the heat and reduce the liquid by half, then add the water. Bring the mixture to the boil, skimming the surface frequently. After 5 minutes' cooking time, add the bouquet garni and simmer, uncovered, for 25 minutes.

Carefully strain the stock into a bowl through a muslin-lined sieve. Leave to cool, then store in the refrigerator for up to 1 week or for several weeks in the freezer.

TO MAKE FISH ASPIC: If the stock is very clear, the addition of a few leaves of gelatine will produce a fish aspic. A few slices of lemon squeezed into the aspic will give it a slightly sharper flavour.

TO MAKE A FISH GLAZE: Simmer the stock gently, skimming the surface frequently, until it has reduced by two thirds. Use the glaze to enrich and add body to certain fish sauces.

ANCHOVY CREAM

Served chilled, this sharp sauce is excellent with fish and, incidentally, also goes well with cold roast beef.

3 tinned anchovy fillets
½ hard-boiled egg yolk
Cayenne pepper
2½ fl oz (60 ml) liquid aspic
2½ fl oz (60 ml) whipped cream

Pound the anchovies to a fine paste with the egg yolk and add cayenne pepper to taste. Stir in the aspic. Pass through a strainer and gradually fold in the cream. Chill until ready to serve.

ANCHOVY SAUCE

Suitable with poached and baked firm white fish.

1 oz (25 g) butter
2½ fl oz (60 ml) double cream
1 tablespoon anchovy essence
1 pint (600 ml) white sauce
Salt and pepper

Add the butter, cream and anchovy essence to the white sauce. Simmer for 5 to 10 minutes, without boiling, to allow the flavours to penetrate. Adjust the seasoning if necessary.

Rabbit Brawn (page 101) with Tomato Bread (page 229)

BUTTER SAUCE

8 fl oz (250 ml) dry white wine
4 fl oz (125 ml) water
2 tablespoons finely chopped shallots
1 tablespoon good-quality wine vinegar
½ teaspoon white pepper
½ teaspoon salt
2 tablespoons double cream
8 oz (250 g) butter, softened

Place all the ingredients except the cream and butter in a pan. Boil and reduce to one third of the original volume. Purée and strain. Add the cream and place on a low heat. Gradually add the butter, beating with a wire whisk. Do not boil; keep warm and re-heat just before serving.

CREAM SAUCE

Excellent with baked and grilled fish, such as trout. Chopped fresh herbs – parsley, chives, coriander, basil and so on – can be added.

1 pint (600 ml) double cream
4 oz (125 g) butter
Salt and pepper

Bring the cream to the boil and cook over gentle heat until slightly reduced. Stir in the butter until melted and thoroughly blended. Season with salt and pepper and serve hot.

My Favourite Kidneys (page 114)

GOOSEBERRY SAUCE

8 oz (250 g) gooseberries
1 oz (25 g) butter
1 oz (25 g) sugar
Nutmeg
Salt

Top and tail the gooseberries and cook in a little water until tender. Pass through a sieve or liquidise. Beat in the butter and sugar, re-heat and season to taste with nutmeg and salt.

HOLLANDAISE SAUCE

$1\frac{1}{2}$ lb (750 g) unsalted butter
6 eggs
Juice of 1 lemon
Pepper

Melt the butter in a pan with a pouring lip. Put the egg yolks and whites with the lemon juice and pepper into a food processor and turn on. Pour the hot melted butter evenly into the whisking eggs until the sauce has thickened. To keep warm, place over a pan of recently boiled water until ready to serve.

For variations you can add blanched sorrel leaves, finely chopped fresh mint and other herbs as you wish.

MAYONNAISE

Use the best olive oil you can afford.

6 whole eggs, at room
  temperature
Juice of 1 or 2 lemons
1 tablespoon wine vinegar
Salt and pepper

Break the eggs into the food processor and add the other ingredients, except the oil. Turn the machine to maximum for 30 or 40 seconds, until the eggs are really foaming. Now pour the oil in

$1\frac{3}{4}$ *pints (900 ml) olive oil (or corn or nut oil), at room temperature*

evenly and slowly for a couple of minutes. If by any chance the mayonnaise is too thick, turn the machine on again at half speed and dribble some tepid water in. I know, I know, you didn't need that amount. The point is you bottle the rest for the coming week.

To Make Tartare Sauce: Add 1 teaspoon each of finely chopped chives, capers, green olives, parsley and gherkins to half a pint (300 ml) of mayonnaise made with an unflavoured oil, such as corn or nut oil, so as not to drown the taste of the herbs.

Shellfish Sauce

When using this recipe to make Lobster Sauce (for example, to accompany Supreme of John Dory with Spring Vegetables on page 60), omit the egg yolks.

*Shellfish of your choice, e.g.
   lobster, prawns
2 oz (50 g) unsalted butter
Dash Cognac
1 pint (600 ml) fish glaze
Salt and pepper
5 fl oz (150 ml) double cream
2 egg yolks*

First boil the shellfish. Remove the flesh from the shell(s) and reserve the flesh. Grind the shells – you need at least 10 oz (300 g) – in a food processor and sauté gently in butter. Flame in the Cognac, add the fish glaze and simmer for 10 minutes or so. Season with salt and pepper. Stir in the cream over a low heat. Strain through muslin, sieve into another pan and beat in the egg yolks over a low heat. Serve at once with the reserved poached shellfish or with poached turbot or cod (in which case, use the shellfish meat as a starter).

COLD PARSLEY SAUCE

Excellent with grilled and fried herring, mackerel and plaice.

*3 oz (75 g) finely chopped
  parsley
½ pt (300 ml) double cream
Salt and pepper
1 teaspoon tabasco*

Whip the cream and fold in the parsley; season to taste with salt, pepper and tabasco.

BASIC BATTER

The consistency of the batter can be varied by adding more or less liquid. A runny batter will produce a light texture, though it will tend to spread. A thick batter will cling better but will be more stodgy.

*4 oz (125 g) plain flour
Pinch salt
1 tablespoon oil
5 fl oz (150 ml) water
2 eggs, separated*

Sift the flour and salt into a bowl and make a well in the centre. Stir in the egg yolk, then add the oil and half the water. Beat until smooth, then gradually add the remaining water. Leave to rest for 30 minutes.

Whisk the egg whites until stiff and fold into the batter just before using. The mixture must be used at once in order to obtain maximum benefit from the aeration.

HAM AND OFFAL

Mr Leopold Bloom ate with relish the inner
organs of beasts and fowls. He liked thick giblet
soup, nutty gizzards, a stuffed roast heart, liver slices
fried with crustcrumbs, fried hencod's roes. Most of
all he liked grilled mutton kidneys which gave to
his palate a fine tang of faintly scented urine.

JAMES JOYCE, *ULYSSES*

Despite the fact that the French have for centuries rated them both for gastronomic pleasure and nutritional value, dishes like tripe and pig's trotters have long been despised in this country because they have been considered suitable only for poor people. Even during the Second World War when it was vital to encourage people to eat such things because of the shortage of meat, the Minister of Food in a broadcast designed to encourage the use of tripe could not disguise the revulsion in his voice whilst extolling its virtues. In Cork where Declan Ryan and his brother are blazing a trail for real food at the Arbutus Lodge Hotel, they have the courage to put trotters and tripe on their menus alongside the classic dishes of modern cuisine. That shows real commitment, for too many Irish people can still remember men being paid partly in money but mostly in tripe for a back-breaking week's work at the docks when Cork was one of the great victualling ports.

Down on Dartmoor my friend Shaun Hill at Gidleigh Park, one of the most sensitively talented chefs I know, who dazzles his well-heeled clients with extravagant dishes, told me that his favourite food was offal – sweetbreads and liver in particular – but the Americans who visit his restaurant are no more keen on it than we Brits.

Another despised dish is the Irish boiled bacon and cabbage. I for one would rather eat it at a dinner party than the roast joint of lean grey beef with frozen vegetables and gravy granule liquid beloved of too many. All you need is a fine piece of rolled loin of bacon about $2\frac{1}{2}$ lb to 3 lb (1.5 kg to 2 kg) which you simmer in a pot of water with a bay leaf or two, a few peppercorns and an onion stuck with about 2 cloves for about 1 hour. Fifteen minutes before the bacon is cooked, you pop into the garden and pick a head of super fresh cabbage, cut it into quarters (remove the thick stalk) and put this into the pot with the ham. Meanwhile, boil some really good spuds in their skins and make some fresh mustard to serve with your bacon.

While we're on the subject, what about improving a piece of boiled or baked ham by making a piquant sauce to pour over the hot slices? All you have to do is make a madeira sauce (see page 157), chop in a few gherkins and capers, give a few twists of the pepper mill and there you are. Then there are the great British faggots, their reputation sadly debased by those funny things you buy in little boxes from supermarket freezer cabinets. My mother makes the best in the world so I've included her recipe in this section.

I think the message is clear: don't be afraid to cook and eat offal whether it's just a grilled pig's trotter or Paul Reed's extravagant Veal Kidney with Fresh Mushrooms and Green Noodles (see page 113).

BOILED HAM WITH PARSLEY SAUCE

This is one of my favourite meals, delicious served with butter beans and a purée of swede.

1 large piece gammon ham, at
*   least 3 lb (1.5 kg)*
2 bay leaves
12 peppercorns
1 celery stick
Onions
Carrots
Dried butter beans
Potatoes, peeled and
*   halved*

For the parsley sauce:
1 oz (25 g) butter
1 oz (25 g) plain flour
¾ pint (450 ml) ham stock
5 fl oz (150 ml) milk
Salt and ground white pepper
1 bunch parsley, finely
*   chopped*

It is very difficult to know in advance the saltiness of a piece of ham. I tend always to buy mine from the same source so that I know what to expect. If in doubt, it is best to cover the ham in cold water and soak it for several hours or overnight.

To cook, place the ham in a large pan and cover with fresh cold water. Add the bay leaves, peppercorns, celery stick and some stalks of parsley from the bunch allowed for the sauce. Cut the onions in half (there is no need to peel as the skins add flavour), and chop the carrots into chunks or sticks and add these to the pan. Bring to the boil and simmer gently, removing any scum as it forms, for 20 to 25 minutes per lb (500 g) of ham. I like to tip in some butter beans, previously soaked overnight, for the last 20 minutes along with some prepared potatoes.

To make the sauce, melt the butter in a saucepan, add the flour and cook for 1 minute. Add the ham stock and whisk well, then add the milk gradually, whisking well between each addition. Add a little more ham stock until you have a good pouring consistency. Check the seasoning – you will need a little white pepper but, depending on the saltiness of the ham, you may not require additional salt. Stir in the chopped parsley.

Lift the ham from the pan and peel off the skin. Serve with some of the onions and carrots, the butter beans and potatoes. Pour over the parsley sauce.

Photograph facing page 105

Baked Ham

Glazes for baked ham:
Brush with home-made
mustard and press on
demerara sugar

Cover with thick-cut orange
marmalade

Baste with dark treacle
thinned with a little dry
cider

Place a clove in each
'diamond' on the fat, press
on brown sugar and baste
with cider

Most cookery books will tell you to wrap your precious piece of ham in foil and bake it in the oven. I feel this dries it out too much. Far preferable is to follow my recipe for boiled ham, but to remove the meat from the pot 30 minutes before the end of the calculated cooking time. Remove the skin, and score the fat into a diamond pattern with a knife. Coat with any of the suggested glazes and pop in the oven to crisp at gas mark 5, 375°F (190°C), for 30 minutes. If the ham is to be served hot for a dinner party, you could do the boiling part in advance and allow the ham to cool in its liquid in the pot, then remove, skin, and finish in the oven at the last minute when your guests arrive.

BLACK PUDDING

Black pudding is known throughout the British Isles, but is especially popular in the Midlands and the North. The chief ingredient, pig's blood, must be drawn immediately the animal is killed and stirred constantly to remove fibres and to prevent clotting. Scalded pig intestines are used for the sausage skins. (Sausage skins, also called 'casings', can be ordered from your butcher. Or – horror of horrors – you can buy artificial ones.) Instead of putting the pudding mixture into sausage skins, however, you can simply turn it into a greased baking tin and bake in the oven at gas mark 5, 375°F (190°C), for 45 minutes.

4 oz (125 g) pearl barley, rice or groats
4 oz (125 g) fine oatmeal
Pinch of salt and pepper
1 pint (600 ml) fresh pig's blood
8 oz (250 g) beef suet or pork fat, diced
2 oz (50 g) onions, finely chopped or minced
Sausage skins or 'casings'

Cook the barley, rice or groats in four times its volume of water until just soft. Mix the oatmeal with salt and pepper and stir to a paste with a little strained blood. Add the cereal, suet or fat, onions and the remaining strained blood to the oatmeal mixture. Put into the skins through a funnel, stirring the mixture frequently to prevent the fat from separating out.

Tie the sausage skins loosely and drop into hot (but not boiling) water; the addition of black pudding dye will ensure an attractive dark finish. Boil for 20 minutes or until no blood comes out when a pudding is pricked with a needle.

To serve, heat the puddings through in hot water for 10 to 15 minutes, or score at intervals and grill for 4 minutes on each side.

Alternatively, cut into rounds and grill or fry in lard. Serve with eggs for breakfast or with a mixed grill for lunch or high tea. In Derbyshire and Staffordshire, black pudding slices are served on oatcakes with fried eggs on top.

HOME-MADE PORK SAUSAGES

1 lb (500 g) lean pork, such as shoulder
8 oz (250 g) pork fat
Salt and pepper
Pinch each nutmeg, ground cloves, mace, thyme
1–2 oz (25–50 g) fresh breadcrumbs
2 egg yolks
Sausage skins

Mince the lean pork and pork fat finely. Season generously with salt, pepper, nutmeg, cloves, mace and thyme. Add the breadcrumbs and egg yolks and mix well.

Refrigerate the mixture to make it easier to handle, then stuff into the skins and twist to secure the ends. If sausage skins are not available, coat with egg and dry breadcrumbs. Serve grilled or fried.

HOG'S PUDDINGS

Groats are unprocessed oats. They look like bird seed, and can be bought from pet shops and health food shops.

1 lb (500 g) groats, soaked in water overnight and drained
2 lb (1 kg) pork (white meat and a little fat), minced
Salt and pepper
Sausage skins

Cook the groats in fresh water, for about one hour and then cool. Mix together the pork, groats and salt and pepper. Stuff into the sausage skins and tie into rings. Boil for approximately 30 minutes.

To serve, grill, fry or bake in the oven at gas mark 5, 375°F (190°C), until the skins are brown and crispy.

CRUBEENS (PIG'S TROTTERS)

4 brined crubeens (pig's
  trotters)
2 carrots
1 stick celery
1 onion
6 fl oz (175 ml) wine vinegar
Melted butter
Dried breadcrumbs
Pinch allspice

Bandage the trotters in pairs on to splints so that they keep their shape while cooking. Put into a pot with the vegetables and cover with water and the vinegar. Simmer for 6 or 7 hours. Allow to cool in the liquid.

To serve, split the trotters in two and roll in melted butter and dried breadcrumbs mixed with a pinch of allspice. Heat slowly under a grill, or in the oven at gas mark 4, 350°F (180°C), until hot and crisp on the outside.

ROAST HEART

Hearts can be stuffed, as here, with sage and onion or with veal forcemeat or an anchovy stuffing. Serve with apple sauce to complement the sage, or with rowan, redcurrant or gooseberry jelly if veal forcemeat is used.

4 lamb's hearts
4 oz (125 g) sage and onion
  stuffing (see page 146)
2 oz (50 g) bacon strips
1 oz (25 g) dripping

Rinse the hearts in cold water to remove any blood and cut away the thick muscular arteries and veins. Soak in cold salted water for 2 hours, wash again and soak for 30 minutes in fresh water. Blanch and refresh. Fill the heart cavities with the stuffing and sew up the openings with fine string.

Lard the hearts with the bacon strips and put in a roasting tin with the dripping. Cover and roast for 1 hour at gas mark 4, 350°F (180°C), basting every 15 minutes. Remove the string before serving the hearts with thickened gravy made from the pan juices.

TRIPE AND ONIONS

*1 lb (500 g) tripe prepared by
  the butcher*
8 oz (250 g) onions, chopped
Salt and pepper
1 pint (600 ml) milk
1 oz (25 g) butter
1 oz (25 g) flour
Chopped parsley to garnish

Simmer the tripe and onions with salt and pepper in the milk in a covered pan for 2 hours or until tender. Strain off the liquid, reserving 1 pint (600 ml).

Melt the butter, stir in the flour and cook for 2 minutes. Remove the pan from the heat and gradually stir in the reserved cooking liquid. Bring to the boil and continue to stir until it thickens. Add the tripe and onions and re-heat. Adjust the seasoning, sprinkle with parsley and serve with pieces of toast or boiled potatoes.

Serves 4

TRIPE HOT-POT

This is one of several super tripe recipes that were given to me by the man from Mr Hey's Tripe Shops in Bradford who has devoted his career to tripe – so I reckon he knows what he's talking about. This one he cooked for me and it was really delicious.

*1 lb (500 g) tripe prepared by
  the butcher*
Salt and pepper
1 oz (25 g) flour
2 lb (1 kg) potatoes, sliced
1 lb (500 g) onions, sliced
3 tomatoes, sliced
Stock
1 tablespoon beef dripping

Wipe the tripe, cut it up and dip in seasoned flour. Fill a greased hot-pot dish with alternate layers of vegetables and tripe, starting and finishing with potatoes, and seasoning each layer with salt and pepper. Pour in the stock so that it comes half-way up the dish, dot the dripping over the top and cover with a lid. Bake in the oven for $1\frac{1}{2}$ hours at gas mark 5, 375°F (190°C), taking off the lid for the last 15 minutes to brown the potatoes.

Rabbit Brawn

1 rabbit, jointed
2 pig's trotters
1 bay leaf
Salt and pepper
2 hard-boiled eggs, sliced

Simmer the rabbit with the pig's trotters, the bay leaf and some salt and pepper for about 2 hours. Leave to cool. Remove the bones and chop the meat finely, reserving the cooking liquid. Arrange the hard-boiled egg slices in the bottom of a mould or terrine and pile the meat on top. Re-heat the cooking liquid and pour a little over the meat. Cover with a saucer and place a weight on it. Leave to set overnight.

Photograph facing page 88

Win Floyd   *Serves a lot of people*

Brawn

Like Potted Beef Cheek (see page 168) this is one of those dishes that, given a French name, would meet with unqualified approval from the well-travelled gastronaut, yet remains unsung or despised in its country of birth. Yet it is very simple and quick to make.

1 pig's head
Onions, chopped
Parsley
Salt and pepper
Nutmeg

Simmer a pig's head very slowly in water with some chopped onions and parsley for several hours until the meat is dropping off the bones. When cooked, leave it in the liquid for an hour or so to cool, but before it gets completely cold, remove the meat to a big bowl and cut it up. While you are doing this, bring the cooking liquid back to simmering point and throw in every bone that you take from the meat. Finally, when all the meat is finely chopped, add salt and pepper and a good grating of nutmeg to it.

Put the meat into as many pudding basins as it will fill. Reduce the liquid in the pan to half and add a small amount to each basin of meat. Leave to set. Any liquid left over can be used as stock for soup.

FAGGOTS

1 pig's caul
1 lb (500 g) pig's fry (liver,
  heart and lights)
8 oz (250 g) pork belly
1 lb (500 g) onions
3 oz (75 g) white
  breadcrumbs
½ oz (15 g) fresh sage, chopped
Salt and freshly ground
  pepper

Soak the caul in tepid water for 1 hour, then drain and dry.

Cover the pig's fry, pork belly and onions with water and simmer for 1 hour. Drain off the liquid and reserve. Mince the pig's fry, pork and onions and add to the breadcrumbs. Add the sage, season with salt and pepper and stir well, adding approximately 2 tablespoons of the cooking liquid to the mixture.

Cut the caul into 4 in. (10 cm) squares. Shape the mixture into balls and cover each with a piece of caul. Place in a baking tin and cook in the oven at gas mark 6, 400°F (200°C), until brown.

Serve with a good, thick, rich gravy made from the reserved cooking liquid and the juices from the tin in which the faggots were cooked. Dried green peas cooked until mushy with a pinch of salt and 1 dessertspoon of sugar, make a delicious accompaniment.

STUFFED PIG'S EARS

4 pig's ears, thoroughly
  cleaned
Oil for frying
½ pint (300 ml) chicken stock
1 oz (25 g) butter
1 oz (25 g) flour
Salt and pepper

Boil the pig's ears for about 2 hours in water. Allow to cool.

Meanwhile, make the stuffing. Mix all the ingredients together and stuff into the cooled pig's ears. Roll the ears up and secure with string. Gently fry the stuffed ears on all sides in a little oil

For the stuffing:
4 oz (125 g) fresh
  breadcrumbs
2 oz (50 g) shredded suet
1 egg, beaten
Rind and juice of 1 lemon
Few sprigs fresh parsley and
  thyme
Salt and pepper

over a medium heat. Transfer to a saucepan and add enough chicken stock to cover. Simmer for about $1\frac{1}{2}$ hours.

Melt the butter, stir in the flour and add the stock in which you poached the pig's ears. Bring to the boil, stirring, and simmer until you have a smooth sauce. Adjust the seasoning if necessary. Serve the stuffed ears with the sauce poured over.

Billy Mackesy   *Serves 8*

PIG'S HEAD AND BOILED CHICKEN

$\frac{1}{2}$ *pig's head*
Bones to enrich the stock
  (optional)
1 baby chicken
2 carrots
2 onions, stuck with cloves
1 stick celery
Parsley
1 bay leaf
1 bouquet garni
Salt and pepper

Soak the pig's head in cold water overnight, changing the water three or four times.

In the morning put the head into fresh cold water with half a dozen bones if used. Bring to the boil and discard the liquor. Cover with fresh water a second time, bring to the boil again and simmer for 45 minutes.

Add the chicken, vegetables, herbs and seasoning to the pot and simmer for 30 to 40 minutes. When the chicken is cooked, carve and serve with slices from the cheek of the pig.

PICKLING AND COOKING AN OX TONGUE

1 × 3½ lb (1.75 kg) ox tongue
Salt
Peppercorns
1 carrot
1 onion
1 bouquet garni

For the pickle:
4 pints (2.3 litres) water
3 oz (75 g) coarse sugar
1 oz (25 g) saltpetre
14 oz (400 g) sea salt

Put all the pickle ingredients into a pan and boil until no more scum rises. Set aside until cold.

Meanwhile, rub the tongue with salt and leave for a few hours to rid it of any blood. When ready, rinse and immerse it in the pickle. Make sure that it is well covered with the pickle: if not, turn it every day. The tongue should be ready in 4 to 5 days, but if it is fairly large leave it for 2 more days.

Remove the tongue from the pickle and wash thoroughly. Tie the meat neatly and put into a pan of cold water. Bring slowly to the boil and skim. Now add a few peppercorns, a carrot, onion and bouquet garni and simmer for 3½ to 4 hours. When cooked, plunge the tongue into cold water and skin. Curl the tongue, put into a 6 in. (15 cm) tin and press with a plate and weight on top. When cold, turn out and serve with one of the chutneys or pickles on pages 244–249.

If you wish to serve the tongue hot, omit the pressing procedure but let it rest for 20 minutes. Slice the tongue and serve with any of the sauces on pages 156–157.

Chicken Livers with Orange Segments, Tarragon and Onion Marmalade (page 102)

COWHEEL PIE

Cheap, nutritious and very filling. Serve with some good freshly made mustard.

1 cowheel
1 large onion
Water or veal or chicken stock
8 oz (250 g) cooked butter beans
Salt and pepper
2 oz (50 g) butter
4 oz (125 g) flour
Milk or beaten egg to glaze

Cut up the cowheel and onion, cover with water or veal or chicken stock and simmer for about 2 hours until tender.

Strain the cowheel, reserving the stock. Arrange in alternate layers with the cooked butter beans in a greased pie-dish, seasoning each layer with salt and pepper and moistening with stock.

Rub the butter into the flour with a pinch of salt and mix to a soft dough with cold water. Roll out rather larger than the dish, damp the edges of the dish, and cover with the pastry. Make a hole in the centre, trim with pastry leaves, decorate the edges and brush the top with milk or egg. Bake in the oven at gas mark 6, 400°F (200°C), for 30 minutes.

Boiled Ham with Parsley Sauce (page 95)

To Prepare Calf's Brain

The method of preparation is similar to that for sweetbread. Soak the brain for 24 hours in cold water. The brain is soft and you will not need anything other than your fingers to trim it. It will easily separate into two large pieces and one smaller piece, which may be discarded. Pinch away the creamy white parts from the underneath of the brain, and any damaged or very dark areas. Put the brain into a saucepan with a little white wine, shallot, black pepper, salt and a squeeze of lemon. Add just enough water to cover, then place a butter paper or circle of greaseproof paper on top. Bring to the boil and remove from the heat. Allow to cool in the cooking liquor. The brain is now ready to use in a recipe such as the one below.

Shaun Hill   *Serves 2*

Calf's Brains in Brown Butter

2 sets prepared calf's brains
8 oz (250 g) unsalted butter
Salt and freshly ground black
  pepper
$\frac{1}{2}$ lemon
Chopped parsley or chervil

Pat the prepared brains dry with kitchen paper.

In a warm pan melt a knob of butter. Just before the butter begins to brown, add the brains and fry until nicely coloured and almost crisped on each side. Lift from the pan and season with salt, pepper and lemon juice; put on to warmed plates.

In the same pan heat the rest of the butter. As it turns brown, strain into a jug or container with the chopped herbs. Pour the foaming brown butter over the brains.

To Prepare Calf's Sweetbreads

Soak overnight in cold water. Carefully cut away most of the membrane from the outside, leaving just enough to hold the sweetbreads together. Place in a saucepan with aromates like slices of onion, leek and carrot, a little salt and black pepper, some sprigs of thyme and a dash of wine vinegar. Add enough water just to cover the sweetbreads, then a buttered piece of paper or circle of greaseproof paper. Use your head when choosing a saucepan: if you use a huge pan that needs gallons of water, you will overcook the sweetbreads by the time the water boils. As soon as the water reaches boiling point, take the pan from the heat and leave the sweetbreads to cool in the cooking liquor. It should then look set but still soft, almost gelatinous to the touch.

Serves 6

Sweetbreads English Style

Calf's sweetbreads are ideal for this dish, but the much less expensive lamb's sweetbreads make an acceptable substitute. They are served grilled on skewers, accompanied by a bowl of bread sauce.

1½ lb (750 g) prepared calf's sweetbreads
12 oz (350 g) smoked streaky bacon rashers
4 oz (125 g) fresh white breadcrumbs
3 oz (75 g) butter

Cut the sweetbreads into thick slices. Remove the rind from the bacon and stretch the rashers around the sweetbreads. Thread on to 6 skewers and cook under a medium-hot grill for 15 to 20 minutes, turning occasionally.

Fry the breadcrumbs in butter until brown and coat the sweetbreads with them. Arrange the sweetbreads on a bed of the remaining crumbs. Serve immediately.

ESCALOPE OF CALF'S SWEETBREADS WITH FRESH FRUIT FLAVOURED WITH A PEPPERED BUTTER SAUCE

1 lb (500 g) calf's sweetbreads
2 oz (50 g) white flour,
   seasoned
1 egg, beaten with a teaspoon
   of water
4 oz (125 g) white
   breadcrumbs
2 oz (50 g) butter

For the fruit garnish:
1 apple
1 orange
6 green and black grapes
12 cranberries

For the sauce:
10 fl oz (300 ml) dry white
   wine
10 fl oz (300 ml) double
   cream
1 oz (25 g) finely snipped
   chives and parsley
$\frac{1}{2}$ oz (15 g) crushed black
   peppercorns
6 oz (175 g) unsalted butter
Juice of $\frac{1}{2}$ lemon

First trim and clean the sweetbreads and place in a saucepan with cold water and a pinch of salt and bring to the boil, so that the sweetbreads heat through and become firm. Remove the saucepan from the heat and leave them in hot liquid for 5 minutes. Re-fresh under cold running water.

Slice each sweetbread thinly and coat with the seasoned flour, eggwash and white breadcrumbs. Meanwhile heat 2 oz of butter in a saucepan until lightly browned. Add the breaded sweetbreads and cook until lightly browned all over. Keep warm in the oven.

To prepare the garnish, firstly peel the apple, remove the core and cut out 6 to 8 segments. Coat in melted butter and place on a tray and cook quickly until they remain a little firm. Fantail each apple segment and keep in a warm place. Now peel the orange and with a sharp knife segment into 6 to 8 pieces. Cut the grapes into fine dice, mix evenly and wash them.

Make the sauce by pouring the white wine into a saucepan and reducing until the liquid has almost evaporated. Add the double cream, chives and parsley, and crushed black peppercorns. Whisk the butter into the reduced liquid. Check for seasoning and add the lemon juice. Keep warm.

Place a few tablespoons of the sauce on a large round plate. Arrange the sweetbreads on either side of the plate on top of the sauce and place 2 fantails of apple and 2 segments of orange on each sweetbread. Arrange the grapes between them and garnish with cranberries.

Shaun Hill

CALF'S SWEETBREADS AND KIDNEY WITH BRAISED LENTILS AND MUSTARD SAUCE

4 oz (125 g) brown lentils
Salt and freshly ground black pepper
1 onion, chopped
2 rashers streaky bacon, cut into small batons
1 carrot, chopped
4 oz (100 g) unsalted butter
5 fl oz (150 ml) reduced veal stock
Dash red wine
1 calf's kidney, sliced
1 lb (500 g) prepared calf's sweetbreads, cut into $\frac{1}{2}$ in. (6 mm) slices (see page 107)
1 tablespoon mustard
5 fl oz (150 ml) cream
Lemon juice (optional)

Soak the lentils overnight in two changes of water. Boil in fresh salted water for about 15 minutes, or until tender, drain and keep hot.

Shallow-fry the onion, bacon and carrot in a little butter. Add the lentils, half the stock and a little red wine. Stir in the rest of the butter, in small pieces, to thicken.

In two hot pans shallow-fry the kidney and sweetbreads separately. In the pan in which you cooked the kidney, make the mustard sauce by whisking or stirring together the mustard and cream. Season with salt and pepper. Allow to boil until the sauce has thickened. Check the seasoning and if necessary add a squeeze of lemon juice.

Serve the kidney on a pool of mustard sauce and the sweetbreads on a bed of lentils.

CHICKEN LIVERS AND POTATO PANCAKES

4 small potatoes, very thinly sliced
Fat for frying
12 oz (350 g) chicken livers, trimmed
Nut oil
4 oz (125 g) green grapes, peeled and de-seeded
4 shallots, roasted
Chives and chervil, chopped

For the sauce:
8 fl oz (250 ml) Sauternes wine
2 oz (50 g) unsalted butter

To make the sauce, reduce the wine by approximately two-thirds and quickly whisk in the butter.

To make the potato pancake, overlap the slices of potato to form a circle. Fry in hot fat until golden, then keep warm.

Meanwhile, toss the chicken livers in the hot oil. When almost cooked, add the grapes and cook a few moments longer.

To present the dish, place the livers and grapes in the centre of a serving plate and top with the potato pancake. Surround with the sauce and garnish with roasted shallots and chopped chives and chervil.

CHICKEN LIVERS WITH ORANGE SEGMENTS, TARRAGON AND ONION MARMALADE

1 lb (500 g) chicken livers
3 oranges, peeled and segmented
3 sprigs fresh tarragon, coarsely chopped
2 oz (50 g) pine kernels, toasted
Selection salad leaves
2 oz (50 g) butter

First make the onion marmalade. Heat the olive oil in a heavy-based pan, add the onions, sugar, salt and pepper. Cover the pan and allow the onions to brown, slowly stirring from time to time with a wooden spoon. After 45 minutes, pour in the vinegar and continue to cook, stirring occasionally, until the marmalade becomes

For the onion marmalade:
2 teaspoons olive oil
3 lb (1.5 kg) onions, finely
  sliced
3 teaspoons sugar
Pinch salt and pepper
6 tablespoons white wine
  vinegar

transparent. Allow to cool.

Trim the chicken livers and put aside. Combine the oranges in a bowl with the tarragon and pine kernels.

Arrange the salad leaves and cooled onion marmalade on six serving plates. Heat 1 oz (25 g) of butter until foaming in a large frying pan. Add half the chicken livers and brown lightly for approximately 2 minutes on either side. Transfer to a warm dish and then repeat the process with the remaining butter and chicken livers. The aim in cooking the livers in batches is to ensure that the temperature of the pan remains high so that they are sealed evenly.

Now arrange the chicken livers on the prepared salad plates and decorate with the oranges, tarragon and pine kernels to serve.

Photograph facing page 104

Serves 1

CALF'S LIVER AND BACON

So simple to cook, but many people and restaurants manage to get it wrong. Here's how to do it.

First of all the calf's liver: it tends to vary quite a lot in colour, some being paler than others. This has no significance where cooking is concerned. All liver should be fresh and clean-looking and have little or no smell. It should be firm: cut away any parts which are sponge-like in texture. Inferior livers will need soaking in milk to remove excess blood. The liver should be sliced about $\frac{1}{4}$ in. (6 mm) thick and all ducts and the outer membrane removed – if the latter is left on, it will pull the liver out of shape as it contracts during cooking. Liver takes such a short time to cook you should make sure that your vegetables are ready and that your diners are sitting down before you start – although I would eat only a few new potatoes with this. If overcooked or left even for a short time after cooking, the liver will be tough and dry.

2 rashers bacon
Butter
Pepper
1 thin slice, approx. 4 oz
  (125 g) calf's liver

Fry the bacon rashers in a little butter in a frying pan until cooked to your liking. Remove and keep warm. Add some more butter to your pan. Grind a little black pepper over your liver and, as soon as the butter is foaming, place it in the pan. When the liver starts to 'bleed' (little drops of blood will appear on the top side), turn it over and cook for the same length of time. This will be a maximum of 2 minutes each side, depending on the thickness. Place on your warmed serving plate with the bacon. Pour over the juices. If you wish, you may add a little stock to the pan and swirl it around with the butter before pouring it over your liver.

Shaun Hill   *Serves 4*

CALF'S LIVER WITH WATERCRESS AND SHALLOT SAUCE

4 oz (125 g) shallots, finely
  chopped
4 oz (125 g) unsalted butter
Dash vermouth
1 bunch watercress, roughly
  chopped
4 × 5 oz (150 g) slices calf's
  liver
Salt and freshly ground black
  pepper
Oil for frying
Cream

In a small saucepan sweat the shallots in a little butter, moisten in vermouth and add the watercress.

Season the liver just before frying with salt and black pepper. Brush with cooking oil and shallow-fry in a frying pan. Remove from the pan and keep warm.

Combine the shallots and watercress with any frying pan juices and residue. Whisk in the softened butter piece by piece, until the sauce has thickened. This is best done off the heat so that the sauce does not separate. If it gets too thick, add a few more drops of vermouth. Finish with a little cream.

To serve, pour the sauce on to warmed plates and place the liver on top.

To Prepare Veal Kidney

Pull away the suet from around the kidney. Then, with your fingertips or a small knife, remove the thin, sausage-skin-like membrane from the kidney. You will see a ball of white fat and nerve at the centre: meticulously cut all of this away. As you do so the kidney will unfold so that it resembles a knobbly steak. The meat should be shiny and a little pale. If not to be used immediately, the kidney should be brushed with a little good-quality oil.

Paul Reed   *Serves 2*

Veal Kidney with Fresh Mushrooms and Green Noodles

10 oz (300 g) veal kidney
1 fl oz (25 ml) white port
2 oz (50 g) wild mushrooms (ceps, morels, oysters or chanterelles), sliced
4 fl oz (125 ml) meat glaze (see page 87)
1 fl oz (25 ml) double cream
2 oz (50 g) butter
½ teaspoon chives, finely chopped
Salt and pepper

For the green noodles:
8 oz (250 g) strong flour
2 oz (50 g) spinach purée
2 eggs
2 tablespoons warm water
Salt

To make the green noodles, mix all the ingredients together to form a dough. Roll out, preferably with a noodle machine, and cut on the fine cutter. Blanch and cook for approximately 3 to 5 minutes in salted and oiled boiling water.

This recipe makes about 14 oz (400 g) noodles. You need 3 oz (75 g) to serve with the kidney; the rest will keep in the refrigerator for 2 to 3 days.

Pan-fry the kidney and remove while still pink. Keep warm.

De-glaze the pan with the port and add the mushrooms, meat glaze and cream. Reduce. When the desired consistency is achieved, beat in the cold butter. Add the chives, salt and pepper.

Finely slice the kidney and arrange on a serving plate. Pour the sauce around and garnish with the freshly cooked noodles.

MY FAVOURITE KIDNEYS

1 pair lamb's kidneys in their
  suet
Salt and pepper
Tabasco sauce or mushroom
  ketchup (see page 249)
2 thick rounds dry toast

Cut the kidneys almost in half and open them out like butterflies. Take out the central core, but don't remove the suet on the outside. Pop the kidneys fat side up under a hot grill till the fat is crisp and golden, then turn over and continue to grill until cooked. Season with salt and pepper and Tabasco sauce or mushroom ketchup, place on the thick slices of toast which absorb the lovely dripping and eat the lot!

Photograph facing page 89

Joan Valsler   *Serves 2*

VEAL KIDNEY STEWED IN CHAMPAGNE

You can also use lamb's kidneys for this recipe, in which case you'll need eight.

1 veal kidney, thinly sliced
1 onion, thinly sliced
2 oz (50 g) butter
5 fl oz (150 ml) Champagne
Mushroom ketchup (see page
  249)
1 tablespoon stock
Salt and pepper
Cream (optional)

Fry the kidney and onion in butter to a nice brown. Transfer to a clean stewpan and add the Champagne, a little mushroom ketchup, the stock and salt and pepper. Stew gently until tender and then serve very hot. A little cream can be added if desired.

GAME

Of the wealth of aliments bestowed on
man by a bountiful Providence for his sustenance
and delectation, none lends a greater grace or ministers
more to the variety of the table than game. The offspring
of wild nature, nursed upon its fruits, its mast, and its
vegetation and exhaling the very essence of its
most secluded recesses, it sheds an added lustre
even upon the most elaborate repast.

GEORGE ELLWANGER, *PLEASURE OF THE TABLE.*

... OF COURSE, THIS IS ONLY A SKETCH
WHAT DO YOU THINK?
YOURS. MANET

If the BBC ever threatens to send me to a desert island I won't go unless they assure me that the woodlands are bursting with pheasants, the hedgerows wild with hares and rabbits, the moors are thick with grouse and partridge, the coast is covered with teal and snipe and wild boar roam the forests. I mean, to hell with the records and the books – just give me the means to catch the game and some matches to light a fire, and I'll be in heaven.

Happily game is no longer the preserve of the landed gentry and, equally pleasingly, attitudes to hanging game till it is rotting and putrid have changed as well. The price of hares, pheasants, wild rabbits *et al* is no longer exorbitant, and since these creatures have a great content of dense and delicious meat, they really do represent genuine good value for the cost-conscious cook. So, whether you dine off snipe and claret or rabbit and cider, you are guaranteed a splendid gastronomic experience.

David Harding   *Serves 4*

RABBIT WITH MUSTARD AND CHAMPAGNE

Oil for frying
2 oz (50 g) butter
1 rabbit, jointed
3 shallots, chopped
2 cloves garlic, chopped
1 pint (600 ml) Champagne
Bouquet garni
Seasoning
½ pint (300 ml) cream
2 tablespoons coarse French mustard
8 oz (250 g) mushrooms, sliced

Heat the oil and butter in a pan and quickly fry the rabbit pieces until golden brown. Add the shallots and garlic and cook for a further minute. Add the Champagne and bouquet garni and season. Cover the pan with a lid and cook at gas mark 5, 375°F (190°C), for approximately 25 minutes, or until the rabbit is tender. Remove the meat from the pan and keep warm. Reserve the liquor.

Add the cream to the cooking liquor and reduce on a fierce heat by half. Next add the mustard and sliced mushrooms. Bring back to a simmer and pour the sauce over the rabbit. Serve immediately.

RABBIT STEWED IN GOOSEBERRY CHAMPAGNE

Margaret Vaughan at the Settle in Frome invited me to a friendly cooking competition: she cooked Cod's Cheeks and Tongues (see page 49), and I chose rabbit and created this simple dish using a bottle of her gooseberry champagne (which is, in fact, commercially available from her).

3 wild rabbits, jointed, giblets
* reserved*
Flour
1 oz (25 g) butter or bacon fat
* or pork fat*
6 oz (175 g) streaky bacon,
* diced*
10 oz (300 g) mixed onions
* and carrots, diced*
Salt and pepper
1 sprig fresh thyme
2 bay leaves
1 rounded tablespoon chopped
* parsley*
2 tablespoons tomato purée
1 bottle gooseberry champagne
* or any dry home-made fruit*
* wine*

Dredge the rabbit pieces in flour. Melt the butter or fat in a large roasting tin or flameproof casserole and fry the rabbit, the diced bacon and vegetables for about 10 minutes till they are golden brown. Season the rabbit with salt and pepper. Now add the herbs and tomato purée, and stir in well. Add the champagne and the rabbit giblets tied in a muslin bag. Cover with a lid or aluminium foil and pop into the oven at gas mark 4, 350°F (180°C), for about 2 hours or until the rabbit is tender. Remove the bag of giblets before serving.

RABBIT STEW

1 × 3 lb (1.5 kg) wild rabbit,
jointed, liver reserved
Lard or bacon fat
Salt and freshly ground
pepper
1 onion, finely chopped
¼ teaspoon chopped rosemary
1 bay leaf
12 fl oz (350 ml) dry cider
Caster sugar
6 salted anchovy fillets
Garlic
1 tablespoon capers
Sprig parsley

Brown the rabbit joints in the fat in a flameproof casserole and season with salt and pepper. Lower the heat and add the onion, rosemary and bay leaf and cook for 5 minutes. Add the cider and a pinch of sugar. Increase the heat, bring the liquid to the boil and simmer for 4 minutes or so. Lower the heat, cover the casserole and simmer for 45 minutes or until the rabbit is tender.

While the rabbit is cooking, blend the anchovies, garlic, capers, parsley and rabbit liver to a purée.

Drain the rabbit pieces one by one and place them on a warmed serving dish. Discard the bay leaf. Add the anchovy mixture to the pan, reduce the heat to very low and whisk for 5 minutes, without letting the liquid come to the boil. Pour this sauce over the rabbit pieces.

RABBIT WITH PRUNES

For the marinade:
2 pints (1 litre) red wine
1 bay leaf
6 peppercorns
2 cloves garlic, crushed
1 tablespoon olive oil

1 wild rabbit, jointed
1½ oz (40 g) butter
Salt and pepper

Prepare the red wine marinade and let the rabbit joints marinate for 24 hours in the refrigerator. Dry them carefully, discarding the marinade.

In a saucepan, melt the butter, add the rabbit joints and sauté them over a high heat for about 10 minutes. Season with salt and pepper. When the rabbit is well browned, sprinkle the joints with the flour and allow the flour to

1 tablespoon flour
8 fl oz (250 ml) red wine
1 lb (500 g) prunes, stoned,
    soaked in water for 4 hours
    and drained
1 tablespoon redcurrant jelly

brown. Pour in the wine. Add the prunes, cover the pan and simmer over a low heat until the meat is tender, about 45 minutes. Remove the rabbit and keep it warm. Stir the redcurrant jelly into the sauce to thicken it and pour it over the meat.

Serves 4

RABBIT IN LENTILS

1 rabbit, jointed
4 oz (125 g) lentils
1 onion, sliced
1 large carrot, sliced
2 sticks celery, sliced
Parsley, thyme, bay leaf
Salt and pepper
Chicken, veal or rabbit stock
    to cover
Chopped parsley

Place the rabbit joints in a pan with the lentils, onion, carrot, celery, herbs and seasoning. Cover with stock, put the lid on the pan and cook gently for about 2 hours until the rabbit and lentils are really tender. Remove the rabbit joints to a warm ovenproof dish.

Rub the vegetables through a sieve or liquidise, adding a little more stock if necessary to make a purée like thick cream. Adjust the seasoning. Coat the rabbit with the purée and re-heat gently in the oven. Sprinkle a little chopped parsley over the dish to serve.

Photograph facing page 137

ROYAL HARE STEW

*1 hare, jointed, blood and
liver reserved*
2 oz (50 g) butter
*2 × 4 oz (125 g) pieces green
streaky bacon, each cut into
12 strips*
*3 medium onions, finely
chopped*
2 tablespoons flour
10 garlic cloves
17 fl oz (500 ml) stock
17 fl oz (500 ml) red wine
Salt and pepper
24 shallots, finely sliced
1 bouquet garni
24 mushrooms

Fry the hare in the butter until lightly browned. Add half the bacon and the onions and mix well. Sprinkle the hare with the flour and cook, stirring and turning the pieces over regularly, for at least 10 minutes or until the flour is well browned. Add 5 of the garlic cloves, crushed, and pour in enough stock and red wine to cover the meat completely. Season with salt and pepper, and add one third of the shallots and the bouquet garni. Reduce the heat to very low and simmer, covered, for about $1\frac{1}{2}$ hours.

Remove the pieces of hare and transfer them to an earthenware casserole with a tightly fitting lid, reserving the rest of the contents. Add the mushrooms, the rest of the bacon, remaining 5 whole garlic cloves and the rest of the shallots to the casserole. Cook for a little while longer until the vegetables are softened.

Remove the bouquet garni from the pan in which the hare was cooked and press the rest of the contents through a sieve over the hare. Cover the casserole and cook in the oven at gas mark $\frac{1}{2}$, 250°F (120°C), until the meat is meltingly tender – about 30 minutes. Stir the reserved blood and the finely minced liver into the hare cooking liquid and warm it over a very low heat, shaking the casserole from time to time. Cook until the sauce begins to thicken, but do not allow it to approach boiling point.

Fillet of Venison with Celeriac and Glazed Apples (page 126)

ROAST HAUNCH OF VENISON

The location in which I cooked this – a vast white-tiled kitchen with teak doors and brass fittings and coal ranges – is the sort of place Escoffier would have been at home in around the turn of the century in some reasonable-sized hotel with a brigade of chefs. But this was just the kitchen of a Scottish laird's house where the green baize door still exists and old retainers make cream in the dairy or pluck game in the larder!!

1 × 6–8 lb (3–4 kg) venison
  joint
1 tablespoon mixed spice
  (cinnamon, nutmeg, etc.)
1 bottle strong red wine
10 fl oz (300 ml) good malt
  vinegar
Juice of 3 lemons
2 oz (50 g) melted butter
Flour
10 fl oz (300 ml) clear mutton
  or game stock
Walnut ketchup (see page
  248)

First season the meat by rubbing it well with the mixed spice and then marinate it for 6 hours in the wine, vinegar and lemon juice. Pop it into a roasting tin and roast in the oven at gas mark 3, 325°F (160°C) for 4 hours. During roasting, baste the meat at least four times with the marinade which has been mixed with melted butter. About 15 minutes before the venison is ready, baste with butter only and sprinkle flour over it. Remove from the roasting tin and keep warm.

Meanwhile, bubble up all the juices in the roasting tin and add the stock and a couple of teaspoons of walnut ketchup. Strain through a sieve, skim off the fat and pour the sauce over the roast.

Pigeon Pie (page 128)

VENISON COLLOPS

Collops is the traditional Scots term for thin slices of meat.

2 lb (1 kg) venison fillet
2 tablespoons butter
1 tablespoon flour
10 fl oz (300 ml) brown
gravy or rich beef stock
10 fl oz (300 ml) water
Salt and black pepper
Pinch ground mace
1 teaspoon redcurrant jelly

Cut the venison into thin slices and fry in hot butter until a rich brown colour on both sides. Remove the meat and stir the flour into the remaining butter. Add the stock and water. Season with salt, pepper and mace. Put the venison back into the pan, cover and simmer very gently until tender. Skim the sauce and add the redcurrant jelly.

Serve the collops with the sauce poured over.

Mike Simpson

CULLODEN HOUSE HIGHLAND GAME PIE

This is a hearty winter pâté baked in a large rectangular dish a good 14 in. (35 cm) long – the kind of thing that's well worth making for a Christmas buffet. You will have to order the venison fillets from your butcher, unless you are lucky enough to own a private hunting lodge!

This is really good served cold with a purée of blackberries, so if you are one of those people who are sensible enough to keep a little bottled fruit from the summer or indeed even a few frozen blackberries, put about 1 lb (500 g) of them in a saucepan with the juice of 1 lemon and a couple of ounces (50 g or so) of caster sugar and simmer them until they are all mushy – don't add any other liquid. Liquidise and strain through a very fine sieve. Allow to cool. To serve, put a little of this sauce on each plate. Lay a slice of the terrine on the sauce and garnish with a finely chopped winter salad – say, endive, crisp lettuce, a bit of frisée and some small pieces of tomato, nicely chopped together in nut oil and a squeeze of lemon juice.

1 lb (500 g) venison, minced
1 lb (500 g) pork, minced
1 lb (500 g) smoked back
   bacon, finely diced
1 tablespoon mixed herbs
   (rosemary, thyme, parsley)
6 juniper berries, crushed
Grated rind of ½ lemon
Grated rind of ½ orange
Salt and pepper
4 tablespoons oil
4 oz (125 g) shallots, finely
   chopped
3 fl oz (75 ml) Cognac
2 × 6–7 in. (15–17.5 cm)
   fillets venison

For the pastry:
2 lb (1 kg) flour
¼ oz (7 g) salt
1 lb (500 g) lard
Water to mix
Beaten egg and milk to glaze

First make the pastry. Sieve the flour and salt and rub in the fat. Add sufficient water to make a firm dough. Roll out the pastry into a large rectangle. Cut out one piece of pastry slightly bigger than the top of the terrine to form a lid. Use the rest of the pastry to carpet the bottom and sides of the terrine, leaving a little overlap on the sides so that later you can pinch the top on.

Meanwhile, with the exception of the 2 fillets of venison, mix all the other ingredients together. Allow to stand for 1 hour at room temperature. Fill half the terrine with the mixture, then lay the venison fillets from end to end down the middle (you might find that you have one long fillet and do not need 2 bits – you can never tell with these things). Now add the rest of the mixture, put on the pastry lid and pinch it with your fingers in an attractive shape all the way around the edges.

Paint the top with an egg and milk wash and pop into the oven at gas mark 3 to 4, 325° to 350°F (160° to 180°C), for about 2 hours. (You may need to cover the pastry with foil to prevent it burning during long cooking.) Check that the pastry is cooked by gently pushing a knife down the side between it and the tin. If it's OK, leave the pie to cool completely before tipping it out and serving.

POT ROAST HAUNCH OF VENISON

Jimmy MacNab is the archetypal Scot – a cheerful kilt-wearing, (occasional) whisky-drinking giant of a man who loves his food and a good yarn at The Creggans Hotel in Stachur (proprietors Sir Fitzroy and Lady Maclean. Some say he was the model of Fleming's James Bond). When Jimmy cooks he does so with gusto, and this old-fashioned recipe is superb for a big dinner party or a Christmas celebration.

2 onions
3 carrots
2 parsnips
2 turnips
1 head celery
2 apples
1 × 10 lb (5 kg) haunch
  venison
Cloves
8 fl oz (250 ml) olive oil
4 oz (125 g) brown sugar
Dried mixed herbs
Fresh thyme, rosemary and
  mint
1½ bottles red wine

Finely chop the vegetables and apples, place in the bottom of a large pot, and set the haunch on top. Make several incisions in the top of the meat, inserting cloves as you go. Rub the olive oil and sugar into the meat, sprinkle over some dried mixed herbs and then some fresh thyme, rosemary and mint. Pour the wine into the pot and leave to marinate in a cool place for 4 days, turning occasionally.

When ready to cook, cover the pot with aluminium foil and place in the oven at gas mark 4, 350°F (180°C). Allow 20 minutes' cooking time for each 1 lb (500 g) of meat.

LOIN OR FILLET OF VENISON WITH A BLACKCURRANT LIQUEUR SAUCE

After the excesses of Jimmy MacNab's mighty roast haunch of venison, I cooked for him a more modern and refined version of this game, based on traditional venison collops (see page 122). He ate the lot, said nothing and poured me a dram of MacPhunn whisky.

Some centuries ago MacPhunn of Drip, a local laird of ancient lineage, fell upon evil times and took to stealing sheep. For this he was carried off to Inverary and hanged and his widow invited to come and collect his corpse. Half-way across Loch Fyne she thought she saw him move and, mixing some of her own milk (she was nursing a baby) with some whisky, forced it between his lips. At this MacPhunn sat up and, not long after, landed as good as new at the cairn which bears his name, a few hundred yards from The Creggans Inn. By law he could not be hanged twice and so he lived happily for many more years and now lies buried in Strachur churchyard.

Such are the life-giving qualities of a really good malt whisky, notably Old MacPhunn.

$1 \times 1\frac{1}{2}$ *lb (750 g) loin or fillet venison*
Butter
1 wineglass blackcurrant liqueur
4 fl oz (125 ml) strong game or beef stock (see pages 151–153)
1 teaspoon tomato purée
Freshly ground black pepper

Bone the venison, if using loin. Cut the venison into 4 in. (10 cm) discs (or collops) and beat lightly with a rolling pin to flatten them. Fry gently in butter for 1 minute or so on each side. Pour in the blackcurrant liqueur and flame. Remove the venison from the pan, put into a serving dish and keep warm.

Meanwhile, as the flames die away from the blackcurrant liqueur, pour in the game or beef stock, and let it bubble for 2 or 3 minutes. Stir in the tomato purée and season well with pepper. At this stage the sauce may be really quite thick and it would be a good idea to add a couple of tablespoons of water and any juices that have seeped from the venison. Dip your finger in to see if it tastes nice and, if you have a good, runny, rich sauce, beat in a knob of butter to make it really rich and shiny, then strain it through a fine sieve over the venison.

FILLET OF VENISON WITH CELERIAC AND GLAZED APPLES

*2 lb (1 kg) venison saddle, on
    the bone*
*4 oz (125 g) carrots, leeks,
    onions, very finely chopped*
1 bouquet garni
6 juniper berries
6 peppercorns
1 clove garlic, crushed
1 bay leaf
2 pints (1 litre) red wine
*Salt and freshly ground black
    pepper*
1 large potato
1 celeriac
4 green apples
8 oz (250 g) caster sugar
2 measures Calvados
2 oz (50 g) butter

You need to start several days ahead. Take the eye of the meat from the bone to produce 2 fillets and put to one side. Chop the bone and cook on top of the stove with the finely chopped carrots, leeks and onions until a very dark colour. Add the bouquet garni, juniper berries, peppercorns, garlic, bay leaf and red wine. Top with cold water, season well, and cook until the maximum flavour is achieved, skimming all the time. When the stock is ready, strain though a fine sieve and reduce to a rich sauce consistency. Coat the venison fillets with this and leave to marinate for several days in a cool place, turning frequently.

To prepare the celeriac, first boil the potato until three-quarters cooked. Remove from the water, allow to cool, then grate. Peel and grate the celeriac: there should be two-thirds celeriac to one-third potato. Mix the two together and season with salt and pepper. Take a round plain cutter, place some of the mixture inside and push down with a spoon until you have made a small pancake shape. When you are almost ready to serve the dish, fry this pancake in butter until golden brown and crispy on both sides.

Next, peel, core, quarter and turn the apples with a small knife into barrel shapes. Put the caster sugar in a heavy-based pan, just cover with cold water and bring to the boil. Let this cook until a caramel colour has been achieved and add the Calvados. Drop the apples into the hot caramel, cook for about 1 minute and then remove.

Take the venison from the marinade, cut into 4 pieces and cook in the butter on the top of the stove for a few minutes on both sides, making sure that you keep the meat medium rare.

Put the marinade into a saucepan and reduce for a few minutes. Add a few knobs of butter if required.

To present the dish, put the celeriac rosti towards the top of the plate and top with the glazed apples. Slice the venison and arrange in a fan below the celeriac, and pour the sauce around it.

Photograph facing page 120

Serves 4

PIGEONS WITH PEAS

This is a superb summer meal and you must use the freshest and crispest herbs and vegetables to appreciate its excellence.

4 young pigeons, drawn
Salt and pepper
Mint
Butter
1 onion, chopped
5 fl oz (150 ml) Rhine wine
5 fl oz (150 ml) stock
1 lb (500 g) peas, shelled
1 bunch spring onions, white
*   bulb only*
2 lettuce hearts, quartered
Lemon juice
Lemon slices and mint leaves
*   to garnish*

Season the pigeons with salt and pepper. Stuff the body cavities with mint leaves, and brown the birds all over in butter. Transfer to a flameproof casserole.

Fry the onion in the remaining butter in the frying pan. Pour on the wine, reduce slightly, then add the stock. Pour over the pigeons in the casserole and cook on top of the stove for about 1 hour.

Fifteen minutes before the pigeons are cooked add the peas, spring onions and lettuce hearts.

To serve, arrange the peas and onions on a warmed dish, sit the pigeons on top and crown with the lettuce. Boil the cooking juices and reduce, stir in some lemon juice and pour over the pigeons. Garnish with lemon slices and mint leaves.

PIGEON PIE

4–5 pigeons, drawn
Salt and pepper
8 oz (250 g) stewing beef
8 oz (250 g) shortcrust pastry
Beaten egg to glaze
1 dessertspoon cornflour
10 fl oz (300 ml) stock (see
  recipe)

Pre-heat the oven to gas mark 4, 350°F (180°C). Joint the birds into two breast joints and two leg joints each and stew the rest of the carcasses in a little water to make stock for the gravy. Cut the beef into small pieces and line a deep 8 in. (20 cm) pie-dish with these. Lay the pigeon joints on top, cover with water, add salt and pepper, then cover the pie-dish with greased paper or aluminium foil. Place in the oven and simmer for 1½ hours.

Remove from the oven and raise oven temperature to gas mark 6, 400°F (200°C). Cover the pie with the shortcrust pastry, brush the top with beaten egg, put back into the oven and bake until the pastry is golden brown.

Make a gravy by mixing 1 dessertspoon of cornflour with a little cold water and add to 10 fl oz (300 ml) of the warmed stock. Allow to thicken while stirring, season and serve with the pie.

Photograph facing page 121

BREAST OF PIGEON WITH HERB RAVIOLI

2 plump pigeons
½ pint (300 ml) chicken stock
1 pint (600 ml) veal stock,
  reduced by half
2 oz (50 g) chicken livers (see
  recipe)
1 oz (25 g) chopped fresh
  herbs

Combine the ingredients for the ravioli paste and allow to rest in the fridge for half an hour.

Remove the breasts from the pigeons and keep the livers, discarding the other giblets. Chop the pigeon bones and legs, then brown them in a pan. Add the chicken and veal stock and reduce by half. Strain through muslin.

For the ravioli paste:
3 oz (75 g) strong flour
1 oz (25 g) semolina flour
1 egg
1 teaspoon oil
Salt and pepper
1 oz (25 g) chopped fresh
    herbs
Nutmeg

Make the ravioli filling by chopping all the livers and mixing with the chopped herbs. Roll out the ravioli paste as thinly as you can. Along one half of the pasta, spoon the filling into 16 mounds at about 2 in. (5 cm) intervals. Fold across the other half of the pasta to cover. Cut out ravioli with a round 2 in. (5 cm) diameter cutter. Press the edges together.

Fry the seasoned pigeon breasts in a pan until golden and then finish in a hot oven for 3–4 minutes until rare.

Poach the ravioli for 1 minute in salted boiling water, then carefully lift out. Slice the pigeon breasts horizontally into thin escalopes and serve with the herb ravioli.

Serves 1

MALLARD IN A CLAY POT

In former times country folk used to bake small game birds wrapped in clay over the ashes of their fires. Today you can achieve the same effect with a chicken brick. You can cook grouse this way as well.

1 mallard, drawn, liver
    reserved
Butter
½ apple
1 rasher fat bacon
2 tablespoons red wine

Soak your chicken brick for several hours in cold water.

Stuff the mallard with a knob of butter, the liver and half an apple to keep the bird moist. Lay the bacon over the breast and put the bird in the clay pot. Spoon over the wine and cover.

Place in a cold oven and turn the temperature control to gas mark 5, 375°F (190°C). Cook for 50 minutes. Serve with fried breadcrumbs, watercress and wafer-thin fried potatoes.

Photograph facing page 136

Pot Roast Mallard

Old grouse and partridge can be cooked the same way.

1 medium swede, diced
2 lb (1 kg) carrots, diced
2 lb (1 kg) parsnips, diced
1 large onion, finely chopped
3 mallards, dressed
1 tablespoon olive oil
2 glasses port
2 tablespoons redcurrant jelly
10 fl oz (300 ml) chicken or
  game stock
Juice of 2 oranges
Fresh rosemary and thyme
Salt and black pepper

Spread the vegetables over the bottom of a deep roasting tin large enough to hold 3 mallards.

Brown the birds evenly, one at a time, in a large frying pan with the olive oil and then place on top of the vegetables in the roasting tin. Pour off any oil remaining in the frying pan and de-glaze with the port. Add the redcurrant jelly to dissolve, and pour over the mallards. Finally add the stock, orange juice, rosemary and thyme and season to taste with salt and pepper. Cover with aluminium foil.

Cook in the oven at gas mark 8, 450°F (230°C), for 30 minutes, then reduce the temperature to gas mark 6, 400°F (200°C), for a further 30 minutes or so, until cooked.

Take the mallards from the oven and split each in two, removing as much of the carcass as possible while still keeping the shape of the half-bird. Serve on to hot plates with generous quantities of the vegetables and cooking liquor.

Roast Pheasant

Grouse and partridge may be roasted in the same way. It's important to get hold of an unhung bird – rotting flesh and thick red floury sauces with stuffing and jam are positively out.

1 plump unhung pheasant,
  drawn
Salt, pepper and thyme
4–5 oz (125–150 g) butter
2 glasses red wine
5 fl oz (150 ml) game glaze
  (see pages 151–152)

Season your bird with salt, pepper and thyme and fry in butter until golden on all sides – don't burn the butter or the pheasant. Then place the bird breast down in a roasting tin with the butter and roast for 15 minutes at gas mark 5, 375°F (190°C), on the left breast and then for a further 15 minutes on the right breast. The breasts stay moist while the tougher legs cook through. Baste frequently! Add more butter if necessary, for the more you baste the better the result.

Now place the bird on its back, add the wine and cook for a further 15 minutes. Jab a fork in a leg to check that it is cooked before removing from the oven to carve. Carefully save any juices that run out as you carve and add to the sauce in the roasting tin. You must now bubble the sauce, with the juices added, on top of the stove for 2 or 3 minutes. Add the game glaze. Taste, season with pepper and whisk in a knob of butter. Pour this sauce over the pheasant and serve with matchstick chips or other fried potatoes.

Serves 2

SPATCHCOCKED PARTRIDGE

2 young partridges, drawn
3 fl oz (75 ml) oil
Salt and pepper
2 bay leaves, crumbled
2 teaspoons chopped thyme
2 teaspoons chopped parsley
8 fl oz (250 ml) rémoulade
  sauce to serve (see page
  133)

Cut the birds almost in two lengthways and flatten out. Marinate them for 2 hours in the oil with the salt, pepper, bay leaves, thyme and parsley, turning them once or twice.

Grill the birds, under a high heat, for 5 minutes on each side. Then reduce the heat and cook for another 10 to 15 minutes, turning them over once or twice. Serve with the rémoulade sauce.

ROAST WOODCOCK OR SNIPE

For me woodcock and snipe are the two best game birds in the entire world. They are quite small: woodcock needs roasting in a hot oven for only about 20 minutes and snipe for even less time. Best of all would be to wrap them in fatty bacon, truss them and spit-roast them over the embers of an open fire. You will probably never do that, so let's go back to the oven plan.

2 woodcock or snipe
Pig's caul or fatty bacon
Butter
1 measure brandy
1 cube frozen game glaze (see
*   pages 151–152)*
Salt and pepper
4 slices bread
Dripping or lard

You must remove the gizzards of the plucked birds when drawing them, but leave the heart and liver inside. Wrap them in either pig's caul or fatty bacon, truss them with string and roast with a knob of butter at gas mark 6, 400°F (200°C). When they are cooked, take off the string, cut them in half, scrape the heart and liver into the juices of the roasting tin and put the birds to one side to keep warm. Add a good dash of brandy to the juices in the roasting tin and, if you have a little cube of frozen game glaze add that too and bubble it all up, mashing in the heart and liver. Add a knob of butter and season with salt and pepper. Set the half-birds on to pieces of bread fried in dripping or lard and pour the sauce over them. This is the classic British way of preparing these delectable birds and a perfect excuse to drink some fine old Burgundy.

SAUCES FOR GAME

Myrtle Allen

BREAD SAUCE

Serve with turkey, chicken and guinea fowl.

10 fl oz (300 ml) milk
5 oz (150 g) breadcrumbs
1 onion stuck with 6 cloves
1 oz (25 g) butter
Salt and pepper
¼ teaspoon ground allspice
1 tablespoon thick cream

Bring all the ingredients except the cream to the boil in a saucepan. Cover and simmer gently on top of the stove or in an ovenproof dish in the oven for 30 minutes. Remove the onion and add the cream before serving.

RÉMOULADE SAUCE

3 or 4 egg yolks
Salt and pepper
1 teaspoon wine vinegar
1–2 teaspoons mustard
17 fl oz (500 ml) olive oil
1 teaspoon chopped shallot
1 teaspoon chopped onion
1 teaspoon chopped parsley
1 teaspoon chopped chervil

Beat the egg yolks in a bowl with the salt and pepper, vinegar and mustard. Add the olive oil drop by drop, whisking constantly. When the mixture is thick, stir in the shallot, onion, parsley and chervil.

REDCURRANT JELLY

Serve with cold meats, turkey, chicken, guinea fowl and game.

Fresh or frozen redcurrants
Sugar
Water

Cover the fruit with cold water. Bring to the boil and cook for about 5 minutes until the fruit is soft. Turn into a strainer placed over a bowl. Leave to stand for about 10 minutes. Do not press the fruit or the juice will become cloudy.

Measure the juice. For every pint (600 ml) of juice, allow 1 lb (500 g) of sugar. Boil the juice and sugar together rapidly until setting point is reached. This will take 5 to 10 minutes. Put a teaspooon of the liquid on a saucer in the refrigerator to test for a set. Pot and cover as for jam. The jelly will keep a year in a cool, dry place.

RED WINE SAUCE

$\frac{1}{2}$ *large onion, diced*
$\frac{1}{2}$ *medium-sized carrot, diced*
1 oz (25 g) unsalted butter
1 clove garlic, crushed
$\frac{1}{2}$ *pint (300 ml) red wine*
Pinch of salt
Pinch of sugar
$\frac{1}{2}$ *pint (300 ml) meat glaze*
  (see pages 151–152)

Cook the onion and carrot gently in a little of the butter for 20 minutes, stirring often; do not let the mixture brown. When this is well cooked, add the garlic. Heat the mixture for a minute and pour in the red wine. Season with a pinch of salt and a pinch of sugar. Reduce the sauce to two-thirds, then add the meat glaze and cook slowly for 20 minutes. Strain through a fine sieve, pushing the vegetables through. Bring the sauce back to the boil; finish away from the flame by adding the rest of the butter.

POULTRY

A Chicken is just a barnyard fowl, and it may
be rightly called the best of all birds covered by
the name of Poultry. It is a more important article
of food, all the world over, than any other
domesticated fowl, and its claim to being the best
of them all rests upon the fact that, like bread,
potatoes and rice, Chicken may be eaten constantly
without becoming nauseating.

ANDRÉ SIMON, *A CONCISE ENCYCLOPEDIA OF GASTRONOMY*.

When I was a boy growing up in Somerset a meal of chicken was a great treat. For a succulent roast and stuffed chicken a plump young bird was chosen from the dozen or so that scratched and clucked around the garden under the apple trees. For stews, soups or pies the oldest, toughest one was summoned to the pot. They had brown and white meat, the neck and giblets were used to make the gravy: they really tasted of something. Today, sadly, the great British free-range chicken is as easy to come by as a dodo steak larded with truffles, but if you take the trouble to seek out a supplier of the real thing and eschew the temptation to pick up a frozen white lump of water-injected, fish-meal fed, anaemic-looking 'meat' from the freezer chests of your local supermarket you will be doing yourself – and the diminishing band of butchers and farmers who care about the good things in life – a favour.

Aidan McCormack   *Serves 1*

PAN-FRIED CHICKEN BREAST

1 free-range chicken breast
Salt and pepper
Butter for frying
1 young slender leek
1 shallot, chopped
1 glass white wine
3 fl oz (75 ml) veal stock
2 tablespoons cream

Bone and skin the chicken breast, season with salt and pepper and fry in butter until cooked. Remove from the pan and keep warm.

Chop the white part of the leek only (reserve the green part) and add, along with the shallot, to the pan in which you fried the chicken. Add the wine and reduce until the leek and shallots are moist. Add the veal stock. Reduce a little until syrupy and add the cream.

Slice the chicken. Lightly cook the reserved green part of the leek and cut into small diamond shapes.

Strain the sauce on to a serving platter. Place the chicken on the platter and decorate with the green leek pieces.

Photograph facing page 152

Mallard in a Clay Pot (page 129)

OLD-FASHIONED ROAST CHICKEN WITH FRESH HERB STUFFING

Allow approximately 1 serving per 12 oz (350 g) chicken.

1 × 3½–5 lb (1.75–2.5 kg)
free-range roasting
chicken, drawn, with neck
and giblets reserved
½ carrot, sliced
½ onion, sliced
1 bouquet garni
Salt and pepper
¼ oz (7 g) butter
1 oz (25 g) good-quality
dripping

For the fresh herb stuffing:
3 oz (75 g) onions, chopped
1½ oz (40 g) butter
5 oz (150 g) soft breadcrumbs
2 tablespoons chopped herbs
(parsley, thyme, chives,
marjoram, savoury)
Salt and pepper

First make a chicken stock by covering the neck, giblets, vegetables and bouquet garni with cold water. Bring to the boil and simmer while the chicken is being prepared and cooked.

Next make the herb stuffing. Sweat the onions gently in butter. When beginning to soften, stir in the crumbs, herbs and a little salt and pepper to taste.

If necessary, wash and dry the cavity of the bird, then season and half-fill with the stuffing. Season the breast and smear with a little butter. Roast in a little dripping in the oven at gas mark 6, 400°F (200°C), for approximately 20 minutes, reducing the heat to gas mark 4, 350°F (180°C), for another 45 minutes to 1 hour more, depending on size. The chicken is done when the juices run clear: to test, prick in the thickest part – between thigh and body.

To make the gravy, spoon the surplus fat from the roasting tin. Deglaze with giblet stock, stirring and scraping well to dissolve the meaty deposits. Boil up well and serve in a warmed gravy boat to accompany the chicken.

Photograph facing page 153

Rabbit in Lentils (page 119)

GLAZED SPRING CHICKEN

6 spring onions, trimmed and
   finely chopped
7 fl oz (200 ml) soy sauce
6 tablespoons dry sherry
1 level teaspoon ground ginger
2½ lb (1.25 kg) free-range
   spring chicken, quartered
2 oz (50 g) butter
Vegetable oil
Clear honey to glaze

Make a marinade from the chopped spring onions, soy sauce, sherry and ginger, mixing together in a large dish. Add the quartered chicken and turn to coat well. Cover and refrigerate overnight, turning the chicken pieces occasionally. Heat the butter and sufficient vegetable oil in a large frying pan and fry the chicken quarters until tender and well browned all over.

When all the quarters are cooked, brush the pieces with a little honey and arrange on a serving dish on a bed of coarsely shredded lettuce. Sprinkle the lettuce with chopped chives if you wish.

CHICKEN FRICASSÉE

This one is for the poor old chicken when it stops laying and has to hit the pot.

1 × 3½ lb (1.75 kg) free-range
   boiling fowl, jointed
2 onions, chopped
2 carrots, sliced
4 oz (125 g) mushrooms,
   sliced
1 bouquet garni
Salt and pepper
2 oz (50 g) butter
2 oz (50 g) plain flour
1 pint (600 ml) chicken stock
   (see page 153)

Put the chicken, onions, carrots and mushrooms into a large pan with enough water to cover. Add the bouquet garni, salt and pepper. Bring slowly to the boil and simmer gently for 1 hour, or until the chicken is tender. Strain the stock, reserving the vegetables and stock separately.

Remove the skin from the chicken, carve the meat and cut it into cubes.

Melt the butter, stir in the flour and cook for 2 to 3 minutes. Remove from

1 egg yolk
3 tablespoons cream
Juice $\frac{1}{2}$ lemon

For the garnish:
4 rashers streaky bacon,
    rinded, rolled and grilled
Parsley sprigs

the heat and gradually add the stock.
Bring to the boil and cook until the
sauce thickens, stirring constantly. Add
the meat and vegetables; remove from
the heat.

Beat together the egg yolk and
cream, add a little of the sauce and
blend well. Pour the mixture back into
the pan and heat through without
boiling. Add the lemon juice. Transfer the fricassée to a warmed
serving dish and garnish with the grilled bacon rolls and parsley
sprigs.

George McCalpine   Serves 4

CHICKEN IN PUFF PASTRY

$1\frac{1}{2}$ lb (750 g) free-range
    chicken breast fillets
Salt and papper
Butter
4 × 5 in. (12.5 cm) discs of
    puff pastry, $\frac{1}{4}$ in. (6 mm)
    thick
Beaten egg to glaze
Parsley to garnish

For the sauce:
1 shallot, chopped
1 oz (25 g) butter
2 fl oz (50 ml) dry white wine
2 fl oz (50 ml) chicken glaze
    (see page 152)
5 fl oz (150 ml) double cream
Salt and pepper
Finely chopped herbs (thyme,
    chives, parsley, chervil)

Season the chicken breast fillets with
salt and pepper and fry in a little butter
until cooked. Set aside and keep warm.

Draw a criss-cross design on the top
of each pastry disc with the point of a
sharp knife. Brush with beaten egg and
bake in the oven at gas mark 6, 400°F
(200°C), until well puffed and golden
brown. Cut off the top to form a lid;
scoop out the uncooked inside and
discard.

To make the sauce, sweat the shallot
in the butter, add the wine and chicken
glaze and reduce. Add the cream and
boil vigorously until the sauce thickens.
Season with salt and pepper and add
the herbs.

Fill the scooped-out pastry discs with
the chicken fillets and coat with the
herb sauce. Garnish the dish with
parsley sprigs.

WELLINGTON CHICKEN WITH CREAM SAUCE

I have named this recipe after my old school in Somerset where the staff very kindly invited me to take the home economics class one merry March day and, despite a few glasses of sherry in the teachers' den beforehand, I came up with this simple but rich dish.

1 plump free-range roasting chicken
Juice of 1 lemon
Salt and pepper
1 large sprig fresh thyme
3 oz (75 g) butter
10 fl oz (300 ml) double cream
6 leaves fresh tarragon
3 egg yolks
Watercress to garnish

Rub the chicken inside and out with lemon juice, salt and pepper. Place the sprig of thyme inside the bird and smear the outside with the butter. Roast, breast down, in the oven at gas mark 5, 375°F (190°C), for about 1 hour. Then turn the chicken on to its back and continue roasting till the skin is golden and crisp. Transfer the bird to a warmed serving dish and keep warm.

Place the roasting tin with all its juices and melted butter on top of the stove over a low heat, stir in the cream and tarragon leaves and bubble up gently for 5 to 7 minutes until you have a rich creamy sauce. Now reduce the heat even lower and beat in the egg yolks. Strain the sauce through a fine sieve over the chicken. Carve, garnish with crisp watercress and serve with boiled new potatoes.

ROAST DUCK

A good duck, roasted well, is always a treat. To give a delicious, crispy skin, ensure that you prick well all over to allow the fat to escape.

*1 × 4 lb (2 kg) free-range
  duck, dressed, giblets
  reserved*
Salt and pepper
1 tablespoon plain flour

For the stock:
1 tablespoon vegetable oil
1 pint (600 ml) water
1 stick celery, chopped
1 onion
1 bay leaf

First make the stock. Heat the oil in a saucepan and brown the duck gizzard and heart. Add the water, vegetables, bay leaf and liver. Bring to the boil, cover and simmer gently for 45 minutes. Strain the giblet stock into a bowl, return it to the pan and bring back to the boil. Boil rapidly until reduced to about 10 fl oz (300 ml). Cool and skim the fat off the surface.

Put the duck on a wire rack in a roasting tin and sprinkle the breast liberally with a mixture of salt and pepper. Rub the seasoning thoroughly into the skin. Prick the skin all over with a sharp fork or skewer. Roast in the oven at gas mark 5, 375°F (190°C), allowing 20 minutes per lb (500 g) and basting occasionally with fat from the tin. Invert the bird half-way through the cooking time.

When the duck is cooked, a skewer pushed into the meat should release clear, not pink, juices. Transfer to a warm plate, remove the trussing string and keep warm.

Drain the fat from the roasting tin and stir the flour into the remaining juices. Cook over moderate heat until it bubbles, stirring all the time to prevent sticking. Gradually stir in the reduced stock. Cook the gravy for about 10 minutes, stirring until smooth and thickened. Season to taste and serve with the duck.

Duck Terrine

This is a grand party dish. The trouble is, when you ask a superb chef for a recipe he tends to give you the sort of quantities he would make, especially as he'll save any surplus for use in another dish as part of the continuing process of the kitchen. I have done my best to scale down Gary's recipe, but you may need to make some further adjustments to fit your own utensils (and don't forget, if you have some ingredients over, you can always put them to good use elsewhere).

8 oz (250 g) veal kidney, minced
Madeira, brandy and port
2 free-range duck breasts
1 pork fillet
12 oz (350 g) chicken livers
Milk
12 rashers streaky bacon
1 oz (25 g) pistachio nuts

For the pastry:
6 oz (175 g) butter
3 eggs
1 egg yolk
2 fl oz (50 ml) orange juice
Orange rind, grated
1 lb (500 g) flour
Salt

For the port jelly:
3 tablespoons redcurrant jelly
15 fl oz (450 ml) port
5 fl oz (150 ml) reduced duck stock
4 leaves gelatine

To make the pastry, melt the butter and add all the wet ingredients and rind. Mix with the flour and salt and knead to a workable paste, adding water if necessary. Allow to rest.

Soak the minced veal kidney in Madeira, the duck breasts in the brandy and the pork fillet in the port for 2 hours. The chicken livers should be soaked in milk to prevent them from becoming bitter. Drain the meats.

To make the terrine, line a large mould or loaf tin with the pastry and lay the rashers of bacon on it, covering the whole of the inside. Place the veal kidney into the base of the mould and lay a duck breast across the top with a sprinkling of pistachio nuts. Place a pork fillet through the centre of the mould and the chicken livers either side. Lay the other duck breast on top and continue to fill with the minced veal kidney and pistachios, seasoning with salt and pepper as you go. When at the top of the mould, fold in the rashers of bacon to cover and place a lid of pastry on top. Make a hole in the centre of the pastry so that the port jelly can be added once the terrine is cooked. Leave to rest.

To cook the terrine, place in the oven at gas mark 6, 400°F (200°C), for 55 minutes to 1 hour. Make the port jelly by heating the redcurrant jelly, port and reduced stock together in a pan. Add the gelatine and stir till it has dissolved. Allow to cool, and as it begins to set pour in through the hole in the pasty lid until the case is filled. Allow to cool, place in the refrigerator and leave to rest for 1 day before serving.

Serves 6 to 8

DUCKLING WITH PEAS

A summer dish in which freshness of ingredients is vital. Use proper hearty English lettuces – none of your icebergs.

2 free-range ducklings, dressed
Salt and pepper
2 oz (50 g) flour
2 oz (50 g) butter
2 pints (1 litre) stock
1¼ lb (625 g) shelled peas
2 lettuces, finely chopped
1 bunch herbs (basil, parsley, mint)
½ teaspoon grated nutmeg
2 egg yolks
5 fl oz (150 ml) double cream
Chopped mint to garnish

Dust the ducklings with seasoned flour and brown in the butter. Roast in the oven in a deep flameproof casserole for 30 minutes at gas mark 4, 350°F (180°C). Pour off the surplus fat and add the stock and some salt and pepper. Bring slowly to the boil and simmer for 15–20 minutes. Add the peas, lettuces and herbs. Cover and simmer for 40 minutes or until the ducks are tender. Remove the bunch of herbs.

Lift out the ducklings and keep warm on a serving dish. Rub the cooking liquid through a sieve or liquidise. Add the nutmeg and blend in the egg yolks beaten with the cream. Heat the sauce through to thicken but do not boil. Season. Pour over the ducklings and serve garnished with mint.

WELSH SALT DUCK WITH LAVERBREAD

This recipe is ideal for an old bird because of the slow, gentle cooking process.

1 good-sized free-range duck,
   dressed
4 oz (125 g) saltpetre
4 oz (125 g) brown
   muscovado sugar
Laverbread, cooked
   (see page 86)

Wipe the duck and place in a deep dish. Rub all over with saltpetre and sugar and leave to stand, covered, in a cool place for 3 days. Turn the duck daily. Rinse the bird before cooking and place in a large pot. Cover with water and bring to the boil, reduce the heat to a very gentle simmer and cook for about 2 hours. Salt duck can be served hot with a white onion sauce, or cold. To serve cold, allow the duck to cool in its cooking liquor. Remove the bird. Skin it and slice into strips. Lay the strips on a platter lined with lettuce leaves. Serve with a purée of laverbread warmed with a little butter and fresh orange juice and grated rind.

Photograph facing page 168

ROAST GUINEA FOWL

This is a pleasing alternative to the strong meat of pheasant or to the insipid taste of modern battery-raised chicken (ugh). There's lots of meat on them, and one guinea fowl happily serves two people.

2 small guinea fowl, drawn,
   giblets reserved
3 oz (75 g) butter
Sprigs tarragon or parsley
12 oz (350 g) streaky bacon
   rashers or pork fat
10 fl oz (300 ml) dry white
   wine

Put the giblets in a pan, cover with water and bring to the boil. Simmer for 1 hour to make stock.
   Put $\frac{1}{2}$ oz (15 g) of butter and a sprig of tarragon or parsley inside each guinea fowl. Melt 1 oz (25 g) of butter and brush liberally over the birds. Cover the breasts with streaky bacon and roast

2½ fl oz (60 ml) sherry
6 oz (175 g) green grapes,
    peeled and de-pipped
Salt and pepper
Juice of 1 lemon

in the oven for 1 hour at gas mark 4,
350°F (180°C). Baste frequently and
remove the bacon for the last 20
minutes to allow the meat to brown.

Remove the guinea fowl from the
oven and carve into joints. Pour most
of the fat from the roasting tin, leaving all the residues, then add the
wine, sherry and stock. Boil through, then add the guinea fowl and
4 oz (125 g) grapes. Season to taste with salt, pepper and lemon juice.

Cover and cook for 15 to 20 minutes in the oven. Remove the
joints from the sauce and place on a warm serving dish. Strain the
sauce and stir in 1 oz (25 g) butter. Pour over the birds and serve
garnished with the remaining grapes.

Serves 4

ROAST GOOSE

No Christmas is complete without roast goose: here is how I prepare
mine. As with all birds, a goose will take longer to cook if stuffed.
For birds that have a high fat content, such as duck or goose, I prefer
to cook a crispy stuffing separately. My favourite for goose is chestnut
stuffing (see page 146).

1 × 6–8 lb (3 kg–4 kg) free-
    range goose, dressed,
    giblets reserved
Salt

For the stock:
½ onion
½ carrot
1 bay leaf
1 bouquet garni

To make the stock, cover the giblets
with water and add the other
ingredients. Allow to simmer slowly
for 2 hours.

Remove any fat from inside the
goose. Prick the bird well all over with
a skewer or fork. Sprinkle with salt and
place, breast down, on a rack in a
roasting tin. Roast in the oven at gas
mark 4, 350°F (180°C), for 25 to 30
minutes per lb (500 g). Drain the fat
periodically from the tin and reserve in a glass bowl. Turn the goose
30 minutes before the end. When the goose is cooked, keep warm.
Skim any fat from the roasting tin and add to the tin the juices that
have settled under the fat in the bowl. Boil the cooking juices rapidly,
add a little of the stock and serve hot with the goose.

Stuffings for Poultry

These are all-purpose stuffings. The quantities given here are enough for a good-sized chicken. If you're stuffing a goose or a turkey multiply the quantities accordingly.

Chestnut Stuffing

2 oz (50 g) bacon, rinded and chopped
8 oz (250 g) unsweetened chestnut purée
4 oz (125 g) fresh white breadcrumbs
1 teaspoon chopped parsley
1 oz (25 g) butter, melted
Grated rind 1 lemon
Salt and pepper
1 egg, beaten

Fry the bacon gently in its own fat until crisp, then drain well on kitchen paper. Combine with the remaining ingredients.

Sage and Onion Stuffing

2 large onions, chopped
1 oz (25 g) butter
Salt and pepper
4 oz (125 g) fresh white breadcrumbs
2 tablespoons chopped sage

Put the onions in a pan and cover with cold water. Bring to the boil and cook for about 10 minutes. Drain and mix with the other ingredients.

CORN AND BACON STUFFING

2 oz (50 g) butter

6 oz (175 g) streaky bacon
    rashers, rinded and chopped

1 onion, chopped

1 small tin sweetcorn kernels,
    drained

½ green pepper, de-seeded and
    chopped

12 oz (350 g) fresh white
    breadcrumbs

2 tablespoons chopped parsley

Salt and pepper

1 egg, beaten

Heat the butter and sauté the bacon and onion together for a few minutes. Add the sweetcorn and green pepper and cook for a few more minutes. Remove from the heat. Stir in the breadcrumbs, parsley and seasoning and mix well. Add enough beaten egg to bind the mixture.

APRICOT AND WALNUT STUFFING

4 oz (125 g) dried apricots

1 oz (25 g) sultanas

3 oz (75 g) fresh white
    breadcrumbs

2 oz (50 g) shelled walnuts,
    finely chopped

¼ teaspoon mixed spice

¼ teaspoon salt

¼ teaspoon pepper

1 tablespoon lemon juice

2 teaspoons grated lemon rind

1 oz (25 g) butter, melted

1 egg, beaten

Soak the apricots overnight. Drain and chop finely. Stir in the remaining ingredients and bind with the egg.

Sausage and Apple Stuffing

1 lb (500 g) pork sausagemeat
Butter
3 cooking apples, peeled,
  cored and chopped
1 onion, chopped
2 sticks celery, chopped
8 oz (250 g) fresh white
  breadcrumbs
2 eggs, beaten
1½ teaspoons salt
Pinch pepper

Brown the sausagemeat in butter and remove from the pan. Pour off all but 4 tablespoons of fat. Add the apples, onion and celery and cook until tender. Return the sausagemeat to the pan with the remaining ingredients and mix well.

6

MEAT

In the latter times some shall depart from
the faith, giving heed to seducing spirits, and
doctrines of devils . . . commanding to abstain
from meats, which God hath created to be received
with thanksgiving of them which
believe and know the truth.

THE BIBLE, *TIMOTHY IV.*

STOCKS

Although a number of dishes in this book have sauces within the recipe, do refer to this section each time a recipe calls for some stock or meat glaze. Throughout the book you'll find many recipes which need, say, 10 fl oz (300 ml) of veal, chicken, or game stock, but you can't really be bothered with all that so you just pour in water or a chicken stock cube, or even abandon the dish altogether. However, if every now and again you are able to spare a couple of hours to make some basic stocks and freeze them in small plastic containers or those little ice-cube trays, when you get to one of these recipes, rather than saying 'Oh my God!', all you have to do is open the freezer door and hey presto! – there is your stock.

The system works in two ways: first of all, you must make a large quantity of veal stock. This is the foundation of everything else. But before you make the veal stock, which will be the one very special effort you must make, let us acquire in advance the ingredients for elaborating the basic veal stock into, say, game or chicken. This will all be explained in due course.

Whenever you have bones left after a meal – carcasses of chickens, pigeons, hares, rabbits – chop them up, pop them into a freezer bag, label and freeze. Do the same with any trimmings not needed in a recipe: for example, if you have made a jugged hare but used only the really fleshy pieces of meat, freeze the trimmings, feet and neck.

To make a basic veal stock which will last you a long time if you freeze it, use the following recipe:

RICH VEAL STOCK

4 lb (2 kg) veal bones
2 calf's feet, halved
8 oz (250 g) carrots, chopped
8 oz (250 g) mushrooms,
  chopped
4 oz (125 g) onions, chopped
1 large celery stalk, chopped
2 cloves garlic
14 fl oz (415 ml) dry white
  wine
7 pints (4 litres) water
8 large tomatoes, skinned, de-
  seeded and chopped
1 large bouquet garni of fresh
  herbs

First of all, brown the veal bones and feet in the oven at gas mark 6, 400°F (200°C), turning from time to time. Transfer to a big saucepan and then put all the chopped vegetables into the roasting tin in which you have cooked the bones.

Set the tin over a medium heat and lightly cook the carrots, mushrooms, onions, celery and garlic until they soften, but don't let them brown. Tip in the wine and continue cooking until the wine has almost all gone, then scrape all the vegetables from the tin into the saucepan with the bones.

Cover with the water and bring the mixture to the boil, turn the heat down immediately and allow to simmer. Skim off any scum and grease that appears on the surface: do this two or three times in the first 30 minutes of cooking. Next add the tomatoes and bouquet garni and continue to cook for at least 3 hours on a low heat. Strain the stock through a very fine mesh into a bowl and allow to cool completely. You can now pour it into small freezer tubs ready for future use.

However, it would be a good idea to take half of the stock that you have made, put it back into the pan and reduce it by three quarters. When it cools it will set to a jelly, and you can pop this into a little freezer tub or ice-cube trays and freeze it. You will find that this rich jelly, which is called a meat glaze, is a wonderful thing to help you make sauces for, say, a steak, whereas the lighter veal stock provides you with a wonderful liquid for making a casserole.

Now, this is how you use your reservoir of veal stock. Supposing you wanted some game stock, perhaps for braising or stewing some pigeons, all you now have to do is take out a few of those game left-overs you have frozen in the deep freeze. De-frost them, chop them into small pieces and brown them in hot oil in a saucepan. Then add a chopped carrot and chopped onion and cook these along with the bits of meat until soft but not brown. Pour in 1 pint (600 ml) of good red wine, chuck in a couple of crushed juniper berries, a bouquet garni, 1 pint (600 ml) of veal stock (not the glaze), and 2 pints (1 litre) of water and simmer the whole thing for a couple of hours at least, skimming off any scum. Strain the stock through a fine mesh. Reserve half as game stock and reduce the other half to two-thirds of its original volume. If you wanted to make a chicken-flavoured or duck-flavoured stock and, of course, subsequently a duck or chicken glaze, you do more or less exactly the same thing; and depending on whether you want a white sauce or a brown sauce, you use red or white wine.

If you take the trouble, perhaps twice a year, to prepare all these stocks and freeze them, on the nights you cook your wonderful meals for your friends you can do so in a very relaxed manner. At least always have some chicken stock and glaze, because all the meat, poultry and game recipes in this book can be made with this. Or use this all-purpose stock.

Makes about 5 pints (3 litres)

MEAT STOCK

This strong stock will keep for up to a week if refrigerated and brought to the boil every 2 days.

2 lb (1 kg) shin or leg of beef
2 lb (1 kg) shin of veal,
  including meaty veal
  knuckle
2 lb (1 kg) chicken backs,
  necks, feet and wing tips
9 pints (5 litres) water

Place a round metal pastry cutter or trivet in the bottom of a large stockpot to prevent the ingredients from sticking. Fit all the meat and bones into the pot and add water to cover by about 2 in. (5 cm). Bring slowly to the boil and skim off the scum that rises. Keep

Pan-fried Chicken Breast (page 136)

1 bouquet garni, bound with
  1 small leek and 1 stick
  celery
1 head garlic
2 medium onions, each stuck
  with 1 clove
4 carrots
Salt

skimming, occasionally adding a glass of cold water, until no more scum rises – this should take about 10 minutes. Add the bouquet garni, the unpeeled garlic, onions, carrots and salt, and skim once more as the liquid returns to the boil. Reduce the heat to very low, cover the pot with the lid ajar and simmer for 5 to 8 hours. If the meat is to be eaten, remove the veal after $1\frac{1}{2}$ hours and the beef after 3 hours.

Ladle the stock into a colander lined with dampened muslin placed over a large bowl. Leave the strained stock to cool completely, then remove the last traces of fat from the surface. If the stock is refrigerated, the solidified fat may be lifted off.

VEAL STOCK: Omit the beef, beef bones and chicken pieces and substitute about 4 lb (2 kg) of meaty veal trimmings (neck, shank or rib tips). For a richer, more gelatinous stock, you can add a calf's foot, cleaned, split and blanched beforehand for 5 minutes in boiling water.

BEEF STOCK: Substitute 4 lb (2 kg) of beef tail, shank or chuck for the shin of veal and the chicken pieces, and simmer the stock for about 5 hours. A veal knuckle or calf's foot can be added to the pot if a more gelatinous stock is desired.

CHICKEN STOCK: Old hens and roosters yield the richest stock. Use about 5 lb (2.5 kg) of carcasses, necks, feet, wings, gizzards and hearts, and simmer for 2 to 4 hours.

LAMB OR MUTTON STOCK: Use about 6–7 lb (3–3.5 kg) of lamb or mutton bones (including shank and middle neck or scrag end) and a veal knuckle. Simmer for 5 to 8 hours.

After they have all been strained and left to cool, if you reduce them by a further two thirds you will have a glaze (or jelly).

Old-fashioned Roast Chicken with Herbs (page 137)

The Grilled Beef Factor

Despite the dramatic progress in cooking and changing tastes, beef in some form or another still remains about the most popular dish in Britain. I suppose the Berni Brothers were responsible for this when thirty-odd years ago they launched their chain of steak houses, and despite the fact that the pretentious gastronauts of the day were disparaging of such places, it was easier then than now to eat a perfectly grilled steak. The trouble today is that people take steak, be it fillet, rump or sirloin, so much for granted that they whack it into a pan or under the grill with no thought or respect for the quality or preparation of the meat, and although there is no disputing the excellence of, say, Entrecôtes Canailles, so brilliantly conceived by *les frères* Roux, there is nothing to beat a simple well-grilled steak.

The most important point to remember when seeking success with this deceptively simple dish is to choose your meat carefully, so you must find a good butcher. The meat must be a deep red – almost vermilion – colour and finely grained. It must be firm, not flabby, and not weeping blood or liquid – it must not be moist. It should be slightly marbled in parts with little bits of fat, and in the case of, say, sirloin steak, the fat on the edge must be creamy white.

The butchering of the meat is also of importance. Always buy fillets from the middle so that they are neatly round, not a scraggy, flabby shape. Ensure that the membrane that surrounds the fillet and any odd bits of sinew are removed.

Unless you happen to be fabulously rich and have a huge cooker or a damned great grill, don't attempt to cook steaks for more than four people at a time. If you must have a dinner party which involves beef for six or more guests, I would recommend a roast joint or casserole – at least this way you will enjoy yourself as well.

With a sirloin steak, again insist upon the middle cut and make sure that the steaks are cut to an even thickness. In between the fat of the sirloin and the meat there is often a tough piece of sinew which must be cut out, and on the outer edge of the fat there is a thin membrane which also must be trimmed off before cooking.

For simple grilled steak, it is best to buy one of those flat, ridged, cast-iron griddles. Some time before you intend to grill your steaks, put this on the gas or the electric hob and let it heat to a very high temperature. Make sure that your meat is at room temperature – in other words, do not attempt to grill a steak that has come straight from the fridge and absolutely never one that has come straight from the freezer.

Make sure that the meat is dry and brush it very, very lightly with a little bland oil. When your griddle is very hot, take the steak between your finger and thumb and press the sides of the steak for a few seconds on to the hot griddle, so that all of the sides are sealed. Next place the steaks on to the griddle for probably not more than 2 minutes on each side if you like them pink in the middle; a little longer if you prefer them more cooked. Only when they have been sealed both front and back and round the sides should you sprinkle them with a little salt. Pepper should be added after they are cooked.

Before you serve the steaks, leave them on warmed plates in a warm part of the kitchen for a minute or two to allow them to 'rest'. This enables the meat to relax again after it has been tortured on the hot griddle, and permits the residual heat of the meat to finish off the cooking process nicely. Steaks cooked this way are great eaten without a sauce or with the kind of sauce that is prepared separately and poured over the meat.

For the more elaborate steak dish with, say, a wine sauce, the cooking process is quite different. Obviously the same rules apply for buying and preparing the meat, but this time you melt some clarified butter in a sauté pan. (It was Albert Roux who convinced me that clarified butter was better than ordinary butter.) You seal the steaks on the edges and both sides in the butter, then add a little salt and continue cooking until they are done to your liking.

Take the steaks from the pan and place them on an upturned saucer which is sitting on a bigger plate, so that any juices that run from the steaks can be collected and poured into the finished sauce. Obviously they must be kept warm during this time.

The pan in which you originally cooked the steaks contains very useful little bits of juice and small particles of meat which will help flavour the ultimate sauce. It is at this stage that if you are making a sauce of, say, wine and mushrooms for the steak, you do what is known as de-glazing the pan. This means simply that you pour a drop of wine into the sauté pan and bubble it up, stirring with a wooden spoon to loosen and mix in all the good things that are stuck to the bottom of the pan. You then proceed with finishing off the sauce, choosing one of the following, but be sure to have read the section on stocks and glazes on pages 150–153 first.

SAUCES FOR GRILLED MEATS

PIQUANT SAUCE WITH ONION, SHALLOT AND GHERKINS

$1\frac{1}{2}$ oz (40 g) butter
$\frac{1}{2}$ medium onion, finely
   chopped
1 large shallot, finely chopped
$1\frac{1}{2}$ tablespoons red wine
   vinegar
5 fl oz (150 ml) meat glaze
2 medium gherkins, chopped
Freshly ground pepper

Heat a little of the butter in a sauté pan, add the onion and shallot and cook slowly until they begin to soften.

Reduce the vinegar by half and add it, with the meat glaze, to the sauté pan. Cook slowly for 15 minutes, remove from the heat and add the rest of the butter, whisking. Finish the sauce by adding the gherkin and some pepper.

MADEIRA SAUCE WITH MUSHROOMS

4 oz (125 g) small very white
   mushrooms
1 oz (25 g) unsalted butter
10 fl oz (300 ml) meat glaze
$\frac{1}{2}$ glass Madeira
Salt and pepper

When cleaning the mushrooms, wash them rapidly: do not let them stand in water or they will turn brown.

Heat a little of the butter in a sauté pan. When it is starting to turn brown, add the mushrooms and sauté over a high heat. Add the meat glaze.

In a separate pan boil the Madeira to reduce it a little; then, away from the heat, add it, slightly cooled, to the sauce. Add the rest of the butter while stirring. Adjust the seasoning before serving.

Hunter's Sauce

1½ oz (40 g) unsalted butter
1 tablespoon oil
2 oz (50 g) firm white
    mushrooms, finely sliced
½ teaspoon shallot, chopped
1–2 ripe tomatoes, skinned,
    de-seeded and coarsely
    chopped
½ glass dry white wine
5 fl oz (150 ml) meat glaze
Chopped chervil and tarragon

In a sauté pan heat 1 oz (25 g) of butter with the oil, add the mushrooms and brown over a high heat. Add the shallot and heat for a few seconds. Add the tomatoes, wine and finally the meat glaze.

Off the heat, just before serving, finish the sauce by adding the rest of the butter and a sprinkling of chopped chervil and tarragon.

Red Wine Sauce with Beef Marrow

½ oz (15 g) unsalted butter
½ teaspoon chopped shallot
½ glass red Bordeaux wine
Pinch crushed peppercorns
1 small piece bay leaf
1 sprig thyme
5 fl oz (150 ml) meat glaze
1 oz (25 g) very fresh beef
    marrow
Salt

In a saucepan, heat half the butter and, when very hot, add the shallot and brown lightly. Add the wine, seasoning and herbs, bring the sauce to the boil, and reduce rapidly until 2 tablespoons remain. Add the meat glaze and boil for 15 minutes. Strain the sauce through a very fine sieve; bring to the boil again, adjust the seasoning and set aside until ready to serve.

Poach the marrow in a bowl of lightly salted hot water for 3 to 5 minutes. Drain and set aside.

When ready to serve, warm the sauce slightly. Off the heat add the rest of the butter to the sauce, stirring continuously with a wooden spoon while adding the marrow.

ROAST BEEF

My personal way of roasting beef that never fails is to rub into the fat a combination of 2 tablespoons of flour, 1 tablespoon of mustard powder and plenty of freshly milled black pepper. You do not have to use all the mixture: it depends on the size of your joint. To minimise shrinkage, meat should always be at room temperature before it is put in the oven.

Heat a little beef dripping in a roasting tin and fry the meat very quickly on each cut side to seal in the juices.

Pre-heat the oven to gas mark 6, 400°F (200°C). Place the meat on a rack in the roasting tin, fat side uppermost so that the fat will run down and baste the joint. Cook for 20 minutes, then reduce the temperature to gas mark 3, 325°F (160°C), and cook for a further 15 to 20 minutes per lb (500 g). Baste frequently. If you like your beef well done, it will require a slightly longer cooking time. Test whether the meat is done by inserting a skewer into the centre and observing the colour of the juices.

Remove the cooked beef from the roasting tin and place on a warmed serving dish. Either leave in the warming oven of the Aga, or near the stove, covered with a little aluminium foil. This is the resting period, an ideal time to increase the oven temperature to cook your Yorkshire pud, or crisp the potatoes.

You can also make the gravy. Skim the fat off the top of the roasting tin. Place over a high heat and add 1 tablespoonful of meat glaze. Stir well to scrape up all the meaty sediment. If you like a rich gravy, whisk in a knob of butter. Strain into a warmed gravy boat and remember to add any juices that may have run from the beef while it was resting. Alternatively, try serving your roast beef with one of the sauces on the preceding pages.

In either case, you'll want to accompany it with a really good Yorkshire pudding. And don't forget the horseradish sauce – home-made is immeasurably better than the bought variety, if you can manage it.

YORKSHIRE PUDDING

The secret of making Yorkshire pudding is to ensure that the oven is very hot, and that the fat in your tin is smoking hot before pouring in the batter.

5 oz (150 g) flour
Pinch salt
1 large egg
10 fl oz (300 ml) milk
Beef dripping

Sift the flour and salt into a bowl. Make a well in the centre, tip in the egg and a little of the milk. Beat well, gradually incorporating the flour, adding more of the milk as necessary until you have a smooth batter the consistency of thick cream. Allow to stand for at least 30 minutes.

Place a teaspoon of good beef dripping in the base of each individual Yorkshire pudding tin, or a tablespoon in a roasting tin if baking in one piece. Put the tins in the top of the oven at gas mark 7, 425°F (220°C), for 5 minutes until the fat is smoking. Working quickly, remove the tins, pour in the batter and pop back into the oven. They are cooked when well risen, puffy and golden brown. Small ones take 10 to 15 minutes; large ones 40 to 45 minutes if cooked in one tin.

HORSERADISH SAUCE

8 fl oz (250 ml) whipped
  cream
2 teaspoons wine vinegar
1 teaspoon lemon juice
$\frac{1}{4}$ teaspoon mustard
$\frac{1}{4}$ teaspoon salt
Pinch pepper
1 teaspoon sugar
$1\frac{1}{2}$ teaspoons grated
  horseradish

Mix all the ingredients together.

ROAST BEEF AND TRENCHERS

A trencher was a wooden platter for serving meat. Sometimes they were made of bread, and then they were eaten up, with all the soaked-in juices and gravy, at the end of the meal. Hence a trencherman was the servant who turned the meat and kept the trenches warm – or else he was a hearty eater who guzzled up all the plates after everyone else had left! That's the end of the history lesson.

8 lb (4 kg) prime English rib
  of beef on the bone
1 lb (500 g) carrots
1 lb (500 g) small onions
1 lb (500 g) parsnips
2 lb (1 kg) potatoes
10 fl oz (300 ml) stock
Salt and pepper

For the trenchers:
½ oz (15 g) sugar
11 fl oz (330 ml) tepid milk
10 fl oz (300 ml) tepid water
2 oz (50 g) fresh yeast
1 oz (25 g) fat
2 lb (1 kg) flour
½ oz (15 g) salt

Put the beef in a large roasting tin and cover with aluminium foil. Roast in the centre of the oven at gas mark 5, 375°F (190°C), for 1 hour. Place the whole vegetables around the joint and baste. Add the stock and seasoning. Put back in the oven, uncovered, and cook for another 45 minutes. Take the meat and vegetables out of the roasting tin and leave to rest in a warm place. Pour the juices from the roasting tin into a sauce/fat separator and keep warm.

To make the trenchers, dissolve the sugar in the milk and water and mix in the yeast. Leave for 10 minutes in a warm atmosphere. Rub the fat into the dry ingredients and stir in the yeast mixture. Cover and leave to prove at room temperature for 45 minutes. Knead and leave for a further 15 minutes.

Divide the dough into 8 equal pieces and roll each piece into a round 8 in. (20 cm) across. Place on well greased plates, prick all over and leave to prove for 20 minutes before the beef is ready. As you remove the cooked joint from the oven, raise the temperature to gas mark 6, 400°F (200°C), and bake the trenchers for 20 to 25 minutes.

To serve, pour some beef gravy on to each trencher, then top witn a good slice of the roast beef accompanied by the roasted vegetables.

Photograph facing page 169

Beef with Anchovies

Salt fish was used in old traditional cooking to add flavour to fresh meat. It is still used often in French country cooking and is brilliant with roast lamb.

10 anchovy fillets, tinned
1 oz (25 g) butter
2 lb (1 kg) rolled topside of beef
2 onions
2 carrots
1 celery
½ swede
1 leek
15 fl oz (450 ml) veal or beef stock

Mash half the anchovies and blend with the butter; brown the beef in this anchovy butter. Lard the meat with the remaining anchovies.

Chop the vegetables coarsely and place in a large casserole. Set the meat on top, pour over the stock, put the lid on the casserole and cook gently for about 2½ hours in the oven at gas mark 3, 325°F (160°C).

Beef and Pigeon Stew

1 lb (500 g) steak and kidney
Flour
Salt and pepper
2 pigeons, drawn and halved
4 bacon rashers
4 oz (125 g) onions, sliced
Dripping
10 fl oz (300 ml) stout
2 tablespoons cider vinegar
1 bunch herbs (thyme, parsley and bay leaf)

Cut the steak and kidney into 1 in. (2.5 cm) cubes and toss in seasoned flour. Wrap each pigeon half in a bacon rasher. Fry the onions lightly in dripping, add the meat and let it brown. Stir in the stout and vinegar and simmer for 15 minutes.

Arrange half the meat and onion mixture in a deep ovenproof dish, lay the pigeons on top, cover with the rest of the meat and onion and pour over the pan juices. Add the herbs and a sprinkling of salt and pepper. Cover well and cook in the oven at gas mark 3, 325°F (160°C), for about 3 hours.

Rich Beef Stew with Dumplings

$1\frac{1}{2}$ lb *(750 g) shin of beef or*
stewing steak
1 lb (500 g) small onions,
sliced
$1\frac{1}{2}$ oz *(40 g) dripping*
1 tablespoon flour
$1\frac{1}{2}$ *pints (900 ml) hot water*
Salt and freshly ground
pepper
1 lb (500 g) carrots, halved
lengthways
1 bay leaf

For the dumplings:
6 oz (175 g) self-raising flour
3 oz (75 g) shredded suet
1 tablespoon chopped parsley
Good pinch salt and pepper
Water to mix

Remove any gristle and surplus fat from the meat and trim into neat $1\frac{1}{2}$ in. (4 cm) cubes.

Fry the meat and onions in the dripping until lightly browned all over. Sprinkle in the flour and mix well. Gradually stir in the water and continue stirring until it boils. Season to taste. Cover and simmer very gently for 1 hour. Then add the carrots and bay leaf and simmer for a further hour, when it will be time to add the dumplings.

To make the dumplings, sieve the flour into a bowl and add the suet, parsley, salt and pepper. Next add enough water to make a soft but not sticky dough – about 3 tablespoons. Lightly flour your hands and roll the dough into 8 small balls. Add to the stew and cook for a further 15 to 20 minutes.

Photograph facing page 200

Collops of Beef with Horseradish Sauce

Before I tell you about the beef, let me digress for a moment in praise of spring greens, which I recommend you serve with it. Late April to early May is the time to enjoy those loose-leaved monochrome greens that are the colour of cabbage white butterflies at the heart and the dark green of a finely polished steam railway engine on the outside. If you do not grow your own, be sure to buy crisp, vibrant, fresh ones. Too many greengrocers offer flabby, tired greens – reject them. Or you won't enjoy this simple treat.

To prepare the greens, peel off the outside leaves, which may be a little coarse, and cut out the stalk at the bottom. Then, with a sharp stainless knife, chop the rest and drop them little by little into boiling salted water for about 2 or 3 minutes, until just cooked. Whip them off the heat, strain (making sure that no water remains) and toss in a pan of foaming melted butter for a couple of seconds with a pinch of freshly ground nutmeg. You then have a superb vegetable to serve with Aidan McCormack's excellent little Collops of Beef with Horseradish Sauce – which I had in the calmly panelled dining room of Middlethorpe Hall in York on a May day when the sun shone so clearly and brightly through the finely polished windows.

Please excuse this wild self-indulgent excursion into gastronomic reportage from our own correspondent on the kitchen front, but on a 3,000-mile, three-week research trip it was really pleasing to get a plate of cabbage, and this fine dish of beef, the recipe for which now follows.

Collops are thin discs of meat cut from the centre of the fillet – your butcher will do this for you.

4 beef collops
1 shallot, finely chopped
Butter
1 large glass port
6 tablespoons creamed
  horseradish
Veal or chicken stock: 6 fl oz
  (175 ml) if in jelly form;
  10 fl oz (300 ml) if liquid
Double cream
Salt and pepper

Fry the collops in butter, then keep them warm while preparing the sauce.

Sauté the shallot in some butter. Add the port and reduce by half. Add the horseradish, then the stock followed by the cream, and finally whisk in a walnut-sized piece of butter. Season to taste.

Serves 6 to 8

SPICED BEEF

This is a traditional dish at the cold Christmas buffet in Ireland. It is usually made with brisket of silverside, but skirt and flank are also suitable.

3 lb (1.5 kg) beef silverside or brisket, boned
8 oz (250 g) coarse salt
2 oz (50 g) brown sugar
½ teaspoon each, allspice, ground cloves and nutmeg
Pinch thyme and pepper
1 bay leaf, crushed
1 tablespoon saltpetre
2 oz (50 g) black treacle
8 oz (250 g) carrots, sliced
2 oz (50 g) onions, finely chopped

Rub the salt into the beef and leave overnight. The following day, mix together the sugar, allspice, cloves, nutmeg, thyme, pepper, bay leaf and saltpetre.

Drain the beef from the salt and wipe dry. Rub the meat thoroughly on both sides with the spice mixture and leave, covered, in a cool place for 2 days. Then pour the warmed treacle over the meat and leave to marinate for a week, turning once a day.

Roll the spiced beef up and tie firmly with string. Put in a pan of boiling water with the carrots and onions and simmer gently for about 3 hours. Leave the meat to cool in the liquid, then remove, place between two boards and press under a heavy weight for 8 hours.

Carve the meat in thin slices and serve with a choice of chutneys, pickles and fluffy mashed potato.

Myrtle Allen   *Serves 3*

STEAK WITH STOUT

1 lb (500 g) stewing steak
2 oz (50 g) butter
2 onions, sliced
Thyme, sage, parsley, bay leaf

Brown the meat in half the butter, taking care not to burn it. Add the onions and cook 2 or 3 minutes more. Add the herbs, tied together, pour over the stout and stock, and season to taste.

4 fl oz (125 ml) stout
  (preferably Murphy's)
8 fl oz (250 ml) beef stock
Salt and pepper
3 potatoes
Roux to thicken (optional)
  made with 1 oz (25 g) flour
  and 1 oz (25 g) butter
Chopped parsley

Top with the whole peeled potatoes. Cover tightly and simmer gently for 2 hours until ready.

The juices may be slightly thickened with a roux and enriched with the remaining butter. Serve the meat surrounded by the potatoes and sprinkled with chopped parsley.

Serves 4

FILLET OF BEEF WITH STOUT AND OYSTERS

I am proud of this dish which I created at Ramores Restaurant and which quite impressed the chef, George!

1 × 1 lb (500 g) piece beef
  fillet, trimmed
5 fl oz (150 ml) stout
  (preferably Murphy's)
5 fl oz (150 ml) strong beef or
  veal stock
2 shallots, chopped
1 bay leaf
1 teaspoon brown sugar
1 oz (25 g) butter
Salt and pepper
16 oysters, shelled

Poach the whole piece of fillet in a mixture of the stout and stock with the chopped shallots and bay leaf for about 10 minutes (the beef should be rare in the middle). Remove the meat and keep warm.

Add the sugar to the stock mixture and reduce by about one third, finally adding the butter to make the sauce thick and shiny. Season to taste with salt and pepper. Pop the oysters into the sauce for 1 minute and then remove.

Pour the sauce on to white plates, then slice the beef thinly and arrange decoratively. Garnish each portion with the poached oysters.

Alternatively, you could garnish the dish with a julienne of carrots and leeks, in which case put a little of this on to each plate and set the oysters on top.

Mrs Floyd's Brisket Pot

This English dish is almost the same as that known in America as New England dinner. The meat must be brisket, thick flank or silverside and it is generally pickled in brine fortified with saltpetre which gives the meat its pinkish tinge.

Wash the meat and tie it if necessary into a compact shape. Place in a pot large enough for both it and the vegetables which are added later. Cover the meat with cold water and bring it to the boil. Boil gently for 5 minutes, when the scum will rise; spoon this off, then cover and simmer gently, with the water hardly moving, until the beef is cooked and tender, allowing 35 minutes per lb (500 g) and 30 minutes over.

If the meat is to be served cold, leave in the pot until lukewarm, then place in a bowl in which the joint fits tightly and put a weight on top. If the meat is to be served hot, skim off the fat 1 hour before the dish is ready and add a number of halved carrots and turnips and one onion per person. Cover again and simmer very gently until cooked. The only seasoning required is freshly ground pepper.

Serve on a large platter with the vegetables around the meat. Pass some of the stock separately. Use the remaining stock as the basis of a good vegetable soup if not too salty.

ROAST FILLET OF BEEF WITH MUSTARD BUTTER

2½ lb (1.25 kg) piece of fillet
1–2 oz (25–50 g) butter

For the mustard butter:
4 oz (125 g) butter
1 teaspoon home-made
  mustard
1 teaspoon finely chopped
  parsley
Squeeze of lemon juice

Pre-heat the oven to gas mark 3, 325°F (170°C).

Place the joint in a roasting tin with the butter. Put in the centre of the oven and roast, allowing 1 hour for a rare joint or 1½ hours for medium rare. Baste often to keep the joint moist.

Meanwhile, prepare the mustard butter. Cream the butter, add the mustard, parsley and squeeze of lemon. Spoon butter onto a square of kitchen foil, shape into a fat roll and twist the ends up like a cracker. Chill until firm.

To serve, cut the meat into thick slices and top each portion with a pat of mustard butter.

To make this dish really supreme, take the juices from the roasting tray, skim off most of the fat and melt into it a little cube of meat glaze. Whisk it up with a knob of butter and serve as an extra, separate sauce.

GROATY PUDDING

A great Black Country dish of yesteryear – served hot as dinner one night and then eaten cold as a kind of savoury cake the next. Try it on bonfire night to supplement those boring old jacket spuds! For a word about groats see page 98.

8 oz (250 g) stewing or shin of beef
2 leeks, chopped
2 onions, chopped
Salt and pepper
8 oz (250 g) groats
1 pint (600 ml) beef stock

Put the meat into an earthenware pot with the leeks, onions and salt and pepper. Lastly add the groats and pour over the stock. Stir all the ingredients together well. Place the lid on the pot and cook in the oven at gas mark 2, 300°F (150°C), for about 6 hours.

POTTED BEEF CHEEK

1 beef cheek, thoroughly cleaned
1 lb (500 g) shin of beef, cubed
1 carrot, chopped
1 onion, chopped
1 bouquet garni
Salt and pepper

Simmer the cheek in water with the shin of beef, carrot, onion and bouquet garni, for 2 hours. Let the meat stand in the cooking juices overnight. Reserve the juices.

Discard all the fat from the cheek, chop the lean roughly and mix with the beef. Season with salt and pepper. Pile the mixture into a large pudding basin and spoon about 6 tablespoons of the reserved cooking liquid over the top. Put a saucer on the top of the basin and weight down. Place in the refrigerator until set.

Welsh Salt Duck with Laverbread (page 144)

Steak and Kidney Pudding

This is one of the oldest puddings, the pride and joy of British classic cooking and something that totally bewilders the French who muddle it with 'le Christmas pudding'. It is traditionally served in its basin, tied round with a white napkin. Accompanied by boiled potatoes, Brussels sprouts and a jug of hot water with which to thin down the rich thick gravy in the pudding after the pastry has been cut, it is an unrivalled feast.

Steak and oyster pudding is a classic version, incorporating 1 dozen chopped oysters – and sometimes 4 oz (125 g) sliced mushrooms – with the layers of beef and kidney; half the stock can be replaced with sherry and a dash of mushroom ketchup (see page 249).

1½ lb (750 g) stewing steak
8 oz (250 g) ox or lamb's
    kidneys
1 oz (25 g) seasoned flour
4 oz (125 g) onions, chopped
1 dessertspoon chopped
    parsley
Salt and pepper
15 fl oz (450 ml) brown stock

For the savoury suet pastry:
12 oz (350 g) flour
1 lb (500 g) fresh breadcrumbs
4 oz (125 g) shredded beef
    suet
½ teaspoon salt
1 teaspoon baking powder

Photograph facing page 185

Mix all the pastry ingredients together and moisten to a stiff dough with water. Roll out and use three quarters of it to line a 3–4 pint (1.7–2.3 litre) pudding basin; shape the remaining quarter to form a lid.

Cut the beef and kidneys into cubes and toss in seasoned flour. Fill the lined basin with alternate layers of beef, kidney and onions, sprinkling each layer with parsley and a little salt and pepper. Add stock to well cover the meat, top with the pastry lid and tie down with buttered foil or greaseproof paper and a pudding cloth. Steam for 4 hours.

Roast Beef and Trenchers (page 160)

LANCASHIRE HOT-POT

*8 × 6 oz (175 g) middle neck
lamb chops*
*4 lamb's kidneys, cored and
sliced*
2 lb (1 kg) potatoes, sliced
8 oz (250 g) onions, sliced
Salt and pepper
*10 fl oz (300 ml) veal or lamb
stock*
1 oz (25 g) lard or dripping

Trim any excess fat from the chops, melt it down and use it to fry the chops and kidneys over a high heat for 3 to 4 minutes. Rinse the potatoes thoroughly in cold water and put a layer of them in a deep ovenproof dish. Lay some of the chops on top and cover with a layer of kidneys and onions. Continue with these layers, seasoning each with salt and pepper, and finishing with a layer of potatoes. Pour over the stock and brush the potatoes with melted lard or dripping, or the melted-down fat from around the kidneys if available.

Cover with a lid and cook in the oven at gas mark 4, 350°F (180°C), for 2 hours. Remove the lid; increase the heat to gas mark 6, 400°F (200°C), place the dish near the top of the oven and cook for 30 minutes more to brown the potatoes.

MUTTON OR LAMB WITH PARSLEY DUMPLINGS

Boiled leg of mutton was a popular nineteenth-century dish, and the dumplings were added to absorb the fat in the juices.

1 lb (500 g) carrots
8 oz (250 g) onions, sliced
2 oz (50 g) butter
2 lb (1 kg) leg of lamb
*1 pint (600 ml) lamb or veal
stock*

Cut the carrots into chips and fry them with the onions in butter for 10 minutes. Arrange over the base of a large pan and place the lamb joint on top. Add the stock, salt, mixed herbs and the bay leaf. Cover with a lid and simmer very

Salt
Mixed herbs
1 bay leaf
Flour
Butter
5 fl oz (150 ml) double cream

For the parsley dumplings:
6 oz (175 g) fresh white
    breadcrumbs
3 oz (75 g) shredded beef suet
2 tablespoons finely chopped
    parsley
Grated rind $\frac{1}{2}$ lemon
Salt and pepper
1–2 eggs, lightly beaten

gently, allowing 20 minutes per lb
(500 g) and 20 minutes extra. Add the
dumplings for the last 15 minutes.

To make the dumplings, mix the
breadcrumbs, suet, parsley and lemon
rind and season with salt and pepper.
Fold in the eggs and mix to a soft
consistency. Form the mixture into
dumplings the size of golfballs.

Lift the cooked meat, vegetables and
dumplings on to a warmed serving
dish. Strain the stock into a clean pan.
Add some flour blended with a little
butter and bring to the boil, stirring
until thickened. Adjust the seasoning,
whisk in a dollop of cream and pour
the sauce over the meat.

Myrtle Allen   *Serves 4*

IRISH STEW

$2\frac{1}{2}$–3 lb (1.25–1.5 kg) mutton
    neck chops
4 medium onions
4 medium carrots
1 pint (600 ml) stock or water
Salt and pepper
4 potatoes
$\frac{1}{2}$ oz (15 g) butter
1 tablespoon chopped chives
1 tablespoon chopped parsley

Cut the excess fat from the chops,
shred it and render it down in a heavy
flameproof casserole. Toss the meat in
the fat until coloured. Cut the onions
and carrots into quarters, add to the
meat and turn in the fat also. Add the
stock and season carefully.

Simmer gently for approximately 2
hours, adding the potatoes halfway
through. When the meat is cooked,
pour off the cooking liquid, de-grease
and re-heat it in another saucepan. Check the seasoning. Swirl in the
butter, chives and parsley and pour back over the stew.

Photograph facing page 184

BOILED MUTTON WITH CAPER SAUCE

Now there is no point in making this classic dish unless you have a real gigot – and a real leg of mutton must be from an animal at least four years old, and preferably from my friend John Noble's estate in Argyll where the weather, as you indeed call this particular kind of beast, grazes undisturbed upon the vast acres of bog myrtle, heather, rosemary, parsley *et al.* to its heart's content. Or until summoned by its lord and master, the laird, to its final resting place upon the battered silver plate that adorns his groaning dinner table, which is where I sat with him in the first-floor dining hall, gorging on this simple feast and glugging fine claret as the winter sun glinted on the loch below. *Should* you have such a thing (and it must be mutton, not lamb) then keep it for two to seven days in a cold larder before cooking as this improves the flavour and tenderness of the meat.

1 leg of mutton (gigot)
6 leeks
2 swedes
6 carrots
4 turnips

For the caper sauce:
1 oz (25 g) butter
1 oz (25 g) flour
5 fl oz (150 ml) warm milk
3–4 tablespoons capers,
  drained
Salt and pepper

Put the gigot in an oval-shaped pot, cover with water and bring to the boil very slowly. Skim the fat off the top. Chop the vegetables and add to the pot. Boil for about 2 hours.

Meanwhile, make the sauce. Melt the butter, add the flour and stir to a creamy paste. Pour in the warm milk and whisk until smooth. Now add about 5 fl oz (150 ml) of the stock that the mutton has been cooking in and simmer gently for about 20 minutes until you have a very smooth sauce. Pop in the capers, check the seasoning and add salt and pepper if necessary.

To serve, garnish the mutton with slices of carrot. Pour the caper sauce over the joint and surround with the boiled vegetables. Mashed turnip or cauliflower makes a delicious accompaniment.

Best End of Lamb with Basil and Turnip

4 × 4 oz (125 g) pieces best
  end of lamb, boned and
  trimmed of fat
Salt and pepper
4 chicken skins
2 oz (50 g) butter
10 fl oz (300 ml) veal stock
2 oz (50 g) turnip trimmings
1 small glass white wine

For the turnip cake:
1 large waxy potato
1 lb (500 g) turnips
Salt and pepper
1 oz (25 g) butter

For the basil mousse:
1 chicken breast
1 egg white
5 fl oz (150 ml) cream
Salt and pepper
1 teaspoon chopped basil

First make the turnip cake. Grate the potato and turnips into a large bowl and season. Melt the butter in an 8 in. (20 cm) round baking tin and place the mixture of potato and turnip in it. Press down very tightly and cook in the oven at gas mark 8, 450°F (230°C), for 5 minutes. Turn the cake and continue cooking for a further 5 minutes. When cooked, turn out and keep warm.

To make the basil mousse, blend the chicken breast and egg white in a food processor. When smooth, add the cream gradually, then season. Fold in the basil.

Season the lamb and spread equal quantities of the basil mousse on to one side of each piece. Lay out the 4 chicken skins, place one of the lamb and mousse pieces in the centre of each, cut off any excess skin, tie both ends of the envelope with string and tie again loosely in the centre.

Melt the butter in a large pan. Place the lamb envelopes in the pan, mousse-side down, and seal for 1 minute. Turn the envelopes and place in the oven at gas mark 5, 375°F (190°C), for 20 minutes in the veal stock, wine and trimmings. Remove from the pan and cut each envelope into 5 slices. Re-heat in the oven.

Cut the turnip cake into 4 pieces and place on plates. Arrange the lamb in a fan around the cake and coat with the strained juices from the dish.

ROAST LEG OF LAMB WITH ROAST GARLIC AND HERB SAUCE

For the herb sauce:
1 *wine glass lime or lemon juice*
1 *wine glass olive oil*
20 *leaves fresh mint, stalks removed*
A smaller quantity fresh parsley, stalks removed
2 *large cloves garlic, crushed*
1 *small bunch fresh chives (half the volume of the parsley)*
1 *teaspoon freshly ground black pepper*

1 × 4 *lb (2 kg) best English or Welsh leg of lamb with thick creamy fat*
Salt and pepper
24 *large cloves garlic*
12 *plump tinned anchovy fillets in olive oil, drained*
10 *fl oz (300 ml) water*
1½ *oz (40 g) butter*

Make the herb sauce by pouring half the lime juice and half the olive oil into a liquidiser. Switch on the machine and add all the other ingredients till they are finely chopped and are well amalgamated with the oil and juice. Turn off the liquidiser and check the consistency of the sauce – it needs to be thick but easily pourable, so if necessary start the machine again and add more juice and oil. Chill the sauce thoroughly before serving.

To roast the lamb, pre-heat the oven to its maximum temperature and meanwhile, in a large hot frying pan, seal the leg all over. Once sealed, season with salt and pepper. Put the cloves of garlic, unpeeled, in a roasting tin, place the lamb on top of them and pop into the oven with nothing else at all. After 30 minutes, take out the lamb, turn it over, place it back on the garlic and lay the anchovy fillets on top of the leg. Pour the water around it and return to the oven (I know the oven's a bit smoky, but don't worry about that). Cook for another 20 minutes.

When the time is up, lift the roasting tin from the oven and whisk the juices in with a fork, making sure to scrape any bits off the side – if the liquid has reduced to almost nothing, simply add another cup or two of water. Remove the garlic cloves from under the meat and keep them warm. Return the meat in the tin to the still-hot oven and switch the oven off. Leave the meat inside for another 15 to 20 minutes.

To serve, put the meat on a warm serving dish with the roasted whole cloves of garlic. Carefully pour all the liquid from the roasting tin into a saucepan and bubble it up on the stove. Whisk in the butter little by little till you have a thin creamy sauce. Strain through a fine sieve over the meat. Serve the chilled herb sauce separately, whisking it with a fork just before bringing it to the table.

Serves 4

MUTTON PIES

Divide the pastry into four and shape each piece round the bottom of a jam jar, reserving enough for lids. Make one pie at a time and keep the rest warm. (Lining muffin tins with the pastry may not be traditional but it is a lot easier. The pies may be wider and shallower, but the taste is the same.)

1 level tablespoon flour
Salt and pepper
Pinch of marjoram
1 lb (500 g) lean lamb, finely
 chopped or minced
1 small onion or shallot, very
 thinly sliced or minced
1 smallish potato, finely diced
1 teaspoon mushroom ketchup
 (see page 249) or
 Worcestershire sauce
4 tablespoons stock
1 lb (500 g) hot-water pastry
 (see page 234)

Season the flour with salt, pepper and a pinch of marjoram and roll the meat in it. Add to the other ingredients in a bowl, mix well and divide into four.

Fill the pastry cases with the mixture one at a time, dampen the edges and pinch the lids on firmly. Make a hole in the centre of each to let out the steam and bake in the oven at gas mark 4, 350°F (180°C), for 45 minutes to 1 hour, or until the filling is cooked. Eat very hot.

ROAST LAMB WITH ROSEMARY AND ANCHOVIES

1 tin anchovies in olive oil
2 tablespoons rosemary leaves
1 leg of lamb
2 cloves garlic
Glass of dry white wine
Lamb or veal stock
Knob of butter

Pre-heat the oven to gas mark 2, 300°F (150°C).

Pound together in a mortar the anchovies and rosemary leaves, adding a little of the anchovy oil if necessary, to form a thick paste. Cut small slits in the lamb and insert slivers of the garlic. Score the lamb with a sharp knife and spread the paste over thickly. Roast uncovered, for 20 to 25 minutes per lb. Then leave to rest for a while in a warm place.

Strain most of the fat from the roasting tray. De-glaze it with a glass of wine, bubble in a drop of stock till it reduces, whisk in a knob of butter and strain it into a sauce boat.

CAWL

Cawl is to Wales what the hot-pot is to Lancashire (see page 170) and the Bakeofe is to Alsace – a slow cooking dish that makes use of local easily available ingredients. It's a great favourite with hungry rugby men, though when I cooked this for the lads of Kidwelly RFC with help from my great mate Ray Gravell, *the* rugby player, they were nearly left hungry as I dropped most of it on the floor of the clubhouse. And without missing a beat they changed the lyrics of the song which they were cheerfully singing to include the words 'silly billy', or something like that!

$1\frac{1}{2}$–2 lb (750 g–1 kg) piece smoked bacon (collar or shoulder)
1 tablespoon lard or bacon fat
2 onions, coarsely chopped

Soak the bacon overnight in cold water, if necessary, to remove some of the salt.

Heat the lard or bacon fat in a large soup pot and brown the onions,

2 parsnips, coarsely chopped
4 carrots, coarsely sliced
1 swede, coarsely chopped
1 lb (500 g) beef brisket or
 neck of lamb (or both)
12 black peppercorns
1 clove
1 bay leaf
Sprig thyme
Lamb or chicken stock, or
 water
1 lb (500 g) potatoes
 (preferably tiny and new)
4 slender leeks, finely chopped

parsnips, carrots and swede. Remove the vegetables and brown the beef or lamb. Return the vegetables to the pot with the meat and add the drained bacon, spices and herbs. Cover with stock. Bring to the boil, skim and simmer for 2–3 hours. If the potatoes are not small and new, cut into pieces. Add to the pot 20 minutes before the end of the cooking time.

To serve, slice the meat and put a piece in each bowl, along with some of the broth and vegetables. Garnish with the finely chopped raw leeks. Eat with a hunk of cheese and some bread.

Serves about 6

WELSH HONEYED LAMB

Chicken or pork can be cooked in the same way.

3–4 lb (1.5–2 kg) shoulder of
 spring lamb
Salt and freshly ground black
 pepper
1 teaspoon ground ginger
2 tablespoons finely chopped
 rosemary
8 oz (250 g) thick honey
10 fl oz (300 ml) cider

First line the roasting tin with foil, as the honey can make it very sticky. Rub the shoulder all over with salt, pepper and the ginger, then put it into the tin and sprinkle half the rosemary over the top. Coat the top skin with honey and pour the cider around. Bake in the oven at gas mark 6, 400°F (200°C), for 30 minutes, then lower the heat to gas mark 3, 325°F (160°C) and cook for a further $1\frac{1}{4}$ hours. Fifteen minutes before the joint is ready, baste carefully and sprinkle over the remaining rosemary. Add a little more cider if it appears to be drying up.

Transfer the cooked joint to a warmed serving dish and leave to rest before carving. Pour off any excess fat from the roasting tin and reduce the remaining gravy slightly on top of the stove, adding more cider if necessary. Serve the sauce in a warmed gravy boat.

PORK WITH APRICOTS

Pork is often served with apples because pigs used to be reared in orchards, but apricots go equally well with it. Tinned or dried fruit may be used outside the season instead of fresh apricots.

3 lb (1.5 kg) leg or loin of pork
10 oz (300 g) apricots, halved and stoned
2 oz (50 g) lard, melted
Salt
2 tablespoons meat glaze

Score the pork rind at narrow intervals to obtain crisp crackling. Make a number of incisions in the meat and insert half an apricot in each. Brush the joint with the lard, rub salt into the rind and roast in the oven, basting frequently with the pan juices. Roast for 20 minutes at gas mark 7, 425°F (220°C), to crisp the crackling, then lower the heat to gas mark 4, 350°F (180°C), and continue roasting, allowing 25 minutes per lb (500 g) and an extra 25 minutes.

Remove the meat from the roasting tin and leave to rest before carving. Skim the fat from the roasting tin and add some meat glaze to the residue. Bubble up, stirring well, and strain into a gravy boat to serve with the pork.

PORK AND PEASE PUDDING

The combination of boiled salted or pickled pork and pease pudding was enjoyed in the Middle Ages, and pease pudding was sold by street vendors well into the nineteenth century – before they invented chips and hot dogs, I suppose! Use a cheap cut of pork such as foreleg or knuckle.

2–3 lb (1–1.5 kg) pickled pork
4 oz (125 g) onions, sliced
2 oz (50 g) carrots, sliced

Put the pork in a large pan of cold water, bring to the boil and skim well. Simmer for 10 minutes, then add the onions, carrots, turnips and celery. Add

8 oz (250 g) turnips, sliced
4 oz (125 g) celery, sliced
12 peppercorns

For the pease pudding:
2 lb (1 kg) split peas, soaked
    overnight
1 oz (25 g) butter
2 egg yolks
Salt and pepper

the peppercorns and simmer gently for about $2\frac{1}{2}$ hours.

To make the pease pudding, tie the soaked peas loosely in a muslin cloth and simmer in the pan with the pork for about $1\frac{1}{2}$ hours. Remove from the pan and rub the swollen peas through a sieve. Dry over gentle heat until thick, then stir in the butter, egg yolks and salt and pepper to taste.

Serve the boiled pork with the vegetables and the pease pudding. Some cooked cabbage tossed in melted butter and nutmeg would go well with this.

George McCalpine   Serves 4

PORK FILLET CHIMNEYS

2 trimmed pork fillets
1 oz (25 g) butter
Salt and pepper
8 oz (250 g) puff pastry
3 oz (75 g) mushrooms
1 oz (25 g) onion
A little egg wash
Fresh parsley to garnish

For the sauce:
1 shallot, chopped
3 oz (75 g) butter
2 tablespoons Madeira
4 fl oz (125 ml) beef glaze

Cut the pork fillet across into medallions $\frac{1}{2}$ in. (1 cm) thick. Lightly fry the medallions in a little butter and season with salt and pepper. Roll out the pastry and cut into 1 × 4 in. (2.5 × 10 cm) rectangles. Wrap a pastry rectangle round each medallion to make a chimney-shaped cylinder. Finely mince the mushrooms and the onion together, and fill the top of each chimney with a little amount. Brush the outsides of the chimneys with egg wash. Bake in the oven at gas mark 5, 375°F (190°C), until the pastry is golden brown.

Meanwhile make the sauce. Fry the shallot in a little of the butter, then add the Madeira and reduce. Add the beef glaze and lastly whisk in the remaining butter.

To present the dish, strain the sauce on to the plates. Place three chimneys in the centre of each plate and garnish with parsley.

RAISED PORK PIE

3 lb (1.5 kg) belly pork
1 tablespoon salt
Pepper
Pinch each dry mustard and
  ground allspice
¼ oz (7 g) gelatine

Hot-water crust:
Made with 1 lb (500 g) plain
  flour (see page 234)

Trim the meat from the bones and chop into small pieces. Put the bones and gristle into a pan with the salt and pepper, cover with water and simmer for 2 to 3 hours to make stock.

Shape the pie crust from three-quarters of the pastry (you can buy special raised pie moulds from kitchen supply shops). Fill with the chopped meat, seasoned with salt, pepper, mustard and allspice. Cover with the pie lid and brush the top with beaten egg, making a hole in the centre of the pastry.

Bake in the oven at gas mark 4, 350°F (180°C), for 2½ hours, reducing the heat after 30 minutes to gas mark 3, 325°F (160°C). Remove from the oven and allow to cool.

Strain the stock, mix with the gelatine dissolved in 1 tablespoon of hot water and pour into the pie. Serve hot or cold.

Photograph facing page 201

PORK AND BEANS

This is one of the oldest known dishes in British cooking, being for centuries the farmworker's mainstay during the winter months. He would have a barrel of salted or pickled pork and a barrel of dried beans. Originally, the two ingredients were boiled separately, probably because of the excessive saltiness of the meat. Parsley sauce was and is the traditional accompaniment.

2–3 lb (1–1.5 kg) pickled
  shoulder of pork
8 oz (250 g) dried butter beans
2 oz (50 g) carrots, sliced
4 oz (125 g) onions, sliced
4 oz (125 g) turnips, sliced
10 peppercorns

Soak the pork for 8 hours in cold
water. Soak the beans separately for
6 hours in cold water. Drain both and
rinse well.

Put the pork in a pan with the
carrots, onions and turnips and enough
water to cover. Bring to the boil, add
the peppercorns and put the lid on the
pan. Simmer for 2 to $2\frac{1}{2}$ hours,
allowing 25 to 30 minutes per lb (500 g) , and add the beans for the
last 50 minutes of the cooking time.

Lift out the pork, carve and arrange on a dish. Serve the beans
separately, dressed with parsley sauce made from the strained cooking
liquid (see the recipe on page 95).

Serves 4

Pork Chops in Beer Sauce

4 pork chops
Salt and pepper
1 oz (25 g) lard or dripping
1 pint (600 ml) beer
1 oz (25 g) capers, drained
2 egg yolks
Pinch nutmeg
Lemon slices and parsley to
  garnish

Season the chops with salt and pepper.
Fry quickly in hot lard in a frying pan
to seal in the juices (or you can trim the
excess fat from the chops, melt it down
and use that). Drain off fat and reserve.
Add most of the beer and more
seasoning to the chops and simmer
gently for 30 to 45 minutes until they
are tender. Remove the chops from
the pan, place on a warm serving
dish and keep warm.

Pour the hot cooking liquid into a basin, add the capers, egg yolks
and nutmeg. Beat thoroughly, adding a little of the drained-off fat.
Return the sauce to the pan and stir until it thickens, but do not boil;
then add a couple of dashes of beer to bring back the flavour. Pour
over the chops and garnish with lemon slices and parsley.

FILLET OF PORK AND GREEN PEPPERCORN TERRINE WITH ORANGE PRESERVE

5 pork tenderloins

4 teaspoons green peppercorns

2 teaspoons brandy

1 teaspoon salt

1 teaspoon each chopped thyme, rosemary and tarragon

1 teaspoon juniper berries, crushed

1 egg, beaten

1 tablespoon flour

8 oz (250 g) streaky bacon rashers

For the orange preserve:

6 oranges

4 oz (125 g) granulated sugar

Trim the pork and cut each tenderloin in two, then slice each piece in half lengthways. In a bowl combine the pork with the green peppercorns, brandy, salt, herbs and juniper berries. Mix thoroughly. Now stir in the egg and flour.

Line a 2 pint (1 litre) terrine or casserole dish with the bacon and overlap the sides. Pack the pork mixture into the terrine and then fold over the bacon. Cover the terrine with a double thickness of foil and place in a deep roasting tin.

Add enough hot water to the roasting tin to reach two thirds of the way up the terrine. Place in the oven at gas mark 2, 300°F (150°C), for $1\frac{1}{2}$ hours or until the terrine is nicely firm and has pulled slightly away from the sides. Weight the terrine with a 3 lb (1.5 kg) weight, let it cool and chill overnight. Serve the terrine in slices at room temperature with the orange preserve.

To make the orange preserve, peel the rind from the oranges very thinly, without the pith, and cut into thin (julienne) strips. Segment the oranges and place with the strips and sugar in a thick-bottomed pan. Bring the mixture to the boil and simmer for 20 minutes, stirring occasionally, until it has reached the consistency of jam. Transfer to a bowl, chill and serve. The preserve will keep in the refrigerator for 3 weeks.

ACCOMPANIMENTS FOR
MEAT DISHES

A SAUCE FOR COLD MEAT

Makes about 2 pints (1 litre)

3 lemons
1½ oz (40 g) salt
1 oz (25 g) allspice
1 oz (25 g) mustard seed
1 oz (25 g) white pepper
1 oz (25 g) grated horseradish
½ oz (15 g) each mace,
　cayenne pepper and cloves
2 pints (1 litre) vinegar

Slice the lemons, remove the pips and rub salt into the slices. Mix the allspice, mustard seed, pepper, horseradish, mace, cayenne and cloves. Put the lemon slices in layers in a jar and sprinkle the mixed spices between each layer. Pour over the vinegar at boiling point. Set aside for 24 hours, squeeze, strain and bottle.

CRUNCHY MUSTARD

2 oz (50 g) white mustard
　seeds
2 oz (50 g) black mustard
　seeds
5 fl oz (150 ml) white wine
　vinegar
3 level tablespoons clear
　honey
¼ teaspoon cinnamon
1 teaspoon salt

Put the mustard seeds and vinegar into a bowl and leave for 36 hours. Place the soaked seeds into a blender with the honey, cinnamon and salt and blend at high speed until thick and creamy. Add more vinegar if the mixture seems too thick. Put into small airtight jars or pots. Seal well or the mustard will dry out quickly.

PICKLE FOR BEEF OR PORK

1½ lb (750 g) coarse salt
1 oz (25 g) saltpetre
6 oz (175 g) brown sugar

Before putting the meat into the pickle, make sure that all the blood has drained from it by rubbing in salt and leaving for a few hours.

Add the pickle ingredients to 1 gallon (4 litres) of water in a large pan. Bring to the boil and boil for 15 to 20 minutes, skimming carefully. Strain the liquid into the container in which you intend to pickle the meat and allow to cool. Put in the meat and cover.

Thick cuts of meat need about 10 days, whereas thinner cuts, or a pig's head split in half, may be sufficiently salted in 4 to 5 days.

Myrtle Allen

MINT SAUCE

1 tablespoon, finely chopped
    mint
2 teaspoons sugar
3–4 tablespoons boiling water
1 tablespoon white vinegar

Put the sugar and mint in a sauce boat. Add the boiling water and vinegar. Allow to infuse for 5 to 10 minutes before serving.

Irish Stew (page 171) with Irish Brown Soda Bread (page 229)

REFORM CLUB SAUCE

Created by Alexis Soyer, the famous French chef of the Reform Club in Victorian days, as an accompanying sauce to lamb cutlets: I have changed it slightly. Of course, you must have beautifully butchered and trimmed best English or Welsh lamb loin chops without too much fat – and don't forget to trim the outside fat of that thin skin that covers it.

3 oz (75 g) wafer-thin ham or tongue, finely chopped
1 small glass sherry
3 oz (75 g) onions, finely chopped
2 oz (50 g) butter
3 oz (75 g) mushrooms, thinly sliced
2 hard-boiled egg whites, thinly sliced
3 oz (75 g) cooked beetroot, finely diced
3 oz (75 g) gherkins, thinly sliced
1 pint (600 ml) meat glaze
Salt, sugar and crushed black pepper
Redcurrant jelly

Soak the ham or tongue in the sherry.

Fry the onions in half the butter until soft, but not coloured. Add the mushrooms and cook for a few more minutes. Stir in the ham or tongue, the hard-boiled egg whites, beetroot and gherkins together with the brown sauce and heat through. Blend in the remaining butter and season with salt, sugar, pepper and redcurrant jelly.

Steak and Kidney Pudding (page 169)

Mushroom Sauce

1 oz (25 g) unsalted butter
3 shallots, chopped
4 oz (125 g) mushrooms,
  cleaned, washed and
  drained
$\frac{1}{2}$ glass dry white wine
$\frac{1}{2}$ pint (300 ml) meat glaze
Sprig of parsley, chopped
Dash of lemon juice

In a sauté pan, heat a little of the butter until light brown; add the shallots and cook slowly. Then add the mushrooms, finely chopped at the last moment to keep them from turning brown. Cook the mushrooms on a very high flame, stirring constantly to let the juices reduce. Add the white wine and reduce it almost completely. Then add the meat glaze.

Simmer over a low flame for 10 minutes. Finish the sauce off the flame by adding the remaining butter and, at the last minute, the chopped parsley and dash of lemon juice. This sauce should be quite thick.

7

VEGETABLES

First he ate some lettuce and some broad beans,
then some radishes, and then, feeling rather sick,
he went to look for some parsley.

BEATRIX POTTER, *THE TALE OF PETER RABBIT*.

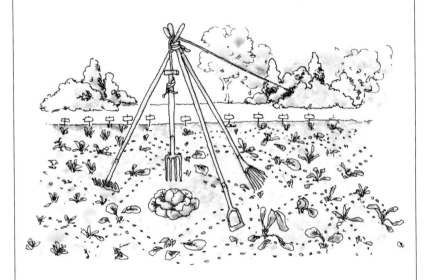

As a result of sophisticated growing methods and refrigerated transport, vegetables are now available outside their natural season and many exotic and previously unheard-of varieties can be found in our shops. There is, however, nothing to beat local fresh vegetables in their natural season. If you are one of those lucky people who have the space to grow a few vegetables in their garden, there is nothing to beat it. The rest of us have to traipse around the supermarkets, gazing at clinically wrapped plastic trays of vegetables that may well have been sitting there for a week. As with all other produce, you cannot be expected to create a delicious meal from inferior ingredients. So spend a little more time over the buying of vegetables: go to a good local greengrocer who shops from the market daily, or perhaps to a market stall. In some country towns they still have the lovely twice-weekly markets where the farmers put on their stalls what they have dug up or picked that week, even if it is a few tons of potatoes.

I cannot stress enough the importance of freshness. I feel a vegetable is at its best a little before it is fully grown, or in some cases when it is very young. Vegetables, like all of us, tend to be slightly tired and past their best in their maturity. As soon as the food supply has been cut off, when they are dug up or picked, this process accelerates. They lose not only their texture and flavour, but also the wonderful nutritional value whose importance we have drummed into us on our mother's knee. I shall never forget my father sending me, blowing hard on my fingers to restore the circulation, into the frosty winter garden to pick the smallest sprouts off the tall stalks only minutes before mum needed them for lunch. I won't go into all the boring chemical processes that take place as the plant cells die – just take it from me that you need to get them young and fresh.

So now we have armfuls of these wonderful vegetables still covered in mud from the garden. How shall we prepare them?

BOILING

Boiling is the most commonly used and abused method of cooking vegetables. How can we forget the limp, colourless, flavourless cabbage that we were served for school dinners (although at my school they favoured butter beans and lentils and my school dinners were by and large good), or the still-common practice of cooking sprouts until they fall apart? If you boil vegetables correctly, they can still retain their colour and nutritive value. There are two schools – or should I say universities? – of thought. Some people add the prepared vegetables to a large pan full of rapidly boiling water; others to just a little boiling water. Certainly the more water used, the faster the vegetables are heated and cooked, and the faster a vegetable is cooked, the more the colour and texture are preserved. This is especially true of the more delicate varieties. The home economist/health argument is that the smaller the amount of liquid used, the greater the retention of the nutritive value. My argument is that I will nearly always use my precious vegetable water to make a stock or gravy, so it is not lost after all. Green vegetables should be boiled uncovered so that they don't go grey and mushy but stay fresh and green.

The methods cited above are normally applicable only to green vegetables as most root vegetables need a longer cooking time to soften. Place roots in cold water and bring to the boil before simmering. Rapid boiling will tend to break up your potatoes.

I will now give you a few hints on boiling times for different vegetables.

The following vegetables should be cooked in a large pan of lightly salted rapidly boiling water:

ARTICHOKES: 20 to 40 minutes, depending on size. Drain upside down.

BEANS, WHOLE GREEN: 2 to 10 minutes.
        RUNNER: 5 to 10 minutes, sliced.
        BROAD: 1 minute if young and shelled, 5 to 15 minutes if older.

BROCCOLI: 5 minutes.

BRUSSELS SPROUTS: 3 to 5 minutes. They will turn a brighter green.

CABBAGE: 5 to 7 minutes. It must be finely shredded.

CAULIFLOWER FLORETS: 3 to 5 minutes.

COURGETTES: 4 minutes. They need to be very small and unpeeled.

PEAS: 3 to 8 minutes depending on size.

POTATOES: 15 to 20 minutes, until just tender. Cook small ones whole.

SPINACH: 1 minute. Push under the water with a wooden spoon. Drain and serve at once. Young spinach leaves are best of all cooked lightly in a closed pan with just a knob of butter, or steamed.

SWEDES: 15 minutes, cubed or sliced.

SWEETCORN: 10 to 15 minutes depending on age and size. Omit the salt but add a little sugar to the water and boil until tender.

The following vegetables need to be cooked in just enough salted water to cover them; the less water the better:

CARROTS: 7 minutes for whole baby carrots. Older carrots may take up to 30 minutes, unless uniformly sliced. Add 1 teaspoon of sugar to the water.

LEEKS: 1 to 2 minutes, sliced. Whole thin leeks 8 minutes.

ONIONS: 15 to 45 minutes, depending on size, peeled and cooked whole. Add 1 teaspoon of sugar to the water.

PARSNIPS: 10 to 15 minutes, cubed.

TURNIPS: 5 to 10 minutes, cubed. When they start to absorb water, drain and stew in a little butter.

STEAMING

This method uses the intense heat of the steam from the boiling water over which they are sitting to cook the vegetables. It is, however, a slower process than boiling and is therefore unsuitable for green vegetables except, say, spinach – just for a moment or two – as too much colour and flavour is lost.

Steaming is most suitable for root vegetables that will not be damaged by the longer cooking time. The vegetables should not come into contact with the boiling water, and to enable this you can buy wonderful expanding metal contraptions that fit inside your saucepans, or you can improvise with a colander. The saucepan must have a tightly fitting lid. You can also use those lidded wicker baskets on top of a saucepan, but make sure the water is boiling like crazy.

Here are a few vegetables suitable for steaming, and their cooking times:

CAULIFLOWER FLORETS: 15 minutes.

PARSNIPS: 20 to 30 minutes, cubed or cut into fingers.

POTATOES: 20 to 30 minutes, cubed.

SWEDES: 30 minutes, cubed.

SHALLOW-FRYING

You can fry almost any vegetable but the method you use has to be adapted for the type of vegetable you are serving. The way the vegetable is prepared is also vitally important.

By rapid shallow-frying in a little fat, often called sautéeing, moist vegetables preserve their crispness as the high heat evaporates any moisture. However, to ensure that the vegetables are cooked through before they burn, you need to prepare them in thin slices or small regular shapes. Large vegetables can be par-boiled and patted dry before frying.

Serves 4 to 6

SAUTÉED POTATOES

As butter burns at a lower temperature than oil, I like to use a combination of butter and oil, which also gives a richer flavour.

$1\frac{1}{2}$–2 lb (750 g–1 kg) potatoes
1 tablespoon oil
$1\frac{1}{2}$ oz (40 g) butter
Salt and freshly ground black
    pepper

Cook the potatoes in boiling salted water for about 15 minutes until just tender. Drain well and remove the skins. Cut the potatoes into $\frac{1}{4}$ in. (6 mm) thick slices with a sharp knife. Heat the oil and butter in a large frying pan and add the potato slices. Cook until golden brown and crisp all over. Drain well on kitchen paper and sprinkle with salt and pepper before serving.

Deep-Frying

In deep-frying the vegetables are cooked purely by the heat of the fat or oil. To ensure that they do not absorb the fat and become greasy, they need to be seared on contact with the oil. The initial temperature of the oil is therefore critical. To test it (unless you have a deep-frying thermometer), drop in a cube of bread or a piece of the vegetable you are about to cook; if it sizzles, the fat is hot enough.

Britain is supposed to be a great chip-eating country, but it is so difficult to find a decent chip or, for that matter, a good potato. To achieve a good chip at home, choose waxy-textured potatoes. Peel and cut each potato into $\frac{1}{2}$ in. (1 cm) thick slices, then cut each slice into $\frac{1}{2}$ in. (1 cm) sticks. Wash them well in plenty of cold water to remove the starch and pat dry in a tea towel or with kitchen paper.

Half-fill a chip pan with oil and heat. Dip in the end of a chip to see if it sizzles. When the oil is the right temperature, about 360°F (167°C), dip the basket into the oil to prevent the chips sticking, then place the chips in the basket and lower gently into the oil. Fry over a moderate heat until they are cooked, but not too browned. Remove from the pan and allow to drain.

Just before serving, increase the heat of the oil until it is about 390°F (180°C) and lower in the basket of chips. Fry rapidly until golden brown. Drain again, sprinkle with salt and serve.

You can fry the chips in one go for approximately 10 minutes, but don't have the fat too hot or they will become too browned before they are cooked.

Most other vegetables need a little protection from the hot fat to prevent them from drying out and burning. The simplest form of batter is made by soaking the prepared vegetables in milk, then dusting in seasoned flour. Shake off the excess flour (this can be done in the frying basket) and lower into the hot fat. Tender young baby courgettes are delicious cooked in this way. Older courgettes should first be peeled in strips lengthways, then very thinly sliced, so that they look like a 20p coin.

Do remember that the thinner you slice the vegetables, the faster they will cook. Bearing this in mind, make sure that your slices or chunks are of uniform size. Also do not overload the basket; rather fry in small batches so that the food has a chance to cook uniformly.

A useful basic coating batter mix is given on page 92.

Purées

Once you have your beautifully cooked tender vegetables, why not turn them into a purée? This is a lovely way for you to alter the textures on your plate.

A purée is made simply by mashing or sieving the cooked vegetable. There are four different ways to achieve this. The first is with the common potato masher, with which you pound the vegetables until you have got rid of all the lumps. For soft root vegetables you can use a kitchen sieve – push them through with a wooden spoon. A posher way to purée is with a food mill: every continental kitchen has one. You pile in the vegetables and turn the handle; different meshes can be fitted to alter the texture. The food mill is particularly suitable for firm-textured vegetables such as cauliflower, onions, peas or beans. An electric food processor is possibly the fastest method, although you need to stop every few seconds to scrape down the sides to ensure a smooth consistency. Do not use one for starchy vegetables, however, as the fast blade tends to make them a little rubbery.

To achieve a firm-textured purée you must drain your vegetables well after boiling or steaming them. Most vegetables retain enough water to produce a moist purée, but some, like potatoes, need a little cream, milk or beaten egg added during the puréeing process. To give all purées a smooth consistency and help to bind them, stir in a little butter with the seasoning. Plenty of salt and freshly ground pepper and nutmeg will enhance the flavour.

Why not experiment with a purée of mixed vegetables – turnips, parsnips, onions and some starchy potatoes to bind it together, with perhaps some chopped chives or mint added at the last moment?

You can prepare your purées in advance for a party. Make them a day or so ahead, cool and put them into buttered ramekins. Keep them covered in the refrigerator, and when required, place the ramekins in a roasting tin half-filled with water (the French call this a *bain-marie*) to warm through in the oven. Invert onto serving dishes for prettiness or scoop out with a tablespoon to form attractive shell shapes. Arrange purées of orange carrot, green Brussels sprouts and yellow swede on a side plate with a few whole sprouts for a contrast in texture and flavour.

BAKING

The joy of baking vegetables is that they require minimal preparation and can be popped in the oven with a roast or casserole and virtually forgotten.

AUBERGINES: Wash and dry. Bake in the oven at gas mark 3, 325°F (160°C), for about 1 hour. They will look puffed up when they come out of the oven as the flesh will have swollen.

BEETROOT: Beetroot take a long time to cook, and are therefore ideal to pop in with a slow-cooking casserole, but you need to prevent them from drying out. Wash them but do not peel or trim, wrap in foil and bake in the oven at gas mark 3, 325°F (160°C), for $3\frac{1}{2}$ to 4 hours. If you increase the oven temperature to speed up the process, you will dry them out. They are done when a skewer slips in easily. Peel before serving.

GARLIC: Baking garlic is an excellent way of cooking it to produce a mild sweet purée. Wrap a bundle of garlic heads in a piece of foil and bake at gas mark 5, 375°F (190°C), for 1 hour. Unwrap the heads, separate into cloves and squeeze the cloves out of their skins into a sieve. Sieve the garlic, add 1 teaspoon of olive oil and a little salt and cream. Serve 1 teaspoon of garlic purée, prettily shaped, on each slice of, say, roast lamb, or on a separate plate of vegetable purées as described above.

ONIONS: Arrange the onions, unpeeled, in an ovenproof dish that holds them snugly in a single layer. Pour just enough water into the dish to cover the bottom and bake in the oven at gas mark 6, 400°F (200°C), for 1 to $1\frac{1}{2}$ hours. If cooked, they should feel slightly soft when squeezed. Carefully peel off the outer skins and serve the onions with salt, freshly milled pepper and butter.

POTATOES: Scrub well, getting all the bits of grit out of the pits. Place on a baking sheet and put into a moderately hot oven. The temperature is not critical, however, for the cooking time can be adjusted accordingly. They will probably take 1 to $1\frac{1}{2}$ hours to cook, depending on size. To serve, cut a cross on the top, push up the sides and drop in a generous lump of butter, or perhaps some soured cream or grated cheese.

Braising

Braised vegetables can be served as a separate course or as an accompaniment to a meat or fish dish. Braising involves cooking the vegetables relatively slowly either on top of the stove or in the oven with a fairly small amount of liquid. Unlike boiling, where the object is to cook the vegetables as quickly as possible to preserve the individual texture and flavour, braising is designed to create different flavours by intermingling the ingredients. The choice of cooking liquid is therefore vitally important, not just for the cooking process but also as a part of the finished dish. Veal or chicken stock is often used (see page 153), but wine can also be added, depending on the required character of the finished dish. The perfect stock for braising vegetables should have sufficient flavour to enhance the dish but not drown the taste of the vegetables. It should also be of good enough quality to reduce to a syrupy texture during the cooking process without an additional thickening agent. Other flavouring elements should be used too, such as garlic, fresh herbs, finely chopped onion or perhaps bacon.

Braised Celery

2 celery hearts
2 onions, chopped
2 carrots, diced
10 fl oz (300 ml) veal stock

Because celery has a very pungent taste it benefits from par-boiling beforehand.
Wash and trim the celery hearts to about 6 in. (15 cm) in length. Halve lengthways and par-boil in salted water for 7 minutes. Drain well. Put the chopped onions and carrots into the bottom of a heavy-based pan or flameproof dish. Lay the celery hearts on top and cover with a good veal stock. Bring to the boil and then braise, uncovered, at gas mark 3 or 4, 160 to 180°C (325 to 350°F), for 1 hour until the celery is very tender. By this time the stock should be of a syrupy consistency. If it is not, remove the vegetables on to a serving dish and keep warm. Boil the stock rapidly until it reaches the right consistency and pour over the vegetables.

Roasting

Root vegetables especially are delicious roasted. Here is my favourite method of cooking roast potatoes.

Peel the potatoes and cut them into large even-sized pieces. Place in cold, salted water and bring to the boil. Cook for at least 10 minutes and drain well. You then need to roughen the outsides, either by shaking the potatoes in the covered pan to rub the corners off and soften them or by running a fork over them.

Heat some lard or dripping in a roasting tin in the oven at gas mark 7, 425°F (220°C). Add the potatoes, season well with salt and pepper, turn over in the fat to ensure that they are well coated, and cook, turning frequently, for about 45 minutes until crispy and golden brown. If roasting a joint at the same time, this should ideally be placed directly on to the wire shelf above the poatoes so that the meat juices can drip over the potatoes.

Other root vegetables such as parsnips are equally good cooked in this manner.

In Praise of Left-over Mashed Potato

Bubble and Squeak (*Photograph facing page 216*): I was rummaging through the freezer chests of a leading supermarket chain recently and I discovered to my horror little blocks of frozen bubble and squeak. What has happened to our life-style that permits us to pay lots of money for a snack that should properly be made from left-overs?

Anyway, I bought one and it wasn't bad, but it did set me thinking about the times when things like bubble and squeak, fishcakes and rissoles were a regular part of my childhood diet, and enjoyable because of the skill that went into cooking them. And the reason they were good was that some simple and elementary rules were followed. For example, bubble and squeak was made of chopped-up cold Brussels sprouts or cabbage mixed with an equal amount of cold mashed potato, well seasoned with salt and lots of pepper.

Its brilliant taste was a direct result of our impecunious family state because, to stretch the budget, off-cuts of smoked bacon were bought from the butcher which were, of course, very cheap but also very, very fatty, and every time the bacon was fried this fat was saved and used to cook the bubble and squeak. Our bubble and squeak was cooked flat in a big frying pan until there was a golden brown crust. Then it was turned over on to a plate and slid back into the pan to brown and crisp the other side. So if you want to enjoy this delicacy, you'd better keep a lot of good bacon fat in your larder.

LAMB OR BEEF RISSOLES: The same principles of sensible economy and good housekeeping are responsible for these little delights. You don't go out of your way to make them, but the day you have a little lamb or beef left over from a roast joint you chop it into small pieces, mince it by hand (not in a food processor) and mix it with an equal quantity of cold mashed potato. Add 1 or 2 teaspoons of freshly chopped parsley and 1 tablespoon of finely chopped onion for each rissole that you are going to make and grind in lots of black pepper. Form the mixture into flat cakes about 2 in. (5 cm) in diameter and fry on both sides in beef or lamb dripping until they are crunchy.

I think the message is becoming clear. These treasures are delicious served with home-made chutney or pickle (see pages 244–249).

FISHCAKES: Do you know, the self-same supermarket that sold frozen bubble and squeak also sold fishcakes – and they weren't even made from real potato? Next time you buy some fish, buy a little extra so that you end up with some left-over poached white fish, because if you don't I can't complete this little potato trilogy.

Flake the cold fish and mix it with an equal quantity of mashed potato. Season well with salt and pepper, put in at least 1 tablespoon of finely chopped parsley per fishcake and form them in the same shape as the rissoles. Fry on both sides in butter, oil or dripping until crunchy and golden.

Anglers, poachers, millionaires and restaurateurs may substitute salmon or bass for the more usual cod, whiting, ling or pollock used in the preparation of fishcakes.

STOVIES

Stovies are pot-roast potatoes enhanced with finely diced leftover roast meat. They are, if you like, Cornish pasties without the pastry.

2 oz (50 g) dripping
2 large onions, sliced
1 lb (500 g) potatoes, sliced
Salt and pepper

Put the dripping into a heavy-based pan and allow to become smoking hot. Add the onions and potatoes with some salt and pepper. Lower the heat. Cover closely and cook gently for a long time (up to 2 hours). When cooked, stir up with a spoon. Good stovies must cook without burning and without the lid being lifted during the cooking. (You're allowed to take a little peep to see if it's ready after an hour or so!)

You can add small cubes of leftover roast meat for extra flavour and pleasure.

POTATO CAKES

I cooked these at the Ulster Folk and Transport Museum with Finnoelle Carragher on an open peat fire with elementary cottage cooking utensils. I wonder how most of us would cope today with just a griddle and a pot suspended over the fire!

Use old potatoes if you can as they are more floury and give the best result.

1 lb (500 g) potatoes
1 tablespoon melted butter
4 oz (125 g) flour

Boil the potatoes in their skins and then peel them. Mash them, but not too smoothly. Add the melted butter and knead in enough flour to make a pliable paste. Roll out and cut into rounds. Bake on a hot griddle or frying pan until brown on both sides.

Eat hot spread with butter and sprinkled with sugar, or fry in bacon fat and eat with bacon for breakfast.

Photograph facing page 216

IRISH POTATO CAKES

8 oz (250 g) potatoes
Salt and freshly ground black
  pepper
½ head fresh garden cabbage,
  finely chopped
6 tablespoons milk
2 oz (50 g) bacon dripping or
  butter, plus extra for frying
4 oz (125 g) wholemeal flour

Boil the potatoes in salted water until cooked. Drain, mash and leave to cool.

Place the cabbage in boiling salted water and cook for a few minutes. Drain and leave to cool.

Place the milk in a saucepan, add the bacon dripping and bring to the boil. Add the cooked potato and cabbage and blend together while the mixture heats through. Fold in the flour until the mixture comes away from the side of the saucepan.

Turn the mixture on to a cold surface and shape into cakes of approximately 2 in. (5 cm) diameter and ½ in. (1 cm) thick. Cook in a little bacon dripping until brown and serve immediately.

Serves 4

ANGLESEY EGGS

6 medium leeks, chopped
Salt and pepper
1 lb (500 g) hot mashed potato
2 tablespoons butter
1 tablespoon flour
10 fl oz (300 ml) warm milk
2 oz (50 g) plus 2 tablespoons
  grated cheese
8 hard-boiled eggs

Cook the leeks in boiling salted water for 10 minutes. Drain very well, and add them to the hot mashed potato. Add half the butter, season to taste and beat until a pale green fluff. Arrange around the edge of an oval or round ovenproof dish and keep warm.

Now heat the rest of the butter, stir in the flour and add the warm milk, stirring well to avoid lumps. Put in the 2 oz (50 g) of grated cheese and mix well.

Cut the eggs in half and place inside the leek and potato ring. Cover with the cheese sauce and sprinkle the remaining cheese on top. Pop into the oven at gas mark 6, 400°F (200°C), until the top is golden brown.

Photograph facing page 216

CHAMP

The noted Irish potato dish.

4 oz (125 g) spring onions,
chopped, or 1½ oz (40 g)
chives, chopped
10 fl oz (300 ml) milk
6–8 potatotes
Salt and pepper
3 oz (75 g) butter

If using onions, simmer these in the milk until soft. Boil the potatoes in salted water until just cooked, then mash. Add the onions and their milk and the chives, if used, together with the milk which you have heated separately. Season to taste with salt and pepper. Let the butter melt over the finished dish.

LEEK PASTRY

1½ lb (750 g) leeks
Shortcrust pastry made with
12 oz (350 g) flour and
6 oz (175 g) fat (see page
232)
8 oz (250 g) bacon or shoulder
ham
2 eggs
4 fl oz (125 ml) milk
Salt and pepper

Cut the leeks into 1 in. (2.5 cm) pieces. Blanch in boiling water for 5 minutes, then drain.

Grease a small shallow roasting tin and line it with half the pastry. Cut the bacon into small pieces and put a layer on to the pastry. Add the leeks. Beat the eggs with the milk (reserving a little to use as a glaze) and season. Pour over the leeks, and cover with the remaining pastry, sealing the edges well. Brush the top of pastry with the reserved beaten egg mixed with a little milk. Place in the oven at gas mark 6, 400°F (200°C), for 25 minutes, then reduce the temperature to gas mark 3, 325°F (160°C), and cook for a further 20 minutes.

Rich Beef Stew with Dumplings (page 163)
Overleaf: Raised Pork Pie (page 180) with Piccalilli (page 246) and Apple
Chutney (page 244)

PUDDINGS

Bring on the dessert. I think I am about to die.

LAST WORDS OF PIERETTE BRILLAT-SAVARIN.

APPLE CAKE

This can be served cold as a cake, but I prefer to have it warm with lots of whipped cream or home-made custard (see page 209) as a pud.

1 lb (500 g) cooking apples
Grated rind and juice of 1
* lemon*
6 oz (175 g) butter
6 oz (175 g) caster sugar
3 eggs
8 oz (250 g) self-raising flour
½ teaspoon baking powder
2 oz (50 g) raisins
½ teaspoon ground cinnamon
2 oz (50 g) flaked almonds

For the icing:
4 oz (125 g) icing sugar
Juice ½ lemon
1 oz (25 g) flaked almonds

Peel, core and thinly slice the apples and sprinkle with the lemon juice.

Cream the butter with all but 1 tablespoon of the sugar until light and fluffy. Add the lemon rind and gradually incorporate the eggs. Sift the flour with the baking powder and slowly fold into the egg mixture.

Spoon half the mixture into a buttered 10 in. (25 cm) deep cake tin and place the apple slices on top. Sprinkle on the raisins, the cinnamon mixed with the remaining sugar, and the flaked almonds. Cover with the rest of the cake mixture and bake in the oven at gas mark 6, 400°F (200°C), for 1 hour. Remove from the oven and leave to cool in the tin for 10 minutes, then turn out.

Make the icing by combining the icing sugar and lemon juice. Pour this over the warm cake and decorate with the flaked almonds.

PRATIE APPLE

This recipe first appeared in *Traditional Irish Recipes* by George L. Thomson.

I cooked this in Veronica Steele's kitchen. Veronica's house is on the most westerly point of Ireland, set in bleak but beautiful countryside. She also makes Milleens cheese, a great Irish cheese similar to the Munster cheese of Alsace – not surprisingly, as Irish monks took the original recipe there.

8 oz (250 g) potatoes
4 oz (125 g) flour
½ teaspoon baking powder
Salt
3 cooking apples, peeled,
  cored and sliced
Sugar
Honey
Butter

Boil and mash the potatoes. Add the flour, baking powder and a little salt to make a dough. Roll out into a large circle and cut into quarters. Divide the apples between two of the pastry triangles. Cover with the other two and seal the edges. Cook in a frying pan, turning once. When browned and cooked, cut a hole in the top of each and put in a generous helping of sugar and honey with a little butter. Allow all of this mixture to melt and serve very hot.

Win Floyd   Serves 4

BAKED APPLE DUMPLINGS

I can remember walking into the kitchen after school and the sweet aroma of these dumplings cooking stirring my tastebuds.

1 lb (500 g) shortcrust pastry
  (see page 232)
4 even-sized cooking apples,
  peeled and cored
2 oz (50 g) sugar
Milk to glaze
Caster sugar

Divide the pastry into four pieces and roll each into a round 8 to 10 in. (20 to 25 cm) across.

Place one apple on each pastry circle and fill the centre with sugar. Moisten the edges of the pastry with water. gather the edges to the top, pressing well, to seal them together. Turn the dumplings over. Brush the tops with milk and sprinkle with caster sugar. Decorate with pastry leaves if desired.

Bake on a greased tray towards the top of the oven at gas mark 7, 425°F (220°C), for 10 minutes and then reduce the temperature to gas mark 3, 325°F (160°C), and continue to cook for a further 30 minutes until the apples are soft.

Eat hot or cold with clotted cream or home-made English custard (see page 209).

Photograph facing page 217

APPLE PIE

There must be countless versions of apple pie, some best forgotten. Here's how I make mine.

8 oz (250 g) shortcrust pastry (see page 232)
1 lb (500 g) cooking apples, peeled, cored and sliced
3 oz (75 g) granulated sugar
3 cloves

Divide the pastry in two and roll out one-half large enough to cover an 8 in. (20 cm) ovenproof plate. Put the apples onto the pastry-lined dish and sprinkle on most of the sugar. Position the 3 cloves strategically. Brush the pastry edges with a little cold water. Roll out the remaining pastry and lift carefully over the apples. Press the edges well together and trim away the excess. With your thumb and finger push up the edges and pinch the top, or use the prongs of a fork. Make a cross in the centre to allow the steam to escape. Use the trimmings to decorate as elaborately as you wish, or have time for. Brush the top with water and sprinkle on the remaining sugar. Bake at gas mark 5, 375°F (190°C) for 40 to 50 minutes until golden brown. Serve with home-made custard (see page 209) or clotted cream.

Declan Ryan   *Serves 4 to 6*

BLACKCURRANT LEAF SORBET

6 oz (175 g) sugar
1 pint (600 ml) water
Grated rind 2 lemons
Juice 3 lemons
3–4 handfuls blackcurrant leaves
A little egg white

Make a mild lemon sorbet base by boiling the sugar and water together for 2 minutes, then adding the lemon rind and juice. Infuse the blackcurrant leaves in the hot sorbet mix. Strain out the leaves when the flavour is strong enough. The leaves discolour the mixture slightly, so add a little egg white to whiten the sorbet before it sets, then leave to freeze.

CHOCOLATE FUDGE PUDDING

6 oz (175 g) self-raising
  flour
4½ oz (135 g) caster sugar
2 oz (50 g) cocoa powder
2 oz (50 g) butter, melted
4 fl oz (125 ml) milk
4 oz (125 g) finely chopped
  walnuts
6 oz (175 g) soft brown sugar
14 fl oz (415 ml) hot water

Mix together the flour, caster sugar and half the cocoa. Pour the melted butter into the milk, then blend with the dry ingredients. Stir in the chopped nuts. Pour the mixture into a greased and lined 9 in. (22.5 cm) square tin. Mix the remaining cocoa into the brown sugar and sprinkle over the top. Pour over the hot water and bake in the oven at gas mark 5, 375°F (190°C), for 35 minutes.

While still hot, cut into squares, invert each on to a serving dish and spoon over the sauce left in the tin. Serve with plenty of whipped cream.

CARROT PUDDING

An unusual warming pudding for frosty winter days that I discovered in Jersey – I thought it never got cold there!

4 oz (125 g) flour
¼ teaspoon bicarbonate of soda
Large pinch mixed spice
4 oz (125 g) suet
4 oz (125 g) currants
4 oz (125 g) raisins
4 oz (125 g) breadcrumbs
4 oz (125 g) potato, grated
4 oz (125 g) carrot, grated
4 oz (125 g) Demerara sugar
1 egg, beaten

Mix the flour, soda and spice well together, add all the remaining ingredients except the egg and blend thoroughly. Bind with the egg, pour into a large pudding basin (remember the mixture will expand in cooking so leave space at the top). Cover with a double layer of greaseproof paper and tie with string. Steam for 3 hours.

Serve with syrup, custard or clotted cream.

CUSTARD TART

This is the *real* thing.

3 eggs
1½ oz (40 g) caster sugar
½ level teaspoon cornflour
½ pint (300 ml) single cream
1 vanilla pod
8 in. (20 cm) sweet pastry
  case, baked blind (see page
  232)
Grated nutmeg

Beat the eggs, add the sugar and cornflour. Continue beating until the sugar has dissolved. Heat the cream with the pierced vanilla pod until it reaches boiling point. Pour onto the egg mixture, whisking continuously. Strain into the flan case and sprinkle with the grated nutmeg.

Bake in a cool oven at gas mark 2, 300°F (150°C) until the custard is set, about 30 minutes. A skewer inserted in the middle should come out clean. Leave to cool before removing from tin. Serve at room temperature.

BREAD PUDDING

A filling cake that keeps well – if eager appetites haven't demolished it first!

2 lb (1 kg) stale bread
8 oz (250 g) shredded suet
1 lb (500 g) granulated or
  brown sugar
1 lb (500 g) mixed dried fruit
3 eggs
2 teaspoons mixed spice
2 oz (50 g) butter

Soak the bread in water for at least 30 minutes, then drain and squeeze out the excess moisture. Mash with a fork and add all the remaining ingredients except the butter. Mix well together and spread the mixture into a greased baking tin. Dot with butter and bake in the oven at gas mark 4, 350°F (180°C), for about 2 hours or until nicely browned.

Photograph facing page 233

INDIVIDUAL BREAD AND BUTTER PUDDINGS

A great traditional British pud, here baked in individual dishes. Quite substantial, so serve after a lightish main course.

15 fl oz (450 ml) milk
15 fl oz (450 ml) double cream
1 vanilla pod
3 eggs
4 oz (125 g) sugar
4 small bread rolls
1¼ oz (30 g) butter
1 oz (25 g) raisins, soaked
1 oz (25 g) sultanas, soaked

Bring the milk and cream to the boil with the vanilla pod. Leave to stand for a few minutes for the flavours to infuse.

Beat the eggs and sugar together and add the milk mixture. Pass through a strainer.

Slice and butter the bread rolls with some of the butter and arrange in 4 ramekins. Scatter over the drained raisins and sultanas. Next pour over the milk mixture and dot the remaining butter on the top. Place the ramekins in a roasting tin filled with enough water to come half-way up their sides and cook in the oven at gas Mark 4, 350°F (180°C), for 30 to 40 minutes. Allow to cool.

Turn out the puddings and serve hot or cold on individual plates with home-made English custard (see page 209) feathered with chocolate, perhaps accompanied by some fresh raspberries.

CHRISTMAS PUDDING

This is the ultimate Christmas pud that my mother has been making for me each year for as long as I can remember.

Makes 3 puddings serving 8, 6 and 4 respectively

12 oz (350 g) fresh white breadcrumbs
12 oz (350 g) plain flour
1 teaspoon salt
½ teaspoon powdered mace
½ teaspoon powdered ginger
½ teaspoon grated nutmeg
½ teaspoon ground cinnamon
12 oz (350 g) suet
1 lb (500 g) soft brown sugar
8 oz (250 g) candied peel, minced
12 oz (350 g) currants
12 oz (350 g) sultanas
1¼ lb (625 g) raisins
8 oz (250 g) apples, peeled, cored and chopped
Grated rind and juice 1 lemon
Grated rind and juice 1 orange
4 tablespoons brandy
3 large eggs, beaten
5 fl oz (150 ml) milk

Mix the first 14 ingredients together in a large bowl along with the orange and lemon rinds. Add the fruit juices and brandy to the beaten eggs, then add to the dry ingredients with enough milk to give a soft dropping consistency. Cover the mixture with a damp cloth and leave overnight.

Half-fill three saucepans with water and put on to boil. Grease 1 pint (600 ml), 1½ pint (900 ml) and 2 pint (1 litre) pudding basins. Stir the mixture and fill the basins with it. Cover with greaseproof paper and then foil. Steam the 1 pint (600 ml) basin over rapidly boiling water for 5 hours, the 1½ pint (900 ml) basin for 7 hours and the 2 pint (1 litre) basin for 9 hours.

When the puddings are cooked, remove them from the basins and allow to cool. Re-cover and store in a cool place. Do not put the foil directly on to the pudding as the fruit eats into it after some weeks. No harm is done to the pudding, but the foil cover ceases to be watertight.

On the day of serving renew the covers and steam as follows: the 1 pint (600 ml) pudding for 2 hours; the 1½ (900 ml) and 2 pint (1 litre) puddings for 3 hours. Serve with thick clotted cream, brandy butter or rum sauce.

HOME-MADE ENGLISH CUSTARD

This is what custard should really taste like, not like that thick nasty stuff they served for school dinners.

8 fl oz (250 ml) milk
5 fl oz (150 ml) double cream
2 egg yolks
1 oz (50 g) caster sugar

Put the milk and cream in a saucepan and bring slowly to the boil. Meanwhile, whisk together the egg yolks and sugar until pale and very creamy. As soon as the milk and cream come to the boil, pour on to the egg mixture and whisk well. Return to the pan and place over a gentle heat, or in a basin over a pan of simmering water, stirring continuously until it has thickened. Serve hot.

Should you need to keep this custard warm, lay a piece of greaseproof paper on the surface to prevent a skin forming.

BAKED RICE PUDDING

Serve this warm with a blob of home-made jam.

2 oz (50 g) short grain rice
½ pint (300 ml) milk
½ pint (300 ml) single cream
1 oz (25 g) caster sugar
Grated nutmeg
½ oz (15 g) butter

Wash the rice well and place in the bottom of a 1½ pint (900 ml) buttered dish. Pour on the milk and allow to soak for 1 hour. Stir in the cream and sugar, sprinkle the top with nutmeg and dot with butter. Bake at gas mark 2, 300°F (150°C) for 2 to 2½ hours until the rice is soft and creamy and the top a crusty golden brown.

CARRAGEEN MOSS PUDDING

Carrageen moss, a brownish black or dark green seaweed, rich in iron and other minerals, grows abundantly on the rocks at low tide. Pick in early summer and bleach in the sun. Wash in plenty of cold water and lay out to dry again. When white and well dried, bring indoors and use in this lovely recipe. Carrageen can also be bought from health food shops.

$\frac{1}{4}$ oz (7 g) clean well-dried
    carrageen
1 *vanilla pod or $\frac{1}{2}$ teaspoon*
    vanilla essence
1$\frac{1}{2}$ *pints (900 ml) milk*
2 *tablespoons sugar*
1 *egg, separated*

Soak the carrageen in tepid water for 10 minutes. Put in a saucepan with milk and the vanilla pod if using. Bring to the boil and simmer very gently for 20 minutes. Pour through a strainer into a mixing bowl. The carrageen will now be swollen and exuding jelly. Rub all this jelly through the strainer and beat it into the milk with the sugar, egg yolk and vanilla essence, if using. Test for a set on a saucer, as with gelatine. Whisk the egg white stiffly and fold it gently into the mixture. It will rise to make a fluffy top. Serve chilled.

DAMSON CRUMBLE

Crumbles can be jazzed up and altered according to the fruit you use. Here is a suggested topping for your damson or plums before the birds and wasps get to them, but if you wanted to make a rhubarb crumble you could add a little ground ginger to the mixture and omit the nuts; or you could use fresh raspberries and all-white flour; or gooseberries with the juice of an orange and the rind stirred into the topping, again omitting the nuts.

2 lb (1 kg) damsons, stoned
Sugar to sweeten
3 oz (75 g) plain flour
3 oz (75 g) wholemeal flour
Pinch salt
3 oz (75 g) butter
3 oz (75 g) caster sugar
½ teaspoon ground cinnamon
2 oz (50 g) chopped walnuts

Place the damsons in a buttered shallow ovenproof dish and sweeten with sugar to taste.

Combine the flours and salt and rub in the butter until the mixture is of a fine crumbly texture. Stir in the sugar, ground cinnamon and chopped nuts. Sprinkle on to the fruit and bake in the oven at gas mark 6, 400°F (200°C), for about 45 minutes until golden brown.

Serve warm with home-made English custard (see page 209).

Paul Reed *Serves 15 to 18*

Dried Fruit Terrine with a Banana Yoghurt Sauce

1 lb (500 g) Agen prunes
10 oz (300 g) dried apple
   rings
12 oz (350 g) dried apricots
12 oz (350 g) dried pears
12 oz (350 g) dried peaches
24 large mint leaves
8 leaves gelatine
2 pints (1 litre) warmed apple
   juice
Fresh strawberries to
   garnish

For the banana yoghurt sauce:
2 oz (50 g) dried bananas
2 × 5 fl oz (150 ml) tubs
   natural yoghurt
4 fl oz (125 ml) stock syrup
   (see page 221)

Blanch the mint for 1 second – no more – in boiling water.

Dissolve the gelatine in the warm apple juice and pour a little in the bottom of a terrine, to a depth of about ⅛ in. (3 mm). Allow to set. Place the blanched mint leaves on top and carefully pour over a little more apple juice mixture. Allow to set.

Now layer the fruit in the terrine, setting each layer as you go with a little more apple juice mixture. When all the fruit has been used, place the terrine in the refrigerator to set fully.

To make the sauce, poach the dried bananas in a little water until very soft, then liquidise. Mix the syrup and yoghurt together and add the banana purée.

To serve the terrine, turn out and slice. Decorate with the banana yoghurt sauce and fresh strawberries.

FRESH FRUIT TERRINE

6 leaves gelatine
1 pint (600 ml) freshly
  squeezed orange juice
2 teaspoons sugar
6 strawberries
2 bananas, sliced and dipped
  in lemon juice
4 oz (125 g) blackcurrants
4 oz (125 g) redcurrants
5 fl oz (150 ml) stock syrup
  (see page 221)
Fine strips orange rind, finely
  chopped mint and small
  bunches redcurrants or
  other soft fruit to decorate

Slowly melt the gelatine in the orange juice with the sugar. Leave until almost set. Spoon one-third of the mixture into a terrine. Arrange the fruit on top. Continue to layer in this way until all the fruit is used. Leave to set. Make up the stock syrup and chill it.

Slice the terrine onto a plate and pour a little stock syrup over. Decorate with fine strips of orange rind and very finely chopped mint. Place a small bunch of redcurrants or a halved strawberry, or two or three raspberries on each plate.

Photograph facing page 241

IRISH MIST AND SWEET GERANIUM SOUFFLÉ

You can use the lemon pulp left over from this recipe in a drink.

10–14 lemons
1 sweet geranium leaf
4 eggs, separated
4 tablespoons caster sugar
1 tablespoon Irish Mist
  liqueur
2 teaspoons gelatine
Whipped cream
Grated peel of 2 small lemons

This mixture can be put into the lemon skins or served as a soufflé. If filling the lemons, cut off the tops and scoop out the insides. Strain off the juice and reserve. Otherwise squeeze the lemons in the ordinary way. If serving as a soufflé, prepare a $1\frac{1}{2}$ pint (900 ml) soufflé dish by tying a collar of greaseproof paper around it to give it another 2 in.

and 1 sweet geranium leaf to
garnish.

(5 cm) in height.

Crush the geranium leaf in your hand and put it in the lemon juice. Beat the egg yolks with the sugar to a thick mousse, beating by hand over a saucepan of boiling water. Add the Irish Mist and beat again.

Melt the gelatine in 2 teaspoons of lemon juice and 1 tablespoon of water. Blend the gelatine and remaining strained lemon juice into the mousse. Put the geranium leaf in too if not enough of its flavour has been extracted. Beat the egg whites until stiff and fold in.

Overfill the soufflé dish with the mixture and freeze for 4 hours. Remove the paper and top the soufflé with a rosette of whipped cream, grated lemon peel and a large geranium leaf.

If you are serving the mixture in lemon skins, fill the skins and freeze for 4 hours.

In both cases the sweet should be served semi-frozen.

Margaret Vaughan

HEDGEROW PUDDING

Margaret Vaughan is of the 'old school', a sadly dying breed, who use anything available to create the most memorable meals.

Simply pick as many blackberries, rosehips, sloes, crab apples and any other edible berries from the hedgerows as you can find. Simmer together over a very gentle heat until the crab apples and sloes are soft and sweeten to taste. Layer the fruit alternately with stale or fresh cake crumbs (breadcrumbs are equally good) in a greased ovenproof dish, finishing with a layer of crumbs. Bake in the oven at gas mark 2, 300°F (150°C), for 1 hour. Sprinkle with brown sugar and return to the top of the oven or place under the grill to crisp. Serve hot or cold with home-made English custard (see page 209).

Ipswich Almond Pudding

15 fl oz (450 ml) milk
5 fl oz (150 ml) double cream
2 oz (50 g) fresh white breadcrumbs
3 oz (75 g) caster sugar
6 oz (175 g) ground almonds
1 teaspoon rose or orange flower water
3 eggs
1 oz (25 g) butter

Warm the milk and cream and pour over the breadcrumbs in a bowl. Stir in the sugar, ground almonds and rose or orange flower water and leave to soak for 15 minutes.

Beat the eggs and blend thoroughly with the breadcrumb mixture. Pour into a 2 pint (1 litre) buttered pie dish and dot with butter.

Place the dish in a roasting tin filled with enough hot water to come half-way up the sides of the dish. Bake in the oven at gas mark 4, 350°F (180°C), for 30 minutes or until the pudding is just set. Serve hot.

Lemon or Lime Posset

Finely grated rind and juice 2 lemons or limes
1 pint (600 ml) double cream
5 fl oz (150 ml) dry white wine
2–3 tablespoons caster sugar
3 large egg whites
Lemon or lime slices to decorate

Add the grated lemon or lime rind to the cream in a large bowl and whisk until stiff. Stir in the dry white wine, then whisk in the lemon or lime juice little by little. Add sugar to taste.

Whisk the egg whites until they form stiff peaks. Fold into the whipped cream mixture. Chill.

Before serving, whisk the posset one more time and spoon into a serving dish or into individual glasses. Decorate with lemon or lime slices.

JUNKET

The name junket comes from the French *jonquette*, the term for the little rush baskets that it was originally made in. It has, however, been made in England since Norman times. I like to top mine with plenty of clotted cream, a combination which is sometimes known as Devonshire junket.

1 pint (600 ml) creamy milk
2 tablespoons caster sugar
1 tablespoon brandy
1 teaspoon rennet
6 oz (175 g) clotted cream

Warm the milk in a heavy-based pan until blood temperature. Add 1 tablespoon of the sugar and stir until dissolved. Stir in the brandy and rennet. Pour into a large glass dish and leave in a cool place (not the refrigerator) for about 5 hours until set, then refrigerate for 1 hour. Spread the clotted cream on top of the junket and sprinkle with the other tablespoon of sugar.

Barry Richardson

LEMON PIE

6 oz (175 g) shortcrust pastry
  (see page 232)
1 tablespoon grated lemon rind
3 tablespoons lemon juice
4 oz (125 g) caster sugar
2 oz (50 g) unsalted butter
4 eggs, beaten

Roll out the shortcrust pastry to line a 7 in. (17.5 cm) pie-dish.
   To make the filling, put the lemon rind, lemon juice, sugar and butter into a small saucepan and heat gently without stirring until the sugar has dissolved. Leave this on one side until it is quite cold.

Strain the beaten eggs and mix them into the cold lemon mixture. Pour gently into the pastry case and bake in the oven at gas mark 6, 400°F (200°C), for 10 minutes, then reduce the temperature to gas mark 4, 350°F (180°C), and cook for a further 15 minutes.
   Serve cold with whipped cream.

ICED ALMOND CREAM WITH BLACKCURRANTS

6 egg whites
9 oz (275 g) sugar
1 lb (500 g) perfumed honey
2¼ pints (1¼ litres) whipped
  cream
7 oz (200 g) flaked almonds
Blackcurrants and sprigs of
  mint to garnish

For the blackcurrant sauce:
6 oz (175 g) blackcurrants,
  prepared
2 oz (50 g) sugar
4 fl oz (125 ml) water

Beat the egg whites with 4 oz (125 g) of the sugar until very stiff. Warm the honey until about 120°F (49°C), pour on to the beaten egg whites and re-whip until stiff. Incorporate the whipped cream into the honey mixture.

Grill the flaked almonds until golden brown. Make a praline mixture with the almonds and remaining sugar by placing them together in a heavy-based pan and heating until the sugar caramelises. Pour on to a greased tray to cool. When cold, crush the praline and add to the cream mixture. Pour into a terrine, stir and place in the freezer for 2 to 3 hours.

To make the blackcurrant sauce, place the fruit, sugar and water in a heavy-based pan. Poach until tender, liquidise and strain back into the pan. Return to the boil and simmer until a syrupy consistency is reached, adding more sugar if necessary. Allow to cool.

When ready to serve, turn out the iced cream and slice as required. Serve each slice with some blackcurrant sauce and decorate with whole blackcurrants and a sprig of mint.

Bubble and Squeak (page 196) with Anglesey Eggs (page 199) and Potato Cakes (page 198)

HEATHER HONEY AND WHISKY
ICE CREAM

4 egg yolks
8 oz (250 g) thick (not clear)
  heather honey
1 pint (600 ml) double cream
5 fl oz (150 ml) whisky

Whisk the egg yolks with the honey until the mixture has doubled in volume. Whisk in the cream and add the whisky to taste. Pour into containers and freeze for 2 to 3 hours. It is not necessary to beat this ice cream during the freezing process: it will set itself.

VANILLA ICE CREAM

2 tablespoons sugar
4 fl oz (125 ml) water
2 egg yolks
½ teaspoon vanilla essence
1 pint (600 ml) whipped
  cream

Boil the sugar and water together till it looks thick and syrupy and when a metal spoon is dipped in it, the last drops of syrup will form thin threads. Allow to cool a little. Beat this a little at a time into the egg yolks. Add the vanilla essence and beat to a thick, creamy white mousse. Fold the cream in. Set to freeze.

Baked Apple Dumplings (page 203)

Jam Roly-Poly

No more jokes about school dinners – try this one tonight.

*8 oz (250 g) self-raising
  flour*
Pinch salt
4 oz (125 g) shredded suet
6–8 tablespoons water
*4 tablespoons raspberry jam,
  warmed*
A little milk
*1 egg, beaten, and caster sugar
  to glaze*

Sift the flour into a bowl with the salt. Add the suet and sufficient water to create a soft but not sticky dough. Turn on to a floured board and roll out to a rectangle about 8 × 12 in. (20 × 30 cm). Brush the pastry with the warmed jam, leaving a $\frac{1}{2}$ in. (1 cm) border all round. Fold in this border and brush with milk. With the short side towards you, roll up the pastry loosely and seal the ends well. Place on a greased baking sheet, with the sealed edge underneath. Brush with the beaten egg and sprinkle with caster sugar. Bake in the oven at gas mark 6, 400°F (200°C), for 35 to 40 minutes until golden brown.

Remove from the oven, sprinkle on a little more sugar and serve hot with home-made English custard (see page 209).

Photograph facing page 232

David Harding *Serves 4*

Hot Lime Tarts

*8 oz (250 g) sweet shortcrust
  pastry (see page 232)*
3 eggs
4 oz (125 g) caster sugar
2 oz (50 g) butter, softened
Juice 1 lemon
Grated rind 1 and juice 2 limes

Use the pastry to line four individual tartlet tins. Fill with baking beans or rice on greaseproof paper and bake blind in the oven at gas mark 4, 350°F (180°C), until golden brown.

Whisk the eggs and sugar until pale. Stir in the butter, citrus juices and rind.

Pour into the tart cases, return to the oven and cook for 15 to 20 minutes until the filling is set and golden brown. Serve hot with whipped cream.

MARMALADE PUDDING

Another family favourite that brings back fond memories of my childhood.

4 oz (125 g) self-raising flour
Pinch salt
4 oz (125 g) shredded suet
*4 oz (125 g) fresh
  breadcrumbs*
1 oz (25 g) brown sugar
6 oz (175 g) marmalade
Milk

Sieve together the flour and salt. Add the suet, crumbs and sugar and mix thoroughly. Add the marmalade and stir well into the dry ingredients with a little milk to make a fairly stiff dough. Pour into a well-greased 1 lb (500 g) pudding basin until it is two thirds full. Cover with greased paper and a lid and steam for $2\frac{1}{2}$ hours. Serve hot with home-made English custard (see page 209).

OLD-FASHIONED SUET-RAISIN PUDDING

A real family favourite, just as my mother makes. It's nicest with the large raisins that need to be stoned.

1 lb (500 g) self-raising flour
Pinch salt
8 oz (250 g) shredded suet
12 oz (350 g) raisins
Milk

Mix the flour, salt, suet and raisins together. Moisten the pudding with sufficient milk to make a stiff dough. Tie it up in a floured cloth, leaving room in the cloth for the pudding to expand during cooking.

Put the pudding into boiling water and boil for 4 hours for a round pudding, $2\frac{1}{2}$ hours for a long shape. Serve hot with home-made English custard (see page 209).

Poached Pear with Tarragon Cream

A savoury dessert for those without an oversweet tooth.

2 large firm pears
10 fl oz (300 ml) stock syrup
  (see opposite)
4 drops green colouring
4 puff pastry crescents to
  decorate

For the tarragon cream:
1 egg, lightly beaten
2 tablespoons caster sugar
3 tablespoons tarragon
  vinegar
Salt and pepper
5 fl oz (150 ml) single cream

Peel, core and halve the pears and poach lightly in the syrup for a few minutes. Add the colouring and leave to cool in the refrigerator.

To make the tarragon cream, place the egg in a small bowl over a pan of simmering water. Add the sugar and vinegar and continue to simmer until thick, stirring occasionally. Season to taste. Lightly whip the cream, and add to the vinegar mixture.

To serve, slice and fan the pears on to a plate. Decorate with the tarragon cream and pastry crescents.

Stoned Cream

This is a very old Lancashire dish. You need a step-ladder in the kitchen to make it and a lot of newspaper on the floor.

1 leaf gelatine
1 pint (600 ml) double cream
Caster sugar
Vanilla essence
3 tablespoons apricot jam
1 wine-glass medium-dry
  sherry
Grated rind and juice 1 lemon

Soak the gelatine in half a cup of water and dissolve over a low heat. Boil the cream for a few minutes with a little sugar, the melted gelatine and a few drops of vanilla essence.

Cover the bottom of a deep glass dish with the apricot jam, sherry, lemon juice and a little grated rind. When the cream has cooled a little, pour it into this dish from as great a height as you can. Let it stand overnight in a cool place before using. In the morning the cream will be all bubbly.

RHUBARB AND ALMOND TARTLETS

These tartlets are also delicious made with raspberries, peeled and de-pipped grapes or peeled and sliced peaches.

2 sticks plump red rhubarb
16 fl oz (475 ml) stock syrup (see below)
3 oz (75 g) butter
3 oz (75 g) sugar
3 oz (75 g) ground almonds
10 fl oz (300 ml) whipped cream

Cut the rhubarb into 1 in. (2.5 cm) lengths and poach in the syrup until just tender, then drain and cool.

Meanwhile, beat the butter, sugar and almonds together to a cream. Put 1 teaspoon of the mixture into each of 16 small patty tins. Bake in the oven at gas mark 4, 350°F (180°C), for approximately 10 minutes, or until golden brown. Cool in the tins but do not allow to set hard before removing to a wire rack.

Just before serving, place a chunk of rhubarb in each tart and top with whipped cream.

STOCK SYRUP

This is as necessary to dessert cooking as meat stocks are to meat cooking. It can be made in advance and kept in a jar in the refrigerator until needed. Stock syrup is often used as a base for sorbets and sauces, as well as for preserving fruit.

1 lb (500 g) sugar
1 pint (600 ml) water

Dissolve the sugar in the water and boil rapidly for 2 minutes. It's as simple as that.

TREACLE TART

This is not the sickly variety you buy in boxes, but a real home-made treacle tart that has a hint of lemon to counteract the sweetness of the syrup.

12 oz (350 g) shortcrust
  pastry (see page 232)
9 tablespoons golden syrup
9 heaped tablespoons fresh
  white breadcrumbs
Grated rind and juice 1 lemon
1 teaspoon ground ginger
Egg wash (1 egg beaten with
  1 teaspoon water)

Roll out two thirds of the pastry and use to line a 10 in. (25 cm) pie plate or flan tin.

Warm the syrup over a gentle heat and add the breadcrumbs, grated lemon rind and 1 tablespoon of the juice, and the ginger. Pour into the pastry case.

Roll out the remaining pastry and cut into strips; use these to create a lattice design on the top of the tart. Decorate the sides of the plate with a fork, being sure to press the ends of the lattice well in. Brush the pastry with the egg wash and bake in the oven at gas mark 5, 375°F (190°C), for 25 to 30 minutes until the pastry is crisp and golden.

Serve with plenty of clotted cream or ice cream.

Photograph facing page 240

TRIFLE

The great British trifle cannot be beaten. I am not talking about the hard set jellied variety, covered in synthetic cream and hundreds and thousands, but the kind our grandmothers knew about. I have not given specific quantities as it depends on the number you are serving and the size of your bowl, but be generous with your fruit and sherry.

1 packet trifle sponge cakes or
  a slightly stale Victoria
  sponge
Plenty of good, preferably
  home-made, raspberry jam
Plenty of good quality dry
  sherry
Fresh raspberries
Bananas, sliced and dipped in
  lemon juice
Home-made custard (see page
  209)
Double cream lightly
  whipped
Toasted flaked almonds

Slice the sponges and spread them generously with the raspberry jam. Line a large glass bowl with them, splash on plenty of dry sherry and leave to soak in. Scatter the raspberries over the sponges together with the banana slices. Cover with the cold home-made custard. Level the top and then spread on the lightly whipped cream. Scatter over the toasted almonds just before serving. The trifle is best made several hours or a day in advance to allow the flavours to intermingle. Allow to reach room temperature before serving.

MERINGUES

Why is it that all bought meringues taste like cardboard? There is no answer, except to make them yourself at home.

3 egg whites
6 oz (175 g) caster sugar

Line a baking sheet with greaseproof paper brushed with oil.

Whisk the egg whites until they stand in peaks. Whisk in half of the sugar until the mixture is thick and shiny, carefully cut and fold in the remaining sugar with a metal spoon. This should be done carefully and only sufficiently to combine the ingredients.

Place tablespoonfuls of the mixture on the baking sheet, or if you are feeling adventurous use a piping bag and create little whirls. Bake in a very cool oven at gas mark $\frac{1}{2}$, 130°F (75°C) for 2 hours if you like a soft middle, or 4 hours if you like them to dry out completely.

Sandwich together with plenty of whipped cream.

QUEEN OF PUDDINGS

A simple winter pudding that is inexpensive to make.

1 pint (600 ml) milk
1 oz (25 g) butter
Grated rind of ½ lemon
3 eggs, separated
7 oz (210 g) caster sugar
3 oz (75 g) fresh white
  breadcrumbs
2 tablespoons good quality
  raspberry jam

Warm the milk in a pan with the butter and lemon rind.

Lightly whisk the egg yolks with 1 oz (25 g) of the sugar and pour in the milk, stirring well. Strain the custard over the breadcrumbs in a greased 2-pint (1 litre) ovenproof dish and leave to stand for 15 minutes.

Bake at gas mark 3, 325°F (170°C) for 25 minutes, until lightly set.

Remove from the oven and spread the top with the warmed jam. Whisk the egg whites until stiff, add half the sugar and whisk again until thick and glossy. Fold in the remaining sugar with a metal spoon. Pile the meringue on top of the pudding and bake at gas mark 4, 350°F (180°C) until the meringue is lightly browned.

Mike Simpson

WHISKY SYLLABUB

2 tablespoons caster sugar
Good dash whisky
Juice 1 lemon
1 pint (600 ml) double cream

Melt the sugar in the whisky and lemon juice until you have a delicious whisky-flavoured syrup. Allow to cool. Whip the cream until thick and frothy and carefully stir into the whisky syrup.

Pour into little pots or glasses and refrigerate before serving.

9

BREAD AND PASTRY

Without wishing in the slightest degree
to disparage the skill and labour of breadmakers
by trade, truth compels us to assert our conviction
of the superior wholesomeness of bread made in
our own homes.

ELIZA ACTON, *MODERN COOKERY FOR PRIVATE FAMILIES.*

BREAD MAKING AND PASTRY

There is a certain mystique surrounding bread and pastry making, and yeast cookery in general. You never fail to overwhelm your family or friends if you produce freshly baked home-made bread with a meal, however simple or complicated the accompanying dish is. I have pinched the recipes in this section from two super people who happen also to be marvellous cooks.

Margaret Vaughan of the Settle Restaurant, an old-fashioned bakery and restaurant in deepest Somerset, uses fruits picked in season from the hedgerows together with good local produce to create the most delicious dishes. She finds bread making both therapeutic and relaxing: nothing clears the brain and focuses the mind better than kneading dough. 'Remember that you need to put a lot of love in – you need to be a good lover to be a good baker!' she says.

Myrtle Allen at Ballymaloe House took lessons with some of the greatest chefs and now runs this delightful country hotel and cookery school in County Cork. Myrtle's aim is to recapture forgotten flavours, or at least to preserve some that may soon otherwise die.

Cooking should be an expression of love that encompasses all one's feelings and emotions and every attention should be paid to the final presentation. Love is no fun if unrequited – we all need someone to appreciate our food, whether customers or loved ones.

WHITE BREAD

3 lb (1.5 kg) strong plain flour
3–4 teaspoons salt
1 oz (25 g) lard
1 oz (25 g) fresh yeast
1½ pints (900 ml) warm water

Sift the flour and salt together into a large bowl and rub in the lard with the fingertips. In a small bowl blend the yeast with 10 fl oz (300 ml) of the water. Make a well in the centre of the flour mixture and pour in the yeast liquid and the remaining water. Work the dough mixture with one hand until it leaves the sides of the bowl clean. If necessary, add a little extra flour.

Turn the dough on to a slightly floured surface and knead it for about 10 minutes until smooth and elastic. Shape it into a round, then set it aside to rise until it has doubled in size.

Grease four 1 lb (500 g) loaf tins. Divide the risen dough into four equal portions on a lightly floured board. Flatten each piece firmly with the knuckles to knock out any air bubbles, then knead for 2 to 3 minutes. Stretch each piece of dough into an oblong the same length as the tin, ease it into the tin and score the dough lightly along the top. Alternatively, fold the dough into three along the long edges or roll it up like a Swiss roll. Tuck the ends under so that the dough, seam downwards, fits the tin.

Brush the top of the dough with lightly salted water. Place the tins in lightly oiled polythene bags and leave in a warm place to rise until the dough reaches the top of the tins. Remove the polythene, brush the top of the dough with salted water again and set the tins on baking trays.

Bake the loaves in the centre of the oven at gas mark 8, 450° F (230° C), for about 30 minutes, or until they have shrunk slightly from the sides of the tin and the upper crusts are a deep golden brown. For really crusty bread, turn the loaves out of the tins on to a baking tray and return them to the oven for a further 5 to 10 minutes. When done, baked loaves sound hollow if tapped on the base. Leave the breads to cool on a wire rack.

FLOWER POT BREAD

1 oz (25 g) fresh yeast
17 fl oz (450 ml) warm water
½ oz (15 g) fat
1 lb 14 oz (900 g) strong flour
½ oz (15 g) salt

Prepare three 6 in. (20 cm) terracotta flower pots by removing last year's geraniums and soil or – better still – buy new ones! Scour thoroughly and grease generously (this is very important). The loaves are less likely to stick if the pots have been sealed by previously baking blind two or three times with the Sunday joint or whenever the oven is in use.

Disperse the yeast in the water. Rub the fat into the dry ingredients and stir in the yeast mixture. Cover and leave to prove at room temperature for 50 minutes. Knead again and leave for a further 25 minutes.

Divide the dough into three, knead gently into balls and place into the prepared flower pots for a further 25 minutes in a warm place to rise. Bake for 30 minutes at gas mark 7, 425° F (220° C).

For a variation on this recipe, simply add 1 large chopped onion to the ingredients to make onion bread. This is better cooked in tins as pots tend to hold the onion flavour.

Photograph facing page 16

IRISH BROWN SODA BREAD

Buttermilk or whey are excellent substitutes for sour milk in this recipe.

1 lb (500 g) wholemeal flour
5 oz (150 g) strong white
_   flour_
2 oz (50 g) oatmeal
1 teaspoon bicarbonate of soda
1 teaspoon salt
_16–24 fl oz (475–725 ml)_
_   sour milk, or fresh milk_
_   soured with juice ½ lemon_

Mix the dry ingredients very well. Moisten with the sour milk to form a soft dough. Knead lightly. Form into a round, mark with a cross and bake for 30–45 minutes in the oven at gas mark 7, 425° F (220° C).

Photograph facing page 184

TOMATO BREAD

1 oz (25 g) fresh yeast
2 tablespoons warm water
1½ lb (750 g) flour
½ oz (15 g) milk powder
½ oz (15 g) sugar
½ teaspoon salt
½ oz (15 g) fat
1 × 14 oz (400 g) tin
_   tomatoes, drained and_
_   chopped_

Disperse the yeast in the water.
    Sift the dry ingredients together, rub in the fat and add the tomatoes and yeast. Leave to prove at room temperature for 45 minutes.
    Knead back and prove for a further 15 minutes. Divide equally into four and knead gently.
    Place in well-greased loaf tins and leave for a further 35 minutes. Bake for 30 to 35 minutes at gas mark 7, 425° F (220° C).

Photograph facing page 88

BALLYMALOE BROWN BREAD

Dried yeast may be used in this recipe intead of baker's yeast. Follow the same method but allow longer to become frothy.

1 lb (500 g) wholemeal flour
2 teaspoons salt
1 teaspoon black treacle
12 fl oz (350 ml) water at
   blood heat
1 oz (25 g) fresh yeast or ½ oz
   (15 g) dried yeast

Mix the flour with the salt and warm it. Mix the treacle with some of the water in a small bowl and crumble in the yeast. Put the bowl in a warm position, such as the back of the stove, until the yeast is risen and frothy. Grease a 1 lb (500 g) loaf tin and put to warm; also warm a clean tea towel.

Stir the risen yeast well, pour it with the remaining water into the flour and mix to make a wettish dough. Put the mixture into the tin and place the tin in the same position as used previously to raise the yeast. Put the tea towel over the tin.

In approximately 20 minutes the loaf will have risen to twice its original size. Now bake it in the oven at gas mark 8, 450° F (230° C), for 40–50 minutes or until it looks nicely browned and sounds hollow when tapped on the base.

WHOLEMEAL BREAD

3 lb (1.5 kg) wholemeal flour
1 tablespoon caster sugar
3–4 teaspoons salt
1 oz (25 g) lard
2 oz (50 g) fresh yeast
1½ pints (900 ml) warm water

Sift the flour, sugar and salt into a large bowl. Cut up the lard and rub it into the flour with the fingertips until the mixture resembles fine breadcrumbs. Blend the yeast in a small bowl with 10 fl oz (300 ml) of the water and pour it into a well in the centre of the flour. Add the remaining water and, using one hand, work the mixture together until the dough leaves the bowl clean. Knead the dough on a lightly floured surface for 10 minutes.

Shape the dough into a large ball and leave it to rise in a lightly oiled polythene bag until it has doubled in size. Turn the dough on to a lightly floured surface and knead again until firm. Divide the dough into two or four equal pieces, depending on how many loaves you want, and flatten each piece firmly with the knuckles to knock out any air bubbles. Stretch and roll each piece of dough into an oblong the same length as the tin; fold it into three or roll up like a Swiss roll. Lift the dough into greased tins, brush the tops with lightly salted water and place each tin inside an oiled polythene bag. Tie the bags loosely and leave to rise until the dough reaches the top of the tins.

Remove the tins from the bags, set them on baking trays and bake in the centre of the oven at gas mark 8, 450°F (230°C), for about 30 minutes, or until the loaves shrink from the sides of the tins. Test by removing from the tins and tapping the bases; they sound hollow when cooked. Cool the loaves on a wire rack.

Shortcrust Pastry

For a plain shortcrust pastry I use a combination of butter and lard. The butter gives a good flavour and the lard produces the crisp short texture. This pastry is ideal for fruit pies.

8 oz (250 g) plain flour
Pinch salt
2 oz (50 g) butter
2 oz (50 g) lard
Cold water to mix

Sift the flour and salt into a mixing bowl. Cut the fat into the flour and then rub between the fingertips until a fine breadcrumb consistency is achieved. Gradually mix in cold water with a knife until the bowl comes clean and the pastry is not crumbly (too dry) or sticky (too wet). Roll into a ball, put in a polythene bag and allow to 'rest' in the refrigerator for 30 minutes before rolling out.

Sweet Shortcrust Pastry

This sweetened shortcrust pastry is used for fruit flans and little open tartlets.

8 oz (250 g) plain flour
Pinch salt
2 oz (50 g) butter
2 oz (50 g) lard
1 oz (25 g) caster sugar
1 egg yolk
Cold water to mix

Follow the method for shortcrust pastry (above) but add the sugar after rubbing in the fat. Mix to a firm dough with the egg yolk and a little water. Allow to 'rest' in the refrigerator for 30 minutes before using.

Jam Roly-Poly (page 218)

Flaky or Rough Puff Pastry

The difference between puff, rough puff and flaky pastry always baffles me. To make a real puff pastry is an exceedingly long and tedious process. The difference between flaky and rough puff is in the fat used and in the way it is incorporated. Generally puff is made with all butter and flaky with half lard, half butter. Both pastries are made up of many layers of fat and air to enable them to rise. You can either flatten the fat and place it on the pastry, fold and roll; or put knobs of the fat on the pastry between each rolling. Here I give you the latter method.

8 oz (250 g) plain flour
Pinch salt
3 oz (75 g) butter and 3 oz (75 g) lard, or 6 oz (175 g) butter
5 fl oz (150 ml) ice-cold water

Sift the flour and salt into a mixing bowl. Divide the fat into four portions – that is, if you are using butter and lard, two of butter and two of lard. Add one of these portions – it doesn't matter which one – to the flour and rub in. Mix in a firm but pliable dough with the water. Knead the dough lightly until smooth, then roll out to an oblong. Cut a portion of the other type of fat into nut-sized pieces and distribute over two thirds of the dough. Fold the dough into three, folding the uncovered portion first. Press the edges and turn the pastry a quarter turn so that the cut edges are now facing you. Roll out the dough again, and repeat the process with another portion of the fat. Repeat once more so that all the fat has been incorporated, then fold and roll again. Chill for 10 minutes, then fold and finally roll out before using.

Bread Pudding (page 206)

HOT-WATER CRUST PASTRY

This is the sort of pastry that you will use to make your raised pies. Work with it while still warm to line your dish, or shape it around a Kilner jar.

1 lb (500 g) flour
1 teaspoon salt
7 oz (200 g) lard
7½ fl oz (225 ml) milk and
water mixed in equal
proportions

Warm a mixing bowl and sift in the flour and salt. Make a well in the centre. Heat the lard in the milk and water until just boiling. Pour into the well in the flour and stir quickly with a wooden spoon until thick. Continue working by hand to a smooth dough. Use now in your recipe as directed.

SAVOURIES

I never worry about diets. The only carrots that
interest me are the number you get in a diamond.

MAE WEST

There is so much good cheese being produced in Britain today (my absolute favourite is the Milleens cheese from the extreme west coast of Ireland) that there is no need to look any further for a fine way to finish a meal than perhaps to revive the old business of savouries (of which the most famous is Welsh Rarebit). So I have included a few of my favourites here. They give you the perfect excuse to open another bottle of red wine or indeed another bottle of port or dry Madeira to finish the meal with – assuming, that is, that you have followed the British and not French system of having your pudding first.

Aidan McCormack *Serves 4*

WELSH RAREBIT

1 oz (25 g) butter
1 oz (25 g) flour
5 fl oz (150 ml) milk
6 oz (175 g) Cheddar cheese, grated
5 fl oz (150 ml) brown ale
1 teaspoon English mustard
2 teaspoons Worcestershire sauce
Salt and pepper
2 egg yolks
4 slices toast

Make a roux with the butter and flour, and leave to cool. Bring the milk to the boil, then whisk it into the roux. Bring to the boil once again, whisking to ensure that it does not burn and also that the sauce is free of lumps. Add the cheese, beat in and remove from the heat.

Reduce the ale, English mustard and Worcestershire sauce. When thick, add this mixture to the cheese sauce. Season well with salt and pepper and beat in the egg yolks.

Spoon on to the slices of toast and grill until bubbling. Serve with extra Worcestershire sauce handed separately.

Scotch Woodcock

1 oz (25 g) butter
4 slices toast, crusts removed
12 tinned anchovy fillets
Pepper and salt
4 egg yolks
5 fl oz (150 ml) double cream

Butter the toast and arrange in an ovenproof serving dish. Pound the anchovy fillets well, add a little pepper and spread on the toast. Keep hot.

Beat the egg yolks well with the cream and season with salt and pepper. Melt $\frac{1}{2}$ oz (15 g) butter in a small saucepan, add the egg mixture and stir, holding just off the heat, until it begins to thicken. It should not boil and should be only a little thicker than double cream. Pour onto the toast and serve.

Marrow on Toast

Marrow from 4 marrow bones
Salt and pepper
1 tablespoon chopped parsley
1 shallot, very finely chopped
4 slices hot dry toast

Remove all the marrow from the bones, cut into pieces about $\frac{1}{2}$ in. (1 cm) square and cook for 1 minute in boiling salted water. Drain, season with salt and pepper, and add the parsley and shallot, mixing all together lightly. Serve hot on the toast.

Savoury Toasts

For each person allow 1 finger of hot buttered toast – about 1 × 3 in. (2.5 × 5 cm) – and top with one of the following:

SARDINES ON TOAST: Grill 1 fresh sardine per person under a hot grill for 1 minute on each side. Place on the toast fingers and sprinkle with cayenne pepper.

DEVILLED SARDINES ON TOAST: Proceed as for Sardines on Toast, but before grilling spread each fish on both sides with a little paste made by combining 2 teaspoons of mustard, a pinch each of cayenne pepper, paprika and turmeric, 1 tablespoon of lemon juice and a walnut-sized piece of softened butter.

KIPPER FILLETS ON TOAST: Grill strips of kipper fillet for 1 minute on each side. Place 1 strip on each toast finger and sprinkle with cayenne pepper.

ANCHOVIES ON TOAST: Make some anchovy butter by working $\frac{1}{2}$ teaspoon of anchovy essence or 2 pounded tinned anchovy fillets into 2 oz (50 g) butter with a pinch of cayenne pepper. Spread this on the toast fingers instead of plain butter and top each one with 3 anchovy fillets, laid lengthways. Just before serving, place under a medium-hot grill for 3 minutes.

MUSHROOMS ON TOAST: Fry 3 whole medium mushrooms per person very gently for about 5 minutes in butter. Arrange on the toast fingers and sprinkle with salt and plenty of freshly ground black pepper.

ASPARAGUS ON TOAST: Spread a little cold hollandaise sauce on each hot dry toast finger (there is no need to butter) and place some hot freshly cooked asparagus tips on top so that the sauce begins to melt.

Scots' Toasts

HERRING ROE TOASTS: Lightly fry some herring roes in butter or dip in olive oil and grill. Then coil each roe on a round of buttered toast, sprinkle with lemon juice and cayenne pepper and garnish with slices of lemon and crisply fried parsley.

FINNAN TOASTS: To 4 oz (125 g) of flaked finnan haddock add a little cayenne pepper, 1 oz (25 g) butter, 2 tablespoons thick cream and 1 dessertspoon of chopped parsley. Heat, spread on buttered toast and sprinkle with chopped parsley and cayenne pepper.

GOOSE LIVER SAVOURIES: Simmer some goose livers in salted water for 10 minutes. Drain thoroughly and pound with a small pat of butter or goose dripping. Season with salt and cayenne pepper. Spread on fingers of buttered toast and garnish each with a buttered mushroom

Serves 4

Devilled Ham Toasts

2 oz (50 g) lean cooked ham, finely minced
2 teaspoons Worcestershire sauce
Pinch cayenne pepper
½ tablespoon French mustard
½ oz (15 g) butter
4 × 2 in. (5 cm) circles hot well-buttered toast
1 tablespoon finely chopped parsley

Thoroughly mix the ham with the Worcestershire sauce, cayenne and mustard. Melt the butter in a small sauce pan and stir the mixture into it until it is very hot. Pile on to the circles of toast, sprinkle with parsley and serve immediately.

DEVILS ON HORSEBACK

2 chicken livers
3 rashers streaky bacon
6 fingers hot buttered toast
Freshly ground black pepper
Cayenne pepper
Paprika

Wash and dry each liver and cut into three. Remove the rind from the bacon and cut each rasher in half. Wrap each piece of liver in bacon and fry or grill for 2 to 3 minutes. Place one roll on each finger of toast. Sprinkle with black pepper and a little cayenne and paprika. Serve very hot.

ANGELS ON HORSEBACK

6 fingers bread
2 oz (50 g) butter
6 oysters
Lemon juice
Cayenne pepper
3 rashers streaky bacon,
   halved

Fry the bread lightly in butter, then keep hot. Trim the beards from the oysters, sprinkle with lemon juice and cayenne and roll each in half a rasher of bacon. Fry quickly in butter just long enough to cook the bacon, turning the rolls so that they are cooked on all sides. This should take only about 2 minutes, during which time the bacon protects the oysters, so that they are not overcooked. Place one roll on each piece of fried bread and serve immediately.

Treacle Tart (page 222)

CLASSIC CHEESE SOUFFLÉ

2 oz (50 g) butter
1½ oz (40 g) plain flour
½ pint (300 ml) milk
4 eggs, separated
3 oz (75 g) Gruyère cheese, grated
1 tablespoon grated Parmesan cheese
¼ teaspoon made mustard
Salt and pepper

Pre-heat the oven to gas mark 5, 375°F (190°C).

Melt the butter in a large pan. Stir in the flour and cook for 1 minute. Remove from the heat and gradually blend in the milk. Heat, stirring, until thickened. Beat in the egg yolks and the cheeses. Season with the mustard, and salt and pepper to taste. Whisk the egg whites until thick. Using a metal spoon, fold a quarter into the cheese mixture, then fold in the remainder. Turn into an oiled 2 pint (1 litre) soufflé dish and bake for 35 to 40 minutes until well risen and golden. Serve immediately.

VARIATIONS: Use only 2 oz (50 g) good flavoured hard cheese. Add 2 oz (50 g) of any one of the following to the basic sauce: chopped chicken or ham; peeled prawns; chopped mushrooms; flaked mackerel.

Fresh Fruit Terrine (page 212)

SAVOURY SCRAMBLED EGGS

Plain scrambled eggs can be transformed into a light luncheon dish or dinner savoury, served on hot buttered toast. Vary the basic scrambled egg mixture of 12 eggs, which serves 3 to 4, by adding any of the following:

4 oz (125 g) diced cooked ham.

8 oz (250 g) sliced button mushrooms, fried in butter, piled on the scrambled eggs and garnished with chopped parsley.

1 tablespoon finely chopped parsley and 1 tablespoon finely chopped chives, tarragon or chervil.

12 oz (350 g) tomatoes, skinned, de-seeded, chopped and fried in 1 oz (25 g) of butter with 1 oz (25 g) of finely chopped onions until all the moisture has evaporated, piled on top of the scrambled eggs.

CHUTNEYS AND PICKLES

With a well-prepared anchovy sauce,
one might eat an elephant.

GRIMOD DE LA REYNIÈRE,
ALMANACH DES GOURMANDS.

Apple Chutney

7 lb (3 kg) sour apples,
    peeled, cored and sliced
1 oz (25 g) garlic, finely
    chopped
2 pints (1 litre) malt vinegar
8 oz (250 g) crystallised
    ginger, chopped
3 lb (1.5 kg) brown sugar
1 lb (500 g) sultanas
1 teaspoon ground mixed spice
1 teaspoon cayenne pepper
1 teaspoon salt

Photograph facing page 201

Place the apples in a pan with the garlic and a small amount of water and cook, covered, until soft.

Add half the vinegar, and all the other ingredients. Bring to the boil, stirring until the sugar has dissolved, then cook, uncovered, until beginning to thicken. Add the remaining vinegar and continue cooking until the desired consistency is reached. Pour into warmed sterilised jars, cover and label.

Bengal Chutney

2 lb (1 kg) cooking apples or
    green gooseberries
8 oz (250 g) onions, sliced
1 clove garlic, chopped
1 lb (500 g) raisins, minced
4 oz (125 g) preserved ginger,
    chopped
1 tablespoon salt
$\frac{1}{4}$ teaspoon cayenne pepper
$1\frac{1}{2}$ pints (900 ml) wine
    vinegar

Peel, core and chop the apples or top, tail and chop the gooseberries. Place with the onions, garlic and a little water in a pan and cook, uncovered, until soft. Add all the remaining ingredients to the pan, bring to the boil and stir until the sugar has dissolved. Simmer gently until the desired consistency is reached. Pour into warmed sterilised jars, cover and label.

DATE AND BANANA CHUTNEY

4 lb (2 kg) bananas
2 lb (1 kg) onions, chopped
1 lb (500 g) dates, chopped
1 pint (600 ml) malt vinegar
Pinch curry powder
8 oz (250 g) crystallised
 ginger, chopped
Pinch salt
1 lb (500 g) black treacle

Peel and slice the bananas, put them in a pan with the onions, dates and vinegar and cook until tender. Beat the mixture to a pulp and add the curry powder, ginger, salt and treacle. Cook the mixture until it turns a rich brown colour. Pour into warmed sterilised jars, cover and label.

GREEN TOMATO CHUTNEY

$\frac{1}{2}$ oz (15 g) root ginger
8–10 chillies
4 lb (2 kg) green tomatoes,
 chopped
1 lb (500 g) apples, peeled,
 cored and chopped
8 oz (250 g) raisins, chopped
$1\frac{1}{4}$ lb (625 g) shallots, chopped
2 teaspoons salt
1 lb (500 g) brown sugar
1 pint (600 ml) malt vinegar

Bruise the ginger and tie in a muslin bag with the chillies. Place all the other ingredients in a preserving pan and suspend the muslin bag among them. Bring to the boil, stirring until the sugar has dissolved, and simmer until the desired consistency is reached. Remove the muslin bag. Pour into warmed sterilised jars, cover and label.

PICCALILLI

2 lb (1 kg) cauliflower
2 lb (1 kg) onions
2 lb (1 kg) shallots
Salt
4 pints (2 litres) malt vinegar
Chillies
1 oz (25 g) turmeric powder
4 oz (125 g) mustard powder
1 tablespoon flour
Sugar to taste

Cut up the cauliflower into small florets and roughly chop the onions and shallots. Sprinkle with a little salt and allow to stand for 24 hours.

Boil together the vinegar, a few chillies and the turmeric. Rinse the vegetables, put them into the vinegar mixture and boil for 10 minutes or until the liquid has reduced quite considerably.

Mix together the mustard and flour with a little cold vinegar. Add this to the vegetable mixture and boil for 2 minutes longer. Add sugar as necessary. Put into warmed sterilised jars, cover and label.

Photograph facing page 201

MARROW CHUTNEY

3 lb (1.5 kg) marrow
2 teaspoons salt
8 oz (250 g) green apples, peeled, cored and chopped
8 oz (250 g) shallots, finely chopped
8 oz (250 g) sultanas
1¼ pints (750 ml) wine vinegar
4 tablespoons sugar
¼ oz (7 g) root ginger
12 black peppercorns

Cut the marrow into chunks and place in a basin. Sprinkle with the salt and leave for 24 hours. Drain and rinse.

Put the marrow, apples, shallots, sultanas, vinegar and sugar into a large pan. Bruise the ginger, place in a muslin bag with the peppercorns and add this to the pan. Bring to the boil slowly and allow to simmer for 1 to 2 hours until it is of the correct consistency. Stir occasionally to prevent burning.

When cooked, remove the muslin bag, then put the chutney into warmed sterilised jars and cover immediately. Label before storing.

MANGO CHUTNEY

2 lb (1 kg) fresh or tinned
  mangoes
1½ lb (750 g) cooking apples,
  peeled, cored and chopped
4 oz (125 g) onions, chopped
4 oz (125 g) tamarinds,
  stoned and chopped
8 oz (250 g) dates, stoned and
  roughly chopped
4 oz (125 g) raisins, roughly
  chopped
Juice of 1 large lemon
1 pint (600 ml) wine vinegar
1 oz (25 g) salt
½ teaspoon cayenne pepper
¼ teaspoon grated nutmeg
3 bay leaves
1½ tablespoons lime juice
2 lb (1 kg) demerara or soft
  brown sugar

Place all the ingredients except the lime juice and sugar in a large bowl, mix thoroughly and leave to stand for at least 3 hours.

Transfer to a preserving pan, bring to the boil and simmer gently until tender, stirring frequently. Add the sugar and lime juice, stir until the sugar is dissolved and continue to simmer until thick. Pour into warmed sterilised jars, cover and label.

WALNUT KETCHUP

If you are lucky enough to have a walnut tree in your garden, it is well worth making this ketchup. You need to pick the nuts when they are young and green.

25 young green walnuts,
  shelled
2 onions, finely chopped
2 cloves garlic, crushed
½oz (15 g) salt
1 pint (600 ml) malt vinegar
4 cloves
2 blades mace
4 black peppercorns
5 fl oz (150 ml) red wine

Bruise and crush the nuts in a non-metallic bowl. Add the onions, garlic, salt and vinegar. Turn the nuts to make sure that they are completely covered. Cover and leave for 2 weeks for all the flavours to be absorbed, stirring occasionally.

On the day of bottling prepare your ketchup bottles. Second-hand ones with screw caps are suitable provided you wash them and their caps thoroughly, then boil them in water for 30 minutes. Drain well.

Strain the liquid from the walnuts, and discard the walnuts. Add the spices and red wine to the liquid and boil for 15 minutes. Strain into a jug, pour into the prepared bottles and label.

Tim Doubleday   *Makes 3 dozen*

PICKLED EGGS

This recipe may also be used to make pickled onions.

10 fl oz (300 ml) malt vinegar
2 teaspoons cayenne pepper
1 handful pickling spice
1 dessertspoon black treacle
4 cloves garlic, chopped
1 teaspoon salt
3 dozen hard-boiled eggs,
  shelled

Boil all the ingredients except the eggs for 15 minutes. Allow the liquid to cool.

Place the eggs and the pickling liquid in a 5 lb (2.5 kg) sterilised jar. Turn upside down to mix well and leave for about 1 month before eating.

MUSHROOM KETCHUP

Mushroom ketchup is a vey useful flavouring to have in your pantry. It is a delicious addition to soups, stews, casseroles and especially steak and kidney pies. Use the large open type of mushrooms for maximum flavour.

3 lb (1.5 kg) large open
mushrooms
2½ oz (65 g) salt
1 pint (600 ml) malt vinegar
½ teaspoon ground ginger
½ teaspoon ground mace
1 teaspoon freshly ground
black pepper
6 tablespoons port
2 tablespoons brandy

Wipe the mushrooms clean and cut off the base of the stalks. Break them into pieces into a bowl, sprinkling each layer with salt. Leave overnight. Rinse well and mash with a potato masher or wooden spoon.

Place the vinegar, spices and pepper into a non-metallic ovenproof bowl, add the mushrooms and mix well. Place in a warm oven for 30 minutes.

Meanwhile, prepare your ketchup bottles. Wash thoroughly and boil with the caps in water for 30 minutes. Remove and drain.

Remove the mushroom mixture from the oven and strain into a jug. Add the port and brandy. Pour the ketchup into the prepared bottles and screw on the caps. Place the bottles in a pan of hot water and simmer for 30 minutes to prevent fermentation. Label before storing.

INDEX